A DESCRIPTIVE
BIBLIOGRAPHY OF
MONTAIGNE'S *ESSAIS*
1580–1700

R. A. SAYCE

AND

DAVID MASKELL

LONDON
The Bibliographical Society
IN CONJUNCTION WITH
The Modern Humanities Research Association
1983

Oxford University Press, Walton Street, Oxford OX2 6DP
London Glasgow New York Toronto
Delhi Bombay Calcutta Madras Karachi
Kuala Lumpur Singapore Hong Kong Tokyo
Nairobi Dar es Salaam Cape Town
Melbourne Wellington
and associate companies in
Beirut Berlin Ibadan Mexico City
Published in the United States by
Oxford University Press, New York

BIBLIOGRAPHICAL SOCIETY PUBLICATION
FOR THE YEAR 1979
PUBLISHED 1983

British Library Cataloguing in Publication Data
Sayce, R.A.
A descriptive bibliography of Montaigne's
Essais, 1580–1700.
1. Montaigne, Michel de – Bibliography
I. Title   II. Maskell, D.
016.844′3   Z8589

ISBN 0-19-721794-X

Printed in Great Britain
by The Alden Press, Osney Mead, Oxford

A DESCRIPTIVE BIBLIOGRAPHY
OF MONTAIGNE'S *ESSAIS*
1580—1700

CONTENTS

LIST OF ILLUSTRATIONS

TITLE PAGES
Reproductions of the title-page or title-pages precede the description of each edition.

PREFACE

When Richard Sayce died on 11 August 1977 he left unfinished a bibliography of Montaigne's *Essais* on which he had been working for some ten years. During that period he had recorded on *fiches* bibliographical details of about seven hundred copies of editions of the *Essais* published before 1701 which are to be found in libraries of Western Europe and the USA. By correspondence with other libraries in France, Eastern Europe and the USSR he had collected information concerning many more copies. He had also drafted a specimen entry for the first edition of 1580.

Shortly after her husband's death Olive Sayce asked me to prepare this material for publication. This I have tried to do with as much fidelity to Richard Sayce's intentions, and as little intervention on my part, as possible. Inevitably, however, the planning and writing of the bibliography have required interpretation of the material he had collected and, in places, further research. At all times I have enjoyed the full cooperation of Olive Sayce, who has been unfailingly helpful in every possible way. Without her this bibliography could not have come into being.

The Bibliographical Society undertook at an early stage to publish this work to honour the memory of Richard Sayce; their generosity in this matter, and also the much valued participation of the Modern Humanities Research Association, provided a great stimulus towards the completion of the work. The lay-out of the book posed considerable technical problems, which were skilfully resolved thanks to the patience and expertise of the Alden Press.

I am also conscious of a very great debt owed to librarians, booksellers, colleagues and friends who have helped Richard Sayce or myself or both of us. The list of over 300 libraries on pp. ix–xviii bears witness to the number of librarians who have cooperated in this venture by permitting access to their collections, by responding with extraordinary helpfulness to questionnaires and queries, and by furnishing the photographs with which the bibliography is illustrated. A number of private owners of copies of the *Essais* have offered them for inspection or loan. Numerous individuals have given advice or assistance. To thank them all by name would be impossible. On behalf of Richard Sayce, and for myself, I gratefully acknowledge the contributions that so many people have made to this work, including the Leverhulme Trust Fund for the award of a Fellowship from 1972 to 1974 to Richard Sayce for research on this bibliography, and the Curators of the Taylor Institution for a generous grant from the Gerrans Memorial Fund to assist with the expenses of publication.

DAVID MASKELL   *January 1981*

When my husband died, leaving unfinished the bibliography on which he had worked for so long, I was faced with a dilemma: whether to deposit the material in a library—the easier course—or to attempt to find someone able and willing to prepare it for publication. With some hesitation, I decided to approach David Maskell, a former graduate student of my husband's. It turned out to be a providential choice. I cannot thank him adequately for the dedication, time, and scholarly effort he has devoted to this exacting task. Without him the bibliography would have remained unpublished, and the fruits of my husband's labours hidden.

OLIVE SAYCE

ABBREVIATIONS

1. LOCATIONS

The numbers refer to the editions of the *Essais* listed in this bibliography

Aar   Aarau, Aargauische Kantonsbibliothek, 26
Aber   Aberdeen University Library, 19, 26
Abbv   Abbeville, Bibliothèque municipale, 16
Agen   Agen, Bibliothèque municipale, 7A
Aix   Aix-en-Provence, Bibliothèque municipale (Méjanes), 29, 33
Albi   Albi, Bibliothèque municipale (Rochegude), 27, 34
Alen   Alençon, Bibliothèque municipale, 25
Ami   Amiens, Bibliothèque municipale, 20, 27, 30, 34
Ams   Amsterdam, Universiteitsbibliotheek, 30, 33
Ang   Angers, Bibliothèque municipale, 30
Ann   Annecy, Bibliothèque municipale, 34
Ant   Antwerp, Museum Plantin-Moretus, 7A, 7A†, 7B, 10, 19, 22
Ariz   University of Arizona, Tucson (Arizona), 25
Arr   Arras, Bibliothèque municipale, 31, 33
Ars   Bibliothèque de l'Arsenal, Paris, 3, 7A, 13, 19, 20, 23, 25, 27,
       28, 29, 30, 31, 32
AS   All Souls College, Oxford, 11, 20
Auch   Auch, Bibliothèque municipale, 16, 20
Aug   Augsburg, Staats- und Stadtbibliothek, 5, 15, 25
Aut   Autun, Bibliothèque municipale, 25, 31
Aux   Auxerre, Bibliothèque municipale, 25
Avig   Avignon, Musée Calvet, 4, 7A, 12B, 20, 23, 24, 25, 30, 32
Avr   Avranches, Bibliothèque municipale, 9

Ball   Balliol College, Oxford, 8
Bar   Bar-le-Duc, Bibliothèque municipale, 1, 10, 14, 24
Barc   Barcelona, Biblioteca Universitaria, 25
Bas   Basel, Universitätsbibliothek, 23, 24, 27, 28, 32
Bayn   Bayonne, Bibliothèque municipale, 25
Bayx   Bayeux, Bibliothèque municipale, 27
Belg   Belgrade, Univerzitetska Biblioteka Svetozar Marković, 28,
       30, 36, 37
Bern   Berne, Stadt- und Universitätsbibliothek, 27
Bes   Besançon, Bibliothèque municipale, 3, 4, 7A, 13, 27, 34

BL   British Library, London, 1, 2, 4, 5, 7A, 8, 9, 10, 11, 13, 14, 16, 17, 19, 20, 22, 23, 24, 25, 26, 27, 28, 30, 31, 33, 34, 35

Blo   Blois, Bibliothèque municipale, 30

BN   Bibliothèque nationale, Paris, 1, 2, 3, 4, 5, 6, 7A, 8, 9, 10, 11, 12, 12A, 12B, 13, 14, 15, 16, 17, 18, 19, 20, 21, 21A, 22, 23, 24, 24A, 25, 26, 27, 28, 29, 30, 31, 32, 33, 34, 35, 36, 37

Boch   Bochum, Universitätsbibliothek, 34

Bod   Bodleian Library, Oxford, 1, 2, 3, 4, 5, 6, 7A, 8, 11, 13, 20, 21, 24, 25, 33, 36

Bol/A   Bologna, Biblioteca Comunale dell'Archiginnasio, 11, 33

Bol/U   Bologna, Biblioteca Universitaria, 3, 32

Bord   Bordeaux, Bibliothèque municipale, 1, 2, 3, 4, 4†, 5, 6, 7A, 8, 10, 12, 13, 19, 20, 21A, 22, 23, 24, 25, 26, 27, 28, 29, 30, 33, 34, 35

Bost   Boston Public Library, Boston (Massachusetts), 25, 32, 34

Boul   Boulogne-sur-mer, Bibliothèque municipale, 26, 31

Bourges   Bourges, Bibliothèque municipale, 23

Bre   Brest, Bibliothèque municipale, 34

Brem   Bremen, Staats- und Universitätsbibliothek, 12

Bresc   Brescia, Biblioteca Civica Queriniana, 17

Brg   Bourg-en-Bresse, Bibliothèque municipale, 13, 30

Bru   Brussels, Bibliothèque royale, 4, 5, 7A, 11, 19, 30, 31, 33

Buc   Bucharest, Academiei Biblioteca, 4, 21, 25, 32, 35, 37

Bud/M   Budapest, Fövárosi Szabó Ervin Könyvtár, 13

Bud/N   Budapest, Országos Széchényi Könyvtár, 10, 13

Bud/U   Budapest, Eötvös Loránd Tudomanyegyetem Könyvtára (Budapesti Egyetemi Könyvtár), 3, 14, 22

Byd   Bydgoszcz, Biblioteka Miejska, 34

Caen   Caen, Bibliothèque municipale, 25, 31

Cam   Cambridge (see under: CUL; Em; Kings; Trin)

Carc   Carcassonne, Bibliothèque municipale, 20

Carl   Carlisle Cathedral Library, 7A

Carp   Carpentras, Bibliothèque municipale (Inguimbertine), 7A, 17, 25

Cass   Bibliothèque de la Cour de Cassation, Paris, 7A, 20, 23, 29, 30, 31

Cath   Bibliothèque de l'Institut Catholique de Paris, 16, 20, 30, 32, 33, 34

CCC   Corpus Christi College, Oxford, 18

Ch   Christ Church, Oxford, 34

Châm   Châlons-sur-Marne, Bibliothèque municipale, 1, 7A, 20, 22,
          24, 26, 27, 32, 33, 36, 37
Chamb   Chambéry, Bibliothèque municipale, 11, 30, 31
Chan/C   Chantilly, Musée Condé, 1, 4, 7A, 16
Chan/F   Chantilly, Les Fontaines, Bibliothèque S.J., 7A, 14, 22, 25, 27
Chap   Chapin Library, Williamstown (Massachusetts), 1, 4, 7A, 22,
          25, 31, 33
Chas   Chalon-sur-Saône, Bibliothèque municipale, 29, 30
Chât   Châtellerault (Vienne), Bibliothèque municipale, 23
Chau   Chaumont (Haute-Marne), Bibliothèque municipale, 1, 16,
          19, 20, 25, 32, 34
Chic/N   Newberry Library, Chicago (Illinois), 1, 9, 25, 27
Chic/U   Chicago University Library (Illinois), 1, 2, 3, 4, 7A, 23, 24,
          25, 27, 30, 31, 32, 35
Clark   Clark Library, Los Angeles (California), 1, 3, 21, 33
Cler   Clermont-Ferrand, Bibliothèque municipale, 25, 29, 30
Cob   Coburg, Landesbibliothek, 11
Cole   New University of Ulster Library, Coleraine, 7A
Colm   Colmar, Bibliothèque municipale, 9, 22, 27, 29, 31
Coln   Cologne, Universitäts- und Stadtbibliothek, 24
Cop   Copenhagen, Det Kongelige Bibliotek, 5, 11, 15, 23, 25, 26,
          28, 34
Coul   Coulommiers, Bibliothèque municipale, 23
Cout   Coutances, Bibliothèque municipale, 13
CUL   Cambridge University Library, 24, 30

Det   Detmold, Lippische Landesbibliothek, 6, 24
Diep   Dieppe, Bibliothèque municipale, 31
Dij   Dijon, Bibliothèque municipale, 7A, 12, 25, 34
Dill   Dillingen, Studienbibliothek, 17
Dôle   Dôle, Bibliothèque municipale, 29
Drag   Draguignan, Bibliothèque municipale, 31
Dub/M   Marsh's Library, Dublin, 30
Dub/T   Trinity College, Dublin, 15, 23, 31
Dub/W   Worth Library, Dublin, 23
Dur   Durham University Library, 14, 26
Düss   Düsseldorf, Universitätsbibliothek, 24
Dut   Musée des Beaux-Arts de la Ville de Paris, Collection Dutuit,
          Petit Palais, Paris, 1
Ed/N   Edinburgh, National Library of Scotland, 2, 7A, 17, 25, 27,
          28

Ed/NB   Library of St Mary College, Blairs, on deposit in National Library of Scotland, 1, 10, 25, 27

Ed/U   Edinburgh University Library, 30

Em   Emmanuel College, Cambridge, 8, 22

Eper   Epernay, Bibliothèque municipale, 5

Epin   Epinal, Bibliothèque municipale, 24

Erl   Erlangen, Universitätsbibliothek, 25, 33

Etam   Etampes, Bibliothèque municipale, 20, 31

Eton   Eton College, Windsor, 23, 25

Eut   Eutin, Kreisbibliothek, 22, 37

Evr   Evreux, Bibliothèque municipale, 22, 31

Ex   Exeter Cathedral Library, 7A

Flo   Florence, Biblioteca Riccardiana, 30

Foix   Foix, Bibliothèque municipale, 8, 34

Frau   Frauenfeld, Thurgauische Kantonsbibliothek, 28, 35

Frei   Freiburg (Breisgau), Universitätsbibliothek, 23, 33

Frib   Fribourg, Bibliothèque cantonale et universitaire, 10

Ful   Fulda, Hessische Landesbibliothek, 6

Gen   Geneva, Bibliothèque publique et universitaire, 6, 10, 17, 29

Gen/B   Biblioteca Bodmeriana, Cologny, Geneva, 1, 2, 3

Ghe   Ghent, Bibliothèque centrale de l'Université, 2, 19

Gla   Glasgow University Library, 8, 24, 36, 37

Gord   Douglas H Gordon, Baltimore (Maryland), 2, 3, 4, 6, 7A

Gött   Göttingen, Universitätsbibliothek, 17, 28, 31, 33, 37

Graz/L   Graz, Steiermärkische Landesbibliothek, 31

Graz/U   Graz, Universitätsbibliothek, 13

Gren   Grenoble, Bibliothèque municipale, 5, 7A, 12, 13, 18, 25, 27, 30

Gron   Groningen, Universiteitsbibliotheek, 28

Hag   Haguenau, Bibliothèque municipale, 37

Hague   The Hague, Koninklijke Bibliotheek, 25, 30

Ham   Hamburg, Stadt- und Universitätsbibliothek, 14, 30

Han   Hanover, Niedersächsische Landesbibliothek, 6, 25, 28

Harv   Harvard University, Cambridge (Massachusetts), 1, 2, 3, 4, 5, 6, 7B, 8, 9, 10, 12, 13, 14, 16, 18, 19, 20, 21, 23, 23A, 24, 25, 26, 27, 30, 31, 32, 33, 34, 35, 36

Heid   Heidelberg, Universitätsbibliothek, 20

Hist   Bibliothèque historique de la Ville de Paris, Paris, 14

Hunt   Henry E Huntington Library, San Marino (California), 1, 8,
           18, 30
Hy   Hyères, Bibliothèque municipale, 31

Ill   University of Illinois, Urbana (Illinois), 8, 14, 16, 18, 20, 25,
           27, 36
Ind   Indiana University, Bloomington (Indiana), 1
Inst   Bibliothèque de l'Institut de France, Paris, 1, 7B, 11, 16, 30,
           31, 34

Jes   Jesus College, Oxford, 16

Kat   Katowice, Biblioteka Śląska, 23
Kilk   Kilkenny, St Canice's Library, 28
Kings   King's College, Cambridge, 7B, 13, 22, 23, 25
Krak/J   Kraków, Biblioteka Jagiellońska, 33
Krak/N   Kraków, Muzeum Narodowe, Biblioteka Zbiory Czartorys-
           kich, 30

Laf   La Flèche, Bibliothèque du Prytanée militaire, 8, 30
Lan   Langres, Bibliothèque municipale, 20
Laon   Laon, Bibliothèque municipale, 27, 37
Laus/P   Lausanne, Bibliothèque des Pasteurs, 10, 14, 29, 30
Laus/U   Lausanne, Bibliothèque cantonale et universitaire, 6, 29
Lav   Laval, Bibliothèque municipale, 29
Leeds   Leeds University, Brotherton Library, 13, 25
Leeuw   Leeuwarden, Provinciale Bibliotheek van Friesland, 6
Leid   Leiden, Universiteitsbibliotheek, 22
Lem   Le Mans, Société d'agriculture, sciences et arts de la Sarthe,
           25
Len/N   Leningrad, Biblioteka Akademii Nauk SSSR, 1, 3, 17, 18, 27,
           30, 34
Len/S   Leningrad, Gosudarstvennaja publičnaja biblioteka im. M E
           Saltykova-Ščedrina, 9, 14, 17, 23, 31, 32, 33, 34, 37
Lep   Le Puy-en-Velay (Haute-Loire), Bibliothèque municipale,
           27, 30
Lich   Lichfield Cathedral Library, 27
LI   Institut français du Royaume-Uni, London, 33
Lille   Lille, Bibliothèque municipale, 25
Linc   Lincoln Cathedral Library, 3
Lju   Ljubljana, Narodna in univerzitetna knjižnica, 33
Liv   Liverpool University Library, 30, 31
LL   The London Library, 6

Loch   Loches, Bibliothèque municipale, 34
Lons   Lons-le-Saunier, Bibliothèque municipale, 2, 18
Louv   Louviers, Bibliothèque municipale, 9
LU   London University Library, Senate House, 1, 2, 4, 11, 14, 24
LUC   University College, Gower Street, London, 25, 31
Lucc   Lucca, Biblioteca Statale, 10, 14, 24, 30
Luz   Lucerne, Zentralbibliothek, 6, 11
Ly   Lyons, Bibliothèque municipale, 4, 5, 6, 7A, 9, 10, 13, 23, 25, 27, 29, 30, 31, 33

Madr   Madrid, Biblioteca Nacional, 11, 23, 25, 29, 30, 32
Magd   Madgalen College, Oxford, 25
Mai   Mainz, Stadtbibliothek, 10
Man   The John Rylands University Library of Manchester, 1, 31, 33
Mars   Marseilles, Bibliothèque municipale, 29
Maz   Bibliothèque Mazarine, Paris, 21, 25, 32
Meaux   Meaux, Bibliothèque municipale, 25
Méd   Bibliothèque de la faculté de médecine, Paris, 4
Mel   Melun, Bibliothèque municipale, 30
Mers   Viscount Mersey, Pulborough, 7A, 27
Mert   Merton College, Oxford, 7A
Metz   Metz, Bibliothèque municipale, 20, 30, 34
Mich   University of Michigan, Ann Arbor (Michigan), 16, 18, 20, 26, 27
Midd   Middelburg, Provinciale Bibliotheek van Zeeland, 5
Mil/A   Milan, Biblioteca Ambrosiana, 27, 33
Mil/B   Milan, Biblioteca Nazionale Braidense, 30, 35, 36
Mil/C   Milan, Biblioteca Comunale, 5
Mn   Manchester College, Oxford, 23
Mod   Modena, Biblioteche Estense e Universitaria, 5, 30, 32, 34, 35, 36
Monb   Montbéliard, Bibliothèque municipale, 7A, 8, 17, 31
Monp   Montpellier, Bibliothèque municipale, 3, 5, 9, 13, 32, 33, 34
Monp/U   Montpellier, Bibliothèque universitaire centrale, 20, 25
Monta   Montauban, Bibliothèque municipale, 7A, 37
Mosc/G   Moscow, Naučnaja biblioteka im. A M Gorkogo, 24, 30
Mosc/H   Moscow, Gosudarstvennaja publičnaja istoričeskaja biblioteka RSFSR, 5, 14, 23, 30, 32, 33, 34, 35
Mosc/L   Moscow, Gosudarstvennaja ordena Lenina biblioteka SSSR im. V I Lenina, 13, 17, 20, 25, 31, 32, 33

Mun   Munich, Bayerische Staatsbibliothek, 23

Nanc   Nancy, Bibliothèque municipale, 5
Nant   Nantes, Bibliothèque municipale, 1, 4, 10, 17, 28, 30
Neuf   Neufchâteau, Bibliothèque municipale, 34
Nev   Nevers, Bibliothèque municipale, 23B, 31
New   New College, Oxford, 30
Newc   Newcastle upon Tyne University Library, 27
Nijm   Nijmegen, Universiteitsbibliotheek, 33
Nîm   Nîmes, Bibliothèque municipale (Séguier), 20, 31
Nio   Niort, Bibliothèque municipale, 1, 23, 33
Nott   Nottingham University Library, 28
Nür   Nürnberg, Germanisches Nationalmuseum, 6, 28
NW   Northwestern University, Evanston (Illinois), 35
NY/M   Pierpont Morgan Library, New York, 1, 4, 5
NY/P   New York Public Library, 2, 4, 7A

Ohio   Ohio State University, Columbus (Ohio), 23
Old   Oldenburg, Landesbibliothek, 23
Ori   Oriel College, Oxford, 12
Orl   Orléans, Bibliothèque municipale, 7B, 10, 30, 33
Oslo   Oslo, Universitetsbibliotek, 27, 30
Ox   Oxford (see under: AS; Ball; Bod; CCC; Ch; Jes; Magd; Mert;
           Mn; New; Ori; Qu; RAS; Sthi; Stj; Tay; Wad; Worc)

Pad/C   Padua, Biblioteca del Museo Civico, 11, 23
Pad/U   Padua, Biblioteca Universitaria, 8, 31, 35
Parm   Parma, Biblioteca Palatina, 14, 32, 33, 36
Pau   Pau, Bibliothèque municipale, 24, 25, 30, 31, 35
Pav   Pavia, Biblioteca Universitaria, 25
Péri   Périgueux, Bibliothèque municipale, 3, 4, 9, 25, 26
Perp   Perpignan, Bibliothèque municipale, 30
Poi   Poitiers, Bibliothèque municipale, 7A, 20, 30, 32
Pom   Pommersfelden, Graf von Schönborn'sche Bibliothek, 17, 27
Poz   Poznań, Biblioteka Uniwersytecka, 12, 25, 37
Pra/M   Prague, Národní muzeum, 23, 31
Pra/S   Prague, Státní knihovna ČSR, 21, 30, 33, 34
Prin   Princeton University, Princeton (New Jersey), 1, 2, 3, 4, 5, 6,
           7A, 8, 10, 12, 13, 15, 19, 20, 21, 23, 24, 25, 26, 28, 30, 31, 37

Qu   Queen's College, Oxford, 27

RAS   R A Sayce,[1] Oxford, 5, 6, 9, 10, 11, 13, 14, 18, 22, 25, 27, 29, 30, 31, 33, 34, 36, 37

Reg   Regensburg, Staatliche Bibliothek, 11, 31

Regg   Reggio Emilia, Biblioteca Municipale, 29

Ren   Rennes, Bibliothèque municipale, 19, 29, 34, 36

Ren/U   Rennes, Bibliothèque de l'Université, 21A, 22, 25, 32, 33

Rhei   Rheims, Bibliothèque municipale, 10, 23

Roa   Roanne, Bibliothèque municipale, 30

Rom/A   Rome, Biblioteca Angelica, 18

Rom/C   Rome, Biblioteca Casanatense, 11, 17

Rom/N   Rome, Biblioteca Nazionale, 8

Rom/V   Rome, Biblioteca Vallicelliana, 14
         See also Vat (Vatican)

Romo   Romorantin, Bibliothèque municipale, 1

Sal   Salins-les-Bains (Jura), Bibliothèque municipale, 22, 30, 31, 33

Scha   Schaffhausen, Stadtbibliothek, 17

Sél   Sélestat, Bibliothèque municipale, 27

Senl   Senlis, Bibliothèque municipale, 14

Sens   Sens, Bibliothèque municipale, 20, 32

Shef   Sheffield University Library, 9

Sol   Solothurn, Zentralbibliothek, 33

Sorb   Bibliothèque de la Sorbonne, Paris, 3, 7A, 23, 25, 27, 28, 30, 35, 36, 37

Spe   Speyer, Altsprachliches Gymnasium, 32

Sta   St Andrews University Library, 25

Stb   Saint-Brieuc, Bibliothèque municipale, 34

Stde   Saint-Denis, Bibliothèque municipale, 25

Stdi   Saint-Dié, Bibliothèque municipale, 5, 10

Ste   Saint-Etienne, Bibliothèque municipale, 25

Stga   St Gall, Stadtbibliothek (Vadiana), 17

Stge   Bibliothèque Sainte-Geneviève, Paris, 3, 13, 14, 25, 29, 30

Sthi   St Hilda's College, Oxford, 9

Stj   St John's College, Oxford, 17, 30, 33, 34

---

[1] These books are at present in the possession of Olive Sayce, who has expressed her intention of donating them to Worcester College, Oxford, together with her husband's notes and papers upon which this bibliography is based. These notes and papers, which are referred to above (p. vii) contain more information about copies of the *Essais* seen by Dr Sayce than can be included here, and also his notes on Montaigne's other works, namely the editions of La Boétie, the translations of Sabunde's *Theologia Naturalis* and the *Journal de Voyage*.

Sto	Saint-Omer, Bibliothèque municipale, 31
Stq	Saint-Quentin, Bibliothèque municipale, 25
Stra	Strasbourg, Bibliothèque nationale et universitaire, 12, 17, 33
Stut	Stuttgart, Württembergische Landesbibliothek, 4, 16, 25
SZ	Sotheby/Zeitlin, 7A†, 7B
Tarb	Tarbes, Bibliothèque municipale, 35
Tay	Taylor Institution, Oxford, 5, 15, 18, 25, 30, 31, 32, 36, 37
Temp	Temple University, Philadelphia (Pennsylvania), 17
Thor	Frederik Thorkelin,[2] Holløselund, Vejby, 2, 4, 7A, 25
Tor	Toruń, Biblioteka Uniwersytecka, 22
Touln	Toulon, Bibliothèque municipale, 25
Touls	Toulouse, Bibliothèque municipale, 4, 13, 25, 30, 33
Tours	Tours, Bibliothèque municipale, 30
Trent	Trento, Biblioteca Comunale, 31
Trin	Trinity College, Cambridge, 5, 9, 11, 16, 22, 27
Tro	Troyes, Bibliothèque municipale, 2, 9, 13, 14, 20, 23, 25, 26, 29, 34
Tüb	Tübingen, Universitätsbibliothek, 6, 27
Ulm	Ulm, Stadtbibliothek, 6, 34
USC	University of Southern California, Los Angeles (California), 23, 31
Utr	Utrecht, Universiteitsbibliotheek, 6, 37
Val	Valence (Drôme), Bibliothèque municipale, 20, 35
Vals	Valenciennes, Bibliothèque municipale, 30, 36
Vat	Biblioteca Apostolica Vaticana, Rome, 16, 21A, 25, 26, 33
Ven	Venice, Biblioteca Nazionale Marciana, 24
Vend	Vendôme, Bibliothèque municipale, 14, 32, 34
Verd	Verdun, Bibliothèque municipale, 13, 31
Vero	Verona, Biblioteca Comunale, 35
Vers	Versailles, Bibliothèque municipale, 2, 3, 4, 7B, 9, 12, 15, 18, 25, 27, 30, 33, 34
Ves	Vesoul, Bibliothèque municipale, 25, 37
Vie	Vienne, Bibliothèque municipale, 31
Vien/N	Vienna, Österreichische Nationalbibliothek, 4, 6, 17, 22, 31, 34
Vien/U	Vienna, Universitätsbibliothek, 31
Virg/S	Virginia State Library, Richmond (Virginia), 33

[2] Mr Thorkelin has expressed his intention of leaving his Montaigne collection to the Kongelige Bibliotek, Copenhagen.

Virg/U   University of Virginia, Charlottesville (Virginia), 1, 7A, 26, 33, 34
Virg/W   College of William and Mary, Williamsburg (Virginia), 3

Wad   Wadham College, Oxford, 7A, 28, 33
Wars/M   Warsaw, Muzeum Narodowe, 23
Wars/N   Warsaw, Biblioteka Narodowa, 17, 22, 29, 31, 34
Wars/U   Warsaw, Biblioteka Uniwersytecka, 24, 30, 36
W/Cong   US Library of Congress (Washington DC), 7A, 10, 12, 30, 31, 36
W/Folg   Folger Shakespeare Library (Washington DC), 5, 6, 7A, 11, 14, 18, 21, 25
Wind   Windsor Castle, Berkshire, 27
Wint   Winterthur, Stadtbibliothek, 33
Wolf   Wolfenbüttel, Herzog August Bibliothek, 11, 16, 18, 20, 22, 25, 30, 32, 34, 37
Worc   Worcester College, Oxford, 30, 33 (See also RAS)
Wroc/O   Wrocław, Biblioteka Zakładu Narodowego im. Ossolińskich, 15, 32
Wroc/U   Wrocław, Biblioteka Uniwersytecka, 6, 9, 24, 26, 30
Wup   Wuppertal, Stadtbibliothek, 24
Würz   Würzburg, Universitätsbibliothek, 5, 29

Xant   Xanten, Stiftsbibliothek, 28

Yale   Yale University, New Haven (Connecticut), 1, 2, 3, 4, 7A, 16, 18, 23, 24, 25, 30, 37

Zof   Zofingen, Stadtbibliothek, 20
Zür   Zürich, Zentralbibliothek, 1, 11, 17, 26

2. OTHER ABBREVIATIONS

BBB   *Bulletin du bibliophile et du bibliothécaire*
BHR   *Bibliothèque d'Humanisme et Renaissance*
BSAM   *Bulletin de la Société des Amis de Montaigne*

caps   capital letters

CW   catch-word

HT   head-title

inits   initials

prelims preliminary leaves

RT   running-title

tp   title-page

type-orns type-ornaments

π unsigned preliminary leaf

$ leaves in each normal gathering (see p. xx)

Italics in the list of copies at the end of each entry indicates that the copy has not been seen.

INTRODUCTION

The aim of this work is to describe all editions of Montaigne's *Essais* published between 1580 and 1700. The conventions used are those recommended by F. Bowers in *Principles of Bibliographical Description* (Princeton, 1949).

Throughout the work editions with a Paris imprint are referred to by date alone, e.g. '1595' means 'the 1595 edition with a Paris imprint'. Other imprints are specified, e.g. '1595 Lyons' means 'the 1595 edition with a Lyons imprint'. Copies are referred to by the abbreviated form of the library in which they are found, e.g. 'Ly' means 'the copy in the Bibliothèque municipale, Lyons'.

Because of the erratic pagination in most editions, reference is made to pages according to their signature. As a page reference 'A1' alone means 'A1 recto', 'A1ᵛ' means 'A1 verso'. 'A1' may also indicate the whole leaf A1, and if ever confusion might arise between the leaf and the page, 'A1ʳ' is used for the page.

All illustrations carry an indication of the height in millimetres of the original. This refers to the height of the printed, engraved or manuscript matter which is reproduced, not to the height of the page which carries it. These measurements must be considered as approximate, since the measurements of the same thing may vary by up to 2% from one copy to another.

The description of each edition starts with facsimile reproductions of the title-page or title-pages. The rest of the description is given under the following headings:

Title-page: Differences between separate or variant title-pages are indicated with reference to the facsimile reproductions.

Collation: This paragraph contains the following information:
(i) Collational formula.
(ii) Number of leaves signed in each normal gathering. '$4 signed' means that the first four leaves of each normal gathering are signed. '$4(5) signed' means that in some gatherings the first four leaves are signed, in others the first five.
(iii) Signature numeration (roman or arabic numerals).
(iv) Missignings found in all copies examined. At the end of this list *variants* indicates missignings found in some copies but corrected in others.

INTRODUCTION

Cet ouvrage a pour objet de décrire toutes les éditions des *Essais* de Montaigne publiées entre 1580 et 1700 selon les principes de F. Bowers dans *Principles of Bibliographical Description* (Princeton, 1949).

Au cours de l'ouvrage les éditions publiées à Paris sont indiquées par le seul millésime, p. ex. '1595' signifie 'l'édition de 1595 publiée à Paris'. Les autres lieux d'impression sont indiqués, p. ex. '1595 Lyons' signifie 'l'édition de 1595 publiée à Lyon'. Les exemplaires sont indiqués par l'abréviation de la bibliothèque dans laquelle ils se trouvent, p. ex. 'Ly' signifie 'l'exemplaire qui se trouve à la bibliothèque municipale de Lyon'.

La pagination de la plupart des éditions est fort irrégulière; aussi les signatures sont-elles employées comme références. 'A1' tout seul indique le recto du feuillet signé A1; 'A1ᵛ' indique le verso du même feuillet. 'A1' peut aussi indiquer le feuillet entier signé A1. Là où il y a possibilité de confondre le feuillet et la page, 'A1ʳ' sert pour signaler le recto de la page.

Toute reproduction photographique est accompagnée d'une indication de la hauteur en millimètres de l'original. Il s'agit toujours de la hauteur de ce qui est reproduit (texte, gravure, manuscrit), non pas de la hauteur du feuillet original. Dans certains cas il peut y avoir une variation de jusqu'à deux pour cent dans les dimensions d'une même chose d'un exemplaire à un autre. Les dimensions données doivent donc être considérées comme approximatives.

En tête de la notice consacrée à chaque édition est placée la reproduction photographique de la page ou des pages de titre. Chaque notice bibliographique comporte les rubriques suivantes:

Title-page: Les différences entre les pages de titre ou les variantes d'un même titre sont indiquées par référence aux reproductions photographiques.

Collation. Ce paragraphe comprend:
   (i) Le formulaire de collation.
   (ii) Le nombre de feuillets signés dans chaque cahier régulier. '$4 signed' signifie que les quatre premiers feuillets de chaque cahier sont signés. '$4(5) signed' signifie que dans certains cahiers les quatre premiers feuillets sont signés, dans d'autres les cinq premiers.
   (iii) Le chiffrage des signatures (chiffres romains ou arabes).

(v) Number of leaves.

(vi) Pagination statement. Totals of unnumbered pages are given in square brackets and italics, e.g. '[*8*]' means '8 unnumbered pages'. In the numbered sequences, the inferred numbering of unnumbered pages is supplied in italics, e.g. '*1* 2–88' etc. means that the first page is not numbered. Misnumbering found in all copies examined is given in the numbered sequence. Where the last numbered page of the series gives an incorrect total for the whole series, the correct total is supplied in square brackets thus: 1129 [= 1087]. Misnumbering corrected in some copies is listed under *variants* at the end of the statement. Pagination is outside in the headline unless otherwise stated.

In some editions the errors of signing, pagination and running-titles are very numerous and so too are the corrections. Examination of further copies will doubtless bring more variants of this nature to light.

Contents: The contents of the book are indicated in summary form. '*Au lecteur*' means Montaigne's preface. Prefaces and notices by others are designated 'Preface' and their authors specified. '*Privilège*' includes *extrait du privilège*. All blank leaves are accounted for. The original French designation of the contents is given in the next section, Head-titles.

Head-titles (HT): Ornamental head-pieces are identified by their chief characteristics. Head-titles are transcribed in quasi-facsimile noting all swash italic capitals and long s.

Running-titles (RT): The verso running-title, placed first, is separated by a vertical stroke from the recto running-title. Then the variations found in all copies examined are listed, followed by variants found only in some copies. Where the variations are very numerous they are summarised or listed in the manner most likely to throw into relief patterns in their occurrence. It is assumed that there are no running-titles on pages with head-titles.

Catch-words (CW): The normal occurrence of catch-words in the main body of the text is indicated as follows. 'Quire' means 'on the verso of the last leaf of each gathering'. 'Leaf' means 'on the verso of each leaf'. 'Unsigned pages' means 'on every page without a signature'. 'Page' means 'on every page'. For each edition a selection of catch-words is given either for identification or to facilitate comparison with related editions.

Measurements: The type-page selected for measurement is identified first.

(iv) Les erreurs de signature notées dans tous les exemplaires examinés. A la fin de cette liste, après le mot *variants*, se trouvent les erreurs de signature particulières à certains exemplaires, mais corrigées dans d'autres au cours du tirage.

(v) Le nombre de feuillets.

(vi) La formule de pagination. Le total des pages non chiffrées est donné entre crochets et en italique, p. ex. '[*8*]' veut dire '8 pages non chiffrées'. Dans la série numérotée le numéro des pages non chiffrées est donné en italique sans crochets, p. ex. '*1* 2–88' signifie que la première page n'est pas chiffrée. Les erreurs de chiffrage notées dans tous les exemplaires examinés se trouvent dans la série numérotée. Là où la dernière page chiffrée donne un total faux pour la série, le vrai total est ajouté entre crochets ainsi: 1129 [=1087]. Les erreurs de chiffrage particulières à certains exemplaires se trouvent à la fin après le mot *variants*. Sauf indication contraire les chiffres de pagination dans les éditions décrites sont placés à l'extérieur de la ligne de tête.

Dans certaines éditions les erreurs et les corrections de signature, de pagination ou de titres courants sont très nombreuses. Par conséquent l'examen d'autres exemplaires permettra sans doute de relever encore de variantes.

Contents: La description complète des matières contenues dans le livre est donnée sous forme abrégée. *Au lecteur*, c'est la préface de Montaigne; les préfaces et les avis d'autres personnes sont désignés 'Preface' avec indication de l'auteur. Tout feuillet blanc est noté. La description des matières telle qu'elle se lit dans l'édition originale est présentée sous la rubrique suivante, Head-titles (titres secondaires).

Head-titles (HT): Les bandeaux sont identifiés par leurs traits les plus caractéristiques. Les titres secondaires sont transcrits avec coupures de lignes, en faisant distinction entre romain et italique, capitales et lettres de bas de casse. Le s long est aussi transcrit.

Running-titles (RT): Le titre courant du verso précède celui du recto, dont il est séparé par un trait vertical. Suivent entre crochets les entorses à la norme notées dans tous les exemplaires examinés, et, après le mot *variants*, les variantes particulières à certains exemplaires. Là où les entorses à la norme sont très fréquentes, les références sont données en forme abrégée ou de façon à mettre en relief toute régularité dans leur distribution. Il n'y a pas de titres courants aux pages qui portent un titre secondaire.

Catch-words (CW): La distribution normale des réclames dans la partie du

'30(+2) lines' means '30 lines of text plus headline and direction-line', i.e. 32 lines for the full type-page. The height of the full type-page is given in brackets after the height of the lines of text alone, e.g. 125(132) × 70 mm. Where appropriate the width with side-notes is given as well.

In all editions the text of the *Essais* is printed in roman type. Latin quotations in the text and the sonnets of La Boétie, where they are present, are in italic type.

Privilège. This section contains a summary of the information contained in the *privilège* or *extrait du privilège,* and also details of the *achevé d'imprimer* or colophon where they occur.

Copies. This is a list of copies examined and of copies whose existence is known at second hand. Copies not seen are indicated by italics. Copies in private individual ownership are not usually included unless reference has already been made to them in other publications. Copies are listed in the order shown in the List of locations by countries, with Paris and London libraries placed first for France and the United Kingdom. Libraries in Cambridge and Oxford are grouped after the abbreviations 'Cam' and 'Ox' respectively.

livre occupée par le texte des *Essais* est indiquée comme suit: 'Quire' signifie 'au verso du dernier feuillet de chaque cahier'. 'Leaf' signifie 'au verso de chaque feuillet'. 'Unsigned pages' signifie 'à chaque page non signée'. 'Page' signifie 'à chaque page'. Le choix de réclames sert soit à distinguer l'édition, soit à faciliter la comparaison entre les éditions de la même famille.

Measurements: En tête est donnée la référence à la page typographique dont les dimensions suivent. '30 (+ 2) lines' signifie '30 lignes de texte plus 2 lignes pour le titre courant et la ligne de pied', c'est-à-dire, 32 lignes pour la page typographique entière. La hauteur de la page typographique entière est donnée entre parenthèses après la hauteur des seules lignes de texte, p. ex. 125 (132) × 70 mm. Le cas échéant, la largeur de la page typographique avec manchettes est signalée aussi.

Dans toutes les éditions décrites dans cet ouvrage le texte des *Essais* est en romain. Les citations latines et les sonnets de La Boétie sont en italique.

Privilège. Sous cette rubrique est noté l'essentiel du privilège ou de l'extrait du privilège, et, le cas échéant, de l'achevé d'imprimer.

Copies: Cette liste donne la localisation des exemplaires vus et non vus. Les exemplaires non vus sont en italique. Les exemplaires appartenant à des particuliers n'y figurent pas sauf dans le cas où des détails ont déjà été publiés à leur sujet. Les exemplaires sont présentés par pays dans l'ordre indiqué ci-après. Les bibliothèques de Paris et de Londres sont placées en tête de celles de la France et du Royaume-Uni. Les bibliothèques de Cambridge et d'Oxford sont groupées après les abréviations 'Cam' et 'Ox' respectivement.

LIST OF LOCATIONS BY
COUNTRIES

FRANCE: BN; Ars; Cass; Cath; Dut; Hist; Inst; Maz; Méd; Sorb; Stge; Abbv; Agen; Aix; Albi; Alen; Ami; Ang; Ann; Arr; Auch; Aut; Aux; Avig; Avr; Bar; Bayn; Bayx; Bes; Blo; Bord; Boul; Bourges; Bre; Brg; Caen; Carc; Carp; Châm; Chamb; Chan/C; Chan/F; Chas; Chât; Chau; Cler; Colm; Coul; Cout; Diep; Dij; Dôle; Drag; Eper; Epin; Etam; Evr; Foix; Gren; Hag; Hy; Laf; Lan; Laon; Lav; Lem; Lep; Lille; Loch; Lons; Louv; Ly; Mars; Meaux; Mel; Metz; Monb; Monp; Monp/U; Monta; Nanc; Nant; Neuf; Nev; Nîm; Nio; Orl; Pau; Péri; Perp; Poi; Ren; Ren/U; Rhei; Roa; Romo; Sal; Sél; Senl; Sens; Stb; Stde; Stdi; Ste; Sto; Stq; Stra; Tarb; Touln; Touls; Tours; Tro; Val; Vals; Vend; Verd; Vers; Ves; Vie

UK: BL; LI; LU; LUC; Aber; Cam: CUL; Em; Kings; Trin; Carl; Cole; Dur; Ed/N; Ed/NB; Ed/U; Eton; Ex; Gla; Leeds; Lich; Linc; Liv; Man; Mers; Newc; Nott; Ox: AS; Ball; Bod; CCC; Ch; Jes; Magd; Mert; Mn; New; Ori; Qu; RAS; Sthi; Stj; Tay; Wad; Worc; Shef; Sta; Wind

AUSTRIA: Graz/L; Graz/U; Vien/N; Vien/U

BELGIUM: Ant; Bru; Ghe

CZECHOSLOVAKIA: Pra/M; Pra/S

DENMARK: Cop; Thor

EIRE: Dub/M; Dub/T; Dub/W; Kilk

GERMANY: Aug; Boch; Brem; Cob; Coln; Det; Dill; Düss; Erl; Eut; Frei; Ful; Gött; Ham; Han; Heid; Mai; Mun; Nür; Old; Pom; Reg; Spe; Stut; Tüb; Ulm; Wolf; Wup; Würz; Xant

HUNGARY: Bud/M; Bud/N; Bud/U

ITALY: Bol/A; Bol/U; Bresc; Flo; Lucc; Mil/A; Mil/B; Mil/C; Mod; Pad/C; Pad/U; Parm; Pav; Regg; Rom/A; Rom/C; Rom/N; Rom/V; Trent; Vat; Ven; Vero

NETHERLANDS: Ams; Gron; Hague; Leeuw; Leid; Midd; Nijm; Utr

NORWAY: Oslo

POLAND: Byd; Kat; Krak/J; Krak/N; Poz; Tor; Wars/M; Wars/N; Wars/U; Wroc/O; Wroc/U

ROMANIA: Buc

SPAIN: Barc; Madr

SWITZERLAND: Aar; Bas; Bern; Frau; Frib; Gen; Gen/B; Laus; Laus/P; Luz; Scha; Sol; Stga; Wint; Zof; Zür

USA: Ariz; Bost; Chap; Chic/N; Chic/U; Clark; Gord; Harv; Hunt; Ill; Ind; Mich; NW; NY/M; NY/P; Ohio; Prin; Temp; USC; Virg/S; Virg/U; Virg/W; W/Cong; W/Folg; Yale

USSR: Len/N; Len/S; Mosc/G; Mosc/H; Mosc/L

YUGOSLAVIA: Belg; Lju

LIST OF EDITIONS OF THE
ESSAIS 1580—1700

1:      1580 Bordeaux, 8° (S Millanges)
2:      1582 Bordeaux, 8° (S Millanges)
3:      1587 Paris, 12° (J Richer)
4:      1588 Paris, 4° (A L'Angelier)
4†:   1588 Paris, 4° (The Bordeaux Copy)
5:      1593 Lyons, 8° (G La Grange)
6:      1595 Lyons, 12° (F Le Febvre)
7A: 1595 Paris, 2° (A L'Angelier, M Sonnius)
7A†:   1595 Paris, 2° (A L'Angelier, fully corrected in ink by Mlle de Gournay)
7B: Re-issue of No. 7A with reset sheets (A L'Angelier)
8:      1598 Paris, 8° (A L'Angelier)
9:      1600 Paris, 8° (A L'Angelier)
10:     1602 Paris, 8° (A L'Angelier)
11:     1602 Leiden A, 8° (J Doreau)
12:     1602 Leiden B or Cologny, 8° (J Doreau, with indexes)
12A: Re-issue of No. 12 as 1609 Geneva (J Can)
12B: Re-issue of No. 12 as 1616 Geneva (P Albert)
13:     1604 Paris, 8° (A L'Angelier)
14:     1608 Paris, 8° (M Nivelle, J Petit-pas, C Rigaud, Veuve D Salis, C Sevestre)
15:     1609 Leiden, 8° (J Doreau)
16:     1611 Paris, 8° (F Gueffier, M Nivelle, J Petit-pas, C Rigaud, C Sevestre)
17:     1616 Cologny or Geneva, 8° (P Albert or no name)
18:     1617 Rouen, 8° (T Daré, J Osmont, M de Preaulx, R Valentin)
19:     [1617] Envers, 8° (A Maire)
20:     1617 Paris, 4° (J Petit-pas, C Rigaud, F Gueffier, M Nivelle, C Sevestre, Veuve D Salis)
21:     1619 Rouen A, 8° (T Daré, Veuve T Daré, J Osmont, A Ouyn, R Valentin, P Daré)
21A: Re-issue of No. 21 as 1620 Rouen (M de Preaulx)
22:     [1619] Rouen B, 8° (N Angot, J Berthelin, J Besongne)
23:     1625 Paris, 4° (Veuve R Dallin, F Targa, R Bertault, N Bessin, R Boutonné, M Collet, E Daubin, C Hulpeau, T de La Ruelle, G Loyson, G and A Robinot, P Rocolet, E Saucié)

23A: Re-issue of No. 23 as 1626 Paris (F Targa)

23B: No. 23 with MS title-page, 1639 Paris (D Douceur)

24:   1627 Rouen, 8° (J Cailloüé, L Du Mesnil, R Féron, G de La Haye, P de La Motte, R Valentin, J Berthelin, J Besongne)

24A: Re-issue of No. 24 as 1632 Paris (P Chevalier)

25:   1635 Paris, 2° (First issue, T Du Bray, P Rocolet; Second issue, J Camusat)

26:   1636 Paris, 8° (M d'Auplet, P Billaine, L Boulanger, M Collet, M Durand, J Germont, N and J de La Coste, S de La Fosse, P L'Amy, G Loyson, J Villery and J Guignard)

27:   1640 Paris, 2° (M Blageart, A Courbé, R Denain)

28:   1641 Rouen, 8° (J Berthelin)

29:   1649 Paris, 8° (M Blageart)

30:   1652 Paris, 2° (A Courbé, E Cousterot, Veuve M Du Puis, Veuve S Huré and S Huré, T Joly, P Le Petit, J-B Loyson, S Piget, P Rocolet)

31:   1657 Paris, 2° (C Angot, D Bechet and L Billaine, E Couterot, Veuve M Du Puis, S Huré and F Leonard, P L'Amy, J and E Langlois, P Le Petit, J-B Loyson, J Piot, P Rocolet, T Jolly)

32:   1659 Paris, 12° (C Journel, J-B Loyson)

33:   1659 Amsterdam, 12° (A Michiels) or Brussels, 12° (F Foppens)

34:   1669 Paris, 12° (L Rondet and C Journel and R Chevillion)

35:   1669 Lyons, 12° (A Olyer, A Besson)

36:   *L'Esprit des Essais*, 1677 Paris, 8° (C de Sercy)

37:   *Pensées*, 1700 Paris, 12° (J Anisson)

1: 1580 Bordeaux

(a) Vol i, first state; without Montaigne's titles [125 mm]

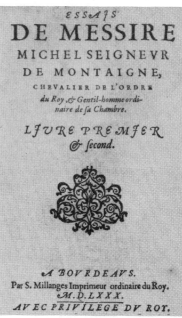

(b) Vol i, second state; with Montaigne's titles [128 mm]

(c) Vol ii, first state; without Montaigne's titles [128 mm]

(d) Vol ii, second state; with Montaigne's titles [132 mm]

(*e*) Vol ii, third state; with Montaigne's
titles and four corrections [132 mm]

Title-page: There are two states of the tp of vol i and three states of the tp
of vol ii. The main difference in both vols is the addition of Montaigne's
titles. Copies without his titles are rare and their addition is more
probable than their suppression.[1] The second state of the tp of vol i
replaces Millanges's device with an arabesque ornament, but all other
states have Millanges's device. The third state of the tp of vol ii has four
corrections: (i) line 3, defective G replaced; (ii) line 4, comma added; (iii)
line 7, *Ɛ* replaced by *E*; (iv) line 7, stop deleted.

(*a*) Vol i, first state, without Montaigne's titles, Millanges's device
(LU, Gen/B 1).

(*b*) Vol i, second state, with Montaigne's titles, arabesque ornament.

(*c*) Vol ii, first state, without Montaigne's titles (Bord 3, Gen/B 1,
Yale, Prin).

(*d*) Vol ii, second state, with Montaigne's titles (LU).

(*e*) Vol ii, third state, with Montaigne's titles and four corrections
(Man).

[1] See F Moureau, 'Sur des exemplaires des *Essais* en vente à la Foire de Francfort
(automne 1581)', *BSAM*, V, 9 (1974), pp 57—9; A Salles, 'Un exemplaire de 1580 coté
600.000 fr.' *BSAM*, II, 2 (1937), pp 85—6.

Collation: 8°: i: π^4 A—2H^8; ii:$^2\pi^2$ 3A—4S^8 [\$5(4)(−X4, 3C4, 3E4, 3P3)
signed, arabic numerals; missigning i: G2 as 2G, 2A5 as A5; ii: 3A5 as
Ii5, 3K2 as kkk2, 3K3 as Kkk 3 (for KKk 3), 3K4 as kkk4, 3Y5 as 2Y5,
4G4 as 3G4, 4K2—5 as Kkkk2(3,4,5), 4Q2 as 2Q2 (*variants*: not signing
3S2, missigning 2A2 as Aa, 4O3 as 30oOO)]; i: 252 leaves; ii: 330
leaves; pp i: [*8*] *1* *2*—37 37 38 40—41 41—42 44—52 35 54—59 19 60
62—117 117—118 120—121 121—122 124—125 125—126 128—240
240—256 259 258—263 294 266—267 298 269—277 *278*—*292* [sonnets]
294—303 *304* 305—319 230 321—322 321—322 325—338 338—408 408
410—468 479 470—485 488 487—496 [*variants*: not numbering 104,
misnumbering 337 338 338 as 337 334 338, and 479 as 496]; ii: [*4*] *1*
2—10 508 12—29 30 [inside HL] 31—41 43 42 *44* 45—55 54 [inside HL]
55 58—59 58—59 62 [inside HL] 63 62 [inside HL] 65—76 77 [inside
HL] 78—84 83 86—87 85 [inside HL] 86 90—91 89—90 95—96 93 93
95—101 72 103—106 167 108—126 125 128—142 133 104 145—186 188
189 189—200 202—203 203—206 208 209 209—210 212—213
213—214 218 217 217 218 220—221 221 223—239 239 243 242 423
244—246 249 248—249 252—253 152 253 256—272 272—274
276—277 270 279 279 281—288 288—314 215 316—335 335—343 345
345 286 347—366 366—408 309 410—438 339 440—472 573—574
475—476 506—507 479—480 510—511 483—484 514—515 487 490
518—519 463 476 522 493—509 509—510 512—513 512—513
516—517 516 571 520—521 520 221 524—526 528 528—530 532
532—535 536 [inside HL] 537—548 349 550—568 529 570—595 566
597—637 639—650 *651*—*653* [=656]. (See note 3)

Contents: i: π1: Title (verso blank); π2: *Au lecteur*; π2^v: Table of contents
Bk I; π4: *Privilège*; π4^v: Errata for Bk I; A1: *Essais* Bk I; ii: $^2\pi$1: Title
(verso blank); $^2\pi$2: Table of contents Bk II; 3A1: *Essais* Bk II; 4S7^v:
Errata for Bk II; 4S8^v: blank.

HT: i: π2   Au lecteur.
       π2^v LES CHAPITRES DV | PREMIER LIVRE.
       π4^v LES PLVS INSIGNES | FAVTES SVRVEN-
              VES | EN L'IMPRESSION | du premier liure.
       A1   [headpiece: 2 central winged putti back to back,
              flowers, foliage] ESSAIS DE | MICHEL DE MON-
              | TAIGNE. | LIVRE PREMIER.
    ii: $^2\pi$2   LES CHPITRES [*sic*] DV | LIVRE SECOND.
       3A1   [headpiece = A1] ESSAIS DE MICHEL DE |

MONTAIGNE.|LIVRE SECOND. (In many copies the headpiece is reversed.)

4S7ᵛ LES FAVTES PLVS GRAN-|DES, QVI SE SONT FAITES|en l'impreſſion du ſecond liure.

RT: ESSAIS DE M. DE MONTA.|LIVRE PREMIER [SECOND]. [There are numerous press-corrections; the following variations are not necessarily found in all copies: ESSIS 4O6ᵛ 4S4ᵛ; MONT 4L6ᵛ 4N8ᵛ 4O5ᵛ 4Q7ᵛ; MONT. once or more in BD—IT—Z 2A—H 3E—HKM—Z 4A—CE—HKLOPS; MONNTA. A5ᵛ C2ᵛ D4ᵛ E4ᵛ; LIBER A6,8; LIRVE 2F3,8 2H6; LIRE 3Y8 4A4 4D5 4F2 4I6 4M3; LVRE 3P1; LIVꓤE 4H1 4K8 4O7 4Q3; PREMIERE. A3,5,7; SECOND. (for PREMIER.) 2F1,5; PREMIER. (for SECOND.) 3A3 3F3 3G6 3N8 3Q7 3S2; SECND. 4B1 4D8; ESSAIS DE M. DE MONTA. 3E7 (verso RT); LIVRE SECOND. 4L3ᵛ (recto RT); LIVRE SECOND.|ESSAIS DE M. DE MONTA. 3G4ᵛ—5ʳ; no RT G4ᵛ T8]

CW: Unsigned pages but with irregularities. i: H3ᵛ ceſte   Q8ᵛ grand 2G4ᵛ de la   ii: 3G8ᵛ nous   3R8ʳ a tort   4L8ᵛ nulle

Measurements (i: P1): 21(+2) lines. 125(133) × 70 mm. 20 lines = 120 mm. (ii: 3P1): 25(+2) lines. 120(129) × 71mm. 20 lines = 97 mm.

Privilège: General *privilège* to Simon Millanges for 8 years dating from the first printing of any book. Paris, 9 May 1579, signed DE PVIBERAL.

Notes: 1. Composition by formes is attested by the presence of long and short pages, some cramped with many abbreviations, some well-spaced; see for example T7ʳ—8ᵛ, 3B5ᵛ—6ʳ, 3B7ᵛ—8ʳ, 3C4ʳ, 3F3ʳ, 3F7ᵛ—8ʳ. The alternation of the number of leaves signed in vol ii strongly suggests the collaboration of two compositors.

$5 signed	$4 signed
3A (signed I15)	3B
3C	3D
3E	3F
3G, 3H, 3I	3K
3L	3M
3N, 3O	3P

3Q, 3R	3S
3T, 3V	3X
3Y, 3Z, 4A	4B
4C, 4D	4E
4F, 4G	4H
4I, 4K	4L
4M	4N
4O, 4P, 4Q, 4R, 4S	

2. Three asterisks on S1 replace the *Discours de la servitude volontaire* of La Boétie which was to have been the centrepiece of Bk I in Chap 28. The 29 sonnets of La Boétie which Montaigne publishes instead as Chap 29 are in italics with no headline or pagination (S3^v—T2^v). The new Chap 29 is wrongly numbered Chap 28 (S2) repeating the chapter number of *De l'amitié* which precedes, and this error continues for the next two chapters *De la moderation* and *Des Cannibales*, which are erroneously numbered 29 and 30 respectively. Chaps 45, 46, 47 are also wrongly numbered 43, 45, 46 on 2D1^v, 2D2^v, 2D7 respectively.

3. The pagination of vol ii is very irregular with so many variants that it is impossible to reconstruct an ideal pagination. Probably no two copies are the same. The pagination statement of Bod is given by way of example.[2]

4. The missigning of 2A2 as Aa means there are two leaves signed Aa, which in Nant and Ed/NB has caused an error of folding. Nant has only six leaves which are in the wrong order. In Ed/NB the order is 2,1,4,3,6,5,8,7.

5. Because of the errors of pagination the Errata often refer to the wrong page. A number of the corrections listed in the Errata have been made in the text, four of which are mentioned by D Martin in his facsimile of the 1580 edition (ii, 654–5); the following is a fuller list of Errata corrections which have been made in the text, though not always exactly as indicated in the Errata. The page and line numbers have been adjusted where necessary and the actual readings in the text are given in brackets (see Plate 1):

i: C1^v p 34 line 1   *for* different   *read* defferent [desferent]
   T5 p 298 line 19 *for* font   *read* foint [foit]

[2] See also A Armaingaud, 'Editions des *Essais* de Montaigne de 1588 et de 1580', *Intermédiaire des chercheurs et des curieux*, 10 June 1902.

	Y7ᵛ	p 350	line 14	*for* deffauts [deffautz]	*read* effects [effaitz]
ii:	3L2ᵛ	p 161	line 2	*after* eftu	*add* de &
			lines 3—4	*delete* de &	[*to read*: eftude &]
			line 15	*for* ideo	*read* adeo
	3L8ᵛ	p 173	line 14	*for* humectat	*read* humectant [humetãt]
	3M5	p 182	line 18	*for* Refes [refes]	*read* Refnes [refnes]
	4K5	p 517	line 24	*for* Bedonius [Bedonins]	*read* Bedoins
	4K8ᵛ	p 524	line 6	*for* retenoit	*read* reieteroit [metteroit]
	4M6ᵛ	p 552	line 8	*for* non	*read* nom

6. J Marchand claims that the Errata of vol ii in the copy which is said to have belonged to Queen Elizabeth has an extra line not found in any other copy.[3] This is not so. In fact the last line has been filled out with an extra erratum: 'pag. 646. lig. 12. pour ie metez, il'. This erratum added in the course of printing can be found in Chau, Nio, LU, Gen/B 2, Chic/U, Chap, and perhaps others (see Plate 2).

7. Besides the press-corrections, already noted, of signature, pagination, running-titles, the last line of the Errata of vol ii and the errata listed in note 5, there are many other press-corrections in the text, eleven of which have been listed by A Salles based on the collation of twelve copies:[4]

			FIRST STATE	CORRECTED STATE
i:	C8	line 7	*potens*	*potens ſui*
	C8	line 17	ne porte, que	ne porte, pas q̃
	O8ᵛ	line 12	moins qui le doit	moins qu'il ne doit
ii:	3A2ᵛ	line 15	nous voirons	nous verriõs
	3A6ᵛ	lines 19—20	il defchargeoit tous	il fe defchargeoit de tous
	3A6ᵛ	line 23	au fenat	du fenat
	3Z1ᵛ	line 5	doit	droit

[3] 'Le Montaigne de la reine Elisabeth d'Angleterre (1580)', *BSAM*, III, 22 (1962), p 23 n3.

[4] 'La première édition des *Essais* de Montaigne (1580): corrections et retouches', *BBB*, 1931, pp 6—12; 'Quelques notes sur l'édition princeps des *Essais* de 1580', *BSAM*, II, 10 (1941), pp 12—13. It is unfortunate that Salles published only a selection of the 140—150 press-variants which he discovered, since the task of collation must be done again. Rochebilière left a copy on which were marked all the variants he had discovered (Claudin, *Bibliographie*, p 285, No 818), but the whereabouts of this copy was unknown to Dr Sayce.

3Z1ᵛ	lines 20–21	nous confeille	nous y confeille
3Z3ᵛ	line 1	[capitalemẽt defendus *omitted*]	capitalemẽt defendus
4G7ᵛ	line 23	vile indice	vilein vice
4K1	line 18	deflogement d'affeurance	deflogement & qu'il eut befoin d'affeurance

These variants have been confirmed in the copies examined except those of 3Z1ᵛ and 3Z3ᵛ (the same forme) where only the corrected state has been found; of course this in no way disproves the existence of the first state. As one would expect, the corrected state occurs much more frequently though not in the case of 4K.

8. A catchword not occurring elsewhere is found in Nio on Q3ᵛ: moins. Since it does not correspond to the text on the following page it was almost certainly suppressed.

9. In about 80% of copies examined 2G3 has the letters *gsit* at the foot of the page. This is doubtless an accident of no significance.

Copies: BN1 (Rés. Z 2764); BN2 (Rés. Z 2765); BN3 (Rés. p.Z 1965); BN4 (Z Payen 1, signature of Mlle de Montaigne, sent by Millanges to Talet); BN5 (Z Payen 2, monogram ER on binding); Dut (J.-A. de Thou, Naigeon and Nodier copy); Inst; Bar; Bord 1 (PF 6925 Rés.); Bord 2 (PF 6926 Rés.); Bord 3 (S 4754 Rés., Lalanne copy, marginal corrections);[5] Châm; Chan/C; Chau; Nant; Nio (lacks both tps); *Romo*[6]; UK: BL; LU; Ed/NB; Man; Ox: Bod.   SWITZERLAND: Gen/B 1 (ML Schiff copy); Gen/B 2; *Zür*.   USA: Chap; Chic/N; Chic/U; Clark; Harv; Hunt; *Ind*; NY/M 1 (E 37 D); NY/M 2 (Heineman 203); Prin; Virg/U; Yale (reproduced in facsimile by D Martin).   USSR: *Len/N*.

---

[5] See on this copy, R Dezeimeris, 'Un nouvel exemplaire annoté des *Essais* de Montaigne', *La Gironde*, 31 August 1881; A Salles, 'Les deux jumeaux de 1580', *BSAM*, II, 3 (1938), pp 23—4, and 'Quelques notes sur l'édition princeps', *BSAM*, II, 10 (1941), pp 12—13.

[6] L Desgraves, *Bibliographie bordelaise*, p 123, No 51. He also mentions a copy at Rennes, Bibliothèque municipale, shelfmark S. 538 (*ibid.*, p 37, No 51) but Dr Sayce was unable to find this copy in either the Bibliothèque municipale or the Bibliothèque de l'Université at Rennes.

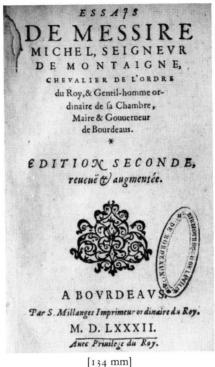

[134 mm]

Title-page: The wording is the same as No 1: 1580 Bordeaux but adds Montaigne's new title *Maire & Gouuerneur de Bordeaus* and *Edition seconde, reueuë & augmentée*. The ornament is the same as on No 1, tp (*b*).

Collation: 8°: *⁴ A—3D⁸ 3E⁴ [\$5 signed, arabic numerals; missigning 2K2 as Klz2, 2K4 as Klz4, 2Y2 as Y2, 2Y3 as Y3 (*variants*: not signing F1, missigning F5 as F, not signing H5, missigning K4 as 4, L2 as L, V2 as Λ2 (or perhaps A2), 2C2 as C2, 2T5 as T5)]; 408 leaves; pp [*8*] *1* 2—88 89 [inside HL] 90—123 224 225 126—127 228 229 230 131—133 234 235 136—164 165 [inside HL] 166—202 103 204—302 305 304—305 *306* 307—*557* 568 559—*657* 650 659—751 724 753—759 750 761—793 795 796 796—797 797 799—806 [*2*] [*variants*: misnumbering 60 as 160, 784 as 788, not numbering 95, 743].

Contents: *1: Title (verso blank); *2: *Au lecteur*; *2ᵛ: Table of contents; *4ᵛ: Errata; A1: *Essais* Bk I; V1ᵛ: blank; V2: *Essais* Bk II; 3E4: *Privilège* (verso blank).

HT: A1 [headpiece: 2 central winged putti back to back, flowers, foliage] ESSAIS DE|MICHEL DE MON-|TAIGNE.| Liure Premier.

V2 [as A1 except] Liure Second.

RT: ESSAIS DE M. DE MONTA. | LIVRE PREMIER [SECOND]. [ESIⱯSS (SAI inverted) 2R7ᵛ 2T8ᵛ; ESSAEIS 2G3ᵛ 2I4ᵛ 2K7ᵛ 2M8ᵛ 2N1ᵛ 2P2ᵛ 2R4ᵛ 2S7ᵛ 2V8ᵛ 2Y8ᵛ 2Z3ᵛ 3B4ᵛ 3C7ᵛ 3D1ᵛ; MONTAI. A5ᵛ C6ᵛ D3ᵛ F2ᵛ G7ᵛ I8ᵛ K1ᵛ M3ᵛ O2ᵛ P5ᵛ R6ᵛ S3ᵛ V4ᵛ X7ᵛ Z8ᵛ 2A1ᵛ 2C5ᵛ E8ᵛ; MON. 2F5ᵛ 2H6ᵛ 2I3ᵛ 2L4ᵛ 2M5ᵛ 2O8ᵛ 2P1ᵛ 2R2ᵛ 2S5ᵛ 2V6ᵛ 2X3ᵛ 2Z2ᵛ 3A8ᵛ 3C1ᵛ; LIARE A4; SECOND. (for PREMIER.) K1, 8; PREMIER (no stop) M5 N2 P2 R6 T7; verso RT on F5, L3 (MONT.), Z4; MONT. once or more in A—KM—Z 2A—2Z 3A—3E; no RT for sonnets L3ᵛ—M3ʳ]

CW: Unsigned pages. E2ᵛ la peur I8ᵛ CHAP. T7ʳ la faut 2F4ᵛ d'orge 2Q4ᵛ Au reſte 3B4ᵛ Alexandre

Measurements (O5): 30(+2) lines. 125(132) × 70 mm. 20 lines = 84 mm.

Privilège: As in No 1: 1580 Bordeaux.

Notes: 1. Set from a copy of No 1: 1580 Bordeaux with MS corrections and additions by Montaigne.[1] The orns on A1 and V2 are the same as on A1 and 3A1 in 1580 Bordeaux. The RTs [ESSAIES] [MONTAI.] [MON.] tend to recur every third forme, e.g.

C	outer	MONTAI. C6ᵛ	E	inner	
C	inner		F	outer	MONTAI. F2ᵛ
D	outer		F	inner	
D	inner	MONTAI. D3ᵛ	G	outer	
E	outer		G	inner	MONTAI. G7ᵛ

2. On K4 in Gord eight words of the last line left of *tel* are inverted.

[1] See M Françon, 'L'édition des *Essais* de 1582', *BSAM*, IV, 14 (1968), pp 3—32 (which is reprinted as the preface to his facsimile edition of the Harvard copy of 1582); 'Notes sur l'édition de 1582', *BSAM*, IV, 7 (1966), pp 82—3; A Salles, 'L'édition de 1582', *BSAM*, II, 4 (1938), pp 27—8.

3. Bord has numerous MS corrections mainly of a proof-reading kind, often of Errata. Some are very similar to Montaigne's method of correcting in No 4†: 1588 The Bordeaux Copy.

Copies:[2] BN1 (Z Payen 3); BN2 (Z Payen 4); BN3 (Z Payen 5); BN4 (Z 19571); BN5 (Rés. Z 2766); BN6 (16° Z 6527); Bord (see note 3); *Lons*; Tro; Vers. UK: BL; LU; Ed/N (lacks *1, 2, gathering L wrongly folded); Ox: Bod. BELGIUM: Ghe. DENMARK: *Thor*. SWITZERLAND: Gen/B. USA: Chic/U (Voltaire's signature above *Au lecteur*); Gord; Harv (reproduced in facsimile by M Françon, lacks 3E4); NY/P; Prin; *Yale*.

3: 1587

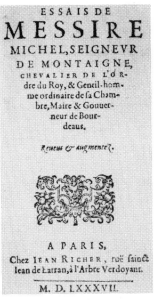

ESSAIS DE
MESSIRE
MICHEL, SEIGNEVR
DE MONTAIGNE,
CHEVALIER DE L'OR-
dre du Roy, & Gentil-hom-
me ordinaire de sa Cham-
bre, Maire & Gouuer-
neur de Bour-
deaus.

Reueus & augmentez.

A PARIS,
Chez IEAN RICHER, ruë sainct
Iean de Latran, à l'Arbre Verdoyant.

M. D. LXXXVII.

[113 mm]

Title-page: The text of the title is the same as No 2: 1582 Bordeaux, but lacks *Edition seconde* and modifies *reueuë & augmentée*. In most copies the tp is conjugate with *4, but in some it has been remounted or the chain-lines differ from *4 (see note 3).

[2] See L Desgraves, *Bibliographie bordelaise*, p 40, No 75 and p 123, No 75.

Collation: 12°: *⁴ A—Z¹² 2A—2Y¹² [$6 signed, roman numerals; missigning 2R4 as R4]; 544 leaves; pp [*8*] 1—393 384 385 396 399 388 389 400 403 392 393 404 405 396 397 408—1075 [*5*] [*variants*: misnumbering 800 as oo].

Contents: *1: Title (verso blank); *2: *Au lecteur*; *2ᵛ: Table of contents; A1: *Essais*. 2Y10ᵛ—12ᵛ: blank.

HT: A1   [headpiece: central putto's head, volutes, fruit] ESSAIS
                 DE | MICHEL DE MON- | TAIGNE. | Liure premier.
     R10ᵛ   [2 rows of 9 arabesque type-orns] [as A1 except] Liure
                 Second.

RT: ESSAIS DE M. DE MONT. | LIVRE PREMIER [SECOND].
[D EMONT. 2X2ᵛ; MONT.t 2Y2ᵛ; PREMIER (no stop) D9 F8 H6 K3;
ESSAIS, LIVRE SECOND. R11; no RT for sonnets K4ᵛ—11ʳ]

CW: Quire. *4ᵛ ESSAIS G12ᵛ fon N12ᵛ Plutarque T12ᵛ longueur
2B12ᵛ chemin 2L12ᵛ les 2V12ᵛ apoplexie:

Measurements (H2): 27 (+2) lines. 113(120) × 58 mm. 20 lines = 84 mm.

Privilège: None.

Notes: 1. This edition is a resetting of No 2: 1582 Bordeaux. It may have been unauthorised or the result of an agreement between Richer and Millanges, the holder of the *privilège*, which did not expire until March 1588.

2. It was probably printed by Jean Du Carroy whose name and address are given in the *achevé d'imprimer* dated 14 September 1587 of Plutarch, *Oeuvres morales*, Paris, Jean Richer, vol ii (Lincoln Cathedral). The press-work of this is similar to Richer's 1587 *Essais*.

3. Jean Marchand has suggested that Richer may have intended to re-issue some copies of this edition with a new tp, perhaps dated 1588, advertising it as the fourth edition. It is certainly true that at least five copies lack the normal tp, which is replaced either by a facsimile or by a MS title, and in other cases the remounted tp or the difference in the chain-lines between the tp and *4 make it suspect. This hypothesis remains tenable, but there is no new evidence in its favour.[1]

---

[1] *Hypothèse sur la quatrième édition des Essais de Montaigne*, Bordeaux, 1937.

4. On R3 the chapter heading of I 55 is *Des Senateurs*, but it is correct in the table of contents.

Copies: BN1 (Rés. Z 2767, tp possibly facsimile); BN2 (Z Payen 6); BN3 (Z Payen 7, two tps); BN4 (8°Z Don 597(1), tp torn and remounted); Ars (near ideal copy); Sorb (lacks gathering I); Stge; Bes; Bord (tp replaced by facsimile, bound in 4 vols); Monp; Péri; Vers.   UK: Linc; Ox: Bod (tp torn, facsimile added, 2R9 torn out and replaced by facsimile). HUNGARY: *Bud/U*.   ITALY: Bol/U.   SWITZERLAND: Gen/B. USA: Chic/U (lacks gathering 2V, bound in 2 vols); Clark (tp remounted); Gord; Harv; Prin (chain-lines on tp possibly different from *4); *Virg/W*; Yale (chain-lines on tp do not match *4).   USSR: *Len/N*.

Note on the missing edition

The next edition to be listed, No 4: 1588, is described on its title-page as the fifth edition but only three are known before it. Possible explanations for this enigma were outlined by Dr Sayce in 1972 and there is no new evidence to modify what he said then:

> What has become of the missing edition? La Croix du Maine, a contemporary witness, speaks of editions printed at Rouen and elsewhere (not later than 1584),[1] but no copy has ever been found and it seems highly unlikely that whole editions of an unbanned book could disappear completely. Strowski mentions a possible Paris edition of 1584 'chez R. Estienne et L'Angelier',[2] but without evidence. More promising is the copy of the 1580 edition which belonged to Guillaume Guizot, with an extra III stamped on the date (therefore 1583),[3] but the most plausible, and technical, explanation is that of M Jean Marchand: starting from the fact that several copies of the 1587 edition have the title-page removed, he supposes that Richer planned a new issue with a cancel title-page, a plan abandoned when Richer heard of the forthcoming l'Angelier edition.[4] To these hypotheses may be added a simpler one: apart from the possibility of mere oversight, the substitution of fifth for fourth edition may have been prompted by the desire to suggest that the book was selling better than it was, a trick not unknown even today.[5]

[1] *Premier volume de la bibliothèque*, Paris, 1584, p 328.

[2] *Les Essais; reproduction en phototypie*, i, 7.

[3] J Le Petit, *Bibliographie des principales éditions originales d'écrivains français*, 1888, p 100.

[4] J Marchand, *Hypothèse*, p 14. See also No 3: 1587, note 3.

[5] R A Sayce, *The Essays of Montaigne*, pp. 11—12. See also A Salles, 'A propos de la troisième (?) édition des *Essais* jusqu'ici introuvable', *BSAM*, II, 1 (1937), pp 12—13; *ibid*., II, 2 (1937), pp 53—4; *ibid*., II, 6 (1939), pp 60—1, with facsimile of the date on the Guizot copy; J. Marchand, 'L'édition des *Essais* de 1587', *BSAM*, II, 9 (1940), pp 57—8.

4: 1588

ESSAIS DE

MICHEL SEIGNEVR

DE MONTAIGNE.

*Cinquiefme edition, augmentée d'vn troi-
fiefme liure: & de fix cens additions aux deux premiers.*

A PARIS,

Chez ABEL L'ANGELIER,
au premier pillier de la grand
Salle du Palais.

Auec Priuilege du Roy.

M . D . LXXXVIII

(*a*) Printed title; date added in MS [134 mm]

Title-page: (*a*) Printed title, date added in MS (NY/M 1).

      (*b*) Engraved title, first state, *orand* for *grand*, no date.

      (*c*) Engraved title, second state, *grand* corrected, date 1588.

    Tp (*a*) without date occupies the lower two-thirds of the page. M.D. LXXXVIII has been added in MS. It is attached to a stub in the only copy known, though tp (*c*) is pasted in from another copy. If (*a*) is genuine, what is the explanation? Perhaps it was a temporary tp for an advance copy before the engraved tp was ready. Perhaps L'Angelier intended to publish an 8vo edition. Perhaps it was a specimen for the engraver to work from, since the engraving follows it closely and in its first state also lacks the date. Perhaps it was intended to print the title in letterpress within the engraved border of (*b*) or (*c*). Some copies with tp (*c*) seem to lack the colon after *liure* but this may be an inking fault (e.g. in Péri, Chan/C). The engraved tp is larger than the printed pages and so is cropped in many copies.

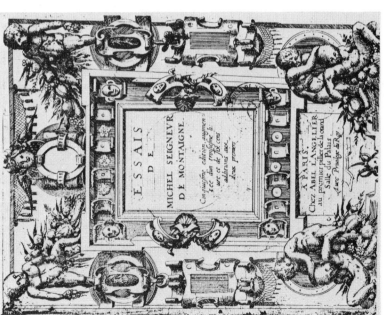

(b) Engraved title; first state, *orand* for *grand*; no date [235 mm]   (c) Engraved title; second state, *grand* corrected; date 1588 [235 mm]

Collation: 4°: ã⁴ A—6L⁴ [$3 signed, roman numerals; missigning 4E2 as 3E2, 4E3 as 4E2, 5P3 as 6P3, 6K1 as Kkkkkk (for KKKKKk), 6K2 as Kkkkkk ij (*variant*: not signing K2)]; 508 leaves; fols [4] 1—38 29 40—59 50 61—82 53 84—97 89 99—105 89 107—111 103 113—129 122 131—154 355 356 357 358 159—160 361 154 363 356 365 366 367 368 569 370 371 372 373 374 375 376 169—270 171 264 273—286 278 288—367 359 369—496 [=504] [*variants*: misnumbering 61 (Q1) as 48, 63(Q3) as 50, 443 as 44 or as 442].

Contents: ã1: Title (verso blank); ã2: *Au lecteur*; ã2ᵛ: Table of contents; ã4ᵛ blank; A1: *Essais* Bk I; 2L4ᵛ blank; 2M1: *Essais* Bks II and III; 6L4ᵛ: *Privilège*.

HT: ã2 [headpiece: central horned head, 2 dogs] Au Lecteur.

A1 [double row of 20 arabesque type-orns] ESSAIS DE MICHEL | DE MONTAIGNE. | Livre Premier.

2M1 [as A1 except] Livre second.

4T4 [as A1 except] Livre troisiesme.

RT: ESSAIS DE M. DE MONTA.|LIVRE PREMIER [SECOND] [TROISIESME]. [MONT. once in BEGKMOQRY 2ADFHKNPRTXZ 3BDFHKMOPSVY 4ACEGILNPRTXZ 5 BDFHKMOQSVY 6ACEGIL; PREMIER. (for SECOND.) 2M2,3,4 2N1,3 (*variant*: IVRE. 6G1); no RT for sonnets T3—X1ᵛ]

CW: Quire. P4ᵛ en 2E4ᵛ ce 3F4ᵛ plus 4G4ᵛ vne 5A4ᵛ *Cum* 6E4ᵛ nous

Measurements (2M3): 32(+2) lines. 191(202) × 121 mm. 20 lines = 120 mm.

Privilège: To Abel L'Angelier for 9 years to publish 'les *Essais du Seigneur de Montagne*, reueus & amplifiez, en plus de cinq cens passages, auec l'augmentation d'vn troisiesme liure'. Paris, 4 June 1588, signed DVDVIT.

Notes: 1. The first two books were presumably set from a copy of No 2: 1582 Bordeaux with MS modifications and additions by Montaigne, and the third book, which appears here for the first time, from the author's MS. This is the last edition published before Montaigne's death on 13 September 1592.

2. After fol 169 (2Y1), which should be numbered 177, the error of 8 leaves is maintained to the end of the book, so that the last leaf should be numbered 504.

3. Bru 1, NY/P and Prin are annotated in contemporary hands. The annotations in Prin are very numerous and may be the work of someone acquainted with Montaigne.[1]

Copies:[2] (*a, b* or *c* indicates state of tp): BN1 (Rés. Z 1113, *c*); BN2 (Rés. Z 1114, *b*); BN3 (Z Payen 8, *c*); BN4 (Z Payen 9, *b*); BN5 (Z Payen 10—12, preface from 1625); BN6 (Z Payen 13, fols. 3—44 only); BN7 (8°Z Don 597(2), *b*); Méd (lacks gatherings ã and A; tp and gathering A made up in MS); Avig (*c*); Bes (gathering ã replaced in facsimile, 2S2.3 inverted, 6L4 back to front); Bord 1 (S 1238 Rés., see No. 4†: 1588, *c*); Bord 2 (S 1238 Bis Rés., *b*); Bord 3(S 1240 Rés., gathering ã and 6L2—4 replaced in facsimile, bound in 3 vols); Chan/C (*c*); Ly 1(319.799, *c*); Ly 2 (409.287, *c*); Nant (ã1—3 detached, *c*); Péri (*c*); *Touls*; Vers (*c*). UK: BL1 (C.79.b.15, *c*); BL2(G.2427, portrait of Montaigne tipped in facing tp, *c*); LU(*c*); Ox:Bod(*c*). AUSTRIA: *Vien/N 1* (BE.4.P.1, *c*); *Vien/N 2*(71.V.51, *c*). BELGIUM: Bru 1 (VI 53716B, *c*); Bru 2(FS IX 80. 6628, *c*). DENMARK: *Thor*.[3] GERMANY: *Stut*. ROMANIA: *Buc*. USA: Chap (full size tp, *b*); Chic/U (full size tp, *c*); Gord (*c*); Harv (tp remounted, *c*); NY/M 1(E37D.2536, *a*); NY/M 2(E37D.18416, *c*); NY/P (*c*); Prin (*c*); Yale (*c*).

---

[1] On these annotations, see A Salles, 'Quelques exemplaires annotés des *Essais*', *BSAM*, II, 1 (1937), pp 39—40; 'A propos de l'exemplaire Le Brun', *BSAM*, II, 3 (1938), p 29, for its location at Princeton; 'Quelques annotations de l'exemplaire Le Brun', *BSAM*, II, 5 (1939), p 28, for some examples of the annotations.

[2] See A Salles, 'Les premières éditions', *BSAM*, II, 2(1937), p 90, for a copy from Montesquieu's library.

[3] F Thorkelin, 'Mon plus cher livre', *BSAM*, V, 10—11 (1974), pp 109—10.

[235 mm]

Title-page: As No 4: 1588 (*c*), but with MS modifications. In the oval cartouche is added *Montaigne*, and beneath ESSAIS DE is added *Ex libris foellient. s. Aussonii burdigalensis*, neither in Montaigne's hand. The five lines *Cinquiesme edition . . . premiers* are deleted and beneath in Montaigne's hand is written *Sixieme edition. Viresque acquirit eundo*.

Collation: As No 4: 1588, K2 signed, misnumbering 61 (Q1) as 48, 63 (Q3) as 50, 443 as 44.

Contents: As No 4: 1588, but ã1ᵛ has MS instructions to the printer; most pages have MS corrections to the text and additions in the margins; the sonnets are deleted.

HT: As No 4: 1588.

RT: A1ᵛ corrected in MS from 'ESSAIS DE M. DE MONTA.' to 'ESSAIS DE MICHEL DE' and A2 corrected in MS from 'LIVRE PREMIER.' to 'MONTAIGNE LIV.I.'. This corresponds to an instruction on ã1ᵛ: '[M]ettez mon nõ tout du long sur chaque face Essais de michel de | [M]ontaigne liu.1.'. 6G1 prints LIVRE.

CW, *Measurements*, *Privilège*: As No. 4:1588.

Notes: 1. The presence of the handwriting of Mlle de Gournay on fol 42ᵛ, continued immediately on the same line by Montaigne, suggests that this addition, and probably those by Mlle de Gournay on fols 47ʳ and 290ᵛ, were written when both were together in or near Paris between June and December 1588. Almost all the other additions and modifications are in Montaigne's hand and continue until some time before his death on 13 September 1592.

2. After Montaigne's death this copy was given to the convent of the Feuillants in Bordeaux.[1] At the time of the Revolution it passed to the municipal library of Bordeaux. It is now referred to as the 'Bordeaux Copy' or 'Exemplaire de Bordeaux'.

Copy: Bord (S 1238 Rés., reproduced in facsimile by F Strowski; see No 4: 1588, Bord 1).

---

[1] 'Manuscrit de Bordeaux', *BSAM*, II, 5 (1939), p 26. See also P. Bonnet, 'L'Exemplaire de Bordeaux et le texte définitif des *Essais*', in *Mémorial du 1er congrès international des études montaignistes* (ed G Palassie), Bordeaux, 1964, pp 94—100, and 'Reinhold Dezeimeris et son exemplaire des *Essais* de Montaigne', *BSAM*, IV, 4 (1965), pp 15—16; A Salles, 'A propos du manuscrit de Bordeaux', *BSAM*, II, 1 (1937), p 19; P Courteault, 'L'exemplaire de Bordeaux au XVIIIᶜ siècle', *BSAM*, II, 9 (1940), pp 54—6.

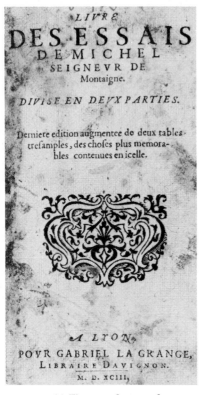

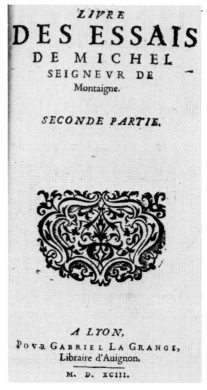

(*a*) First part [140 mm]   (*b*) Second part [138 mm]

Title-page: (*a*) First part. (*b*) Second part. Imprint of Gabriel La Grange on both tps but with different settings.

Collation: 8°: †⁸ **⁸ *†*⁴ **†*² A—3F⁸ a—z⁸ 2*A*⁸ [$5(−A5) signed, arabic numerals; missigning †4, †5 as *4, *5, 2C5 as C3, 2K5 as kk5 (for KK5), z1—4 as Z 1, 2, 3, 4, z5 as Z5 (*variants*: missigning **2 as **5, not signing E2)]; 630 leaves; pp [*44*] 1—62 65 64—243 224 245—499 454 501—505 606 507—511 478 513—514 495 516—518 483 520—524 425 428 527—529 930 531—552 523 544 555—571 672 563 574 576 566 567 578 579 570 571 582 583 580 575 586 587 578 579 590 591 582 593 594 595 596 597 598—603 694 605—615 516 617 718 619—825 798 827—829 [5] 3—46 64 48—154 555 156—236 137 238—289 390 291—358 357 360 [*24*] [*variant*: misnumbering 678 as 677].

Contents: †1: Title (*a*) (verso blank); †2: *Au lecteur*; †2ᵛ: Table of contents for Bks I—II; †5 (signed *5): Index to Bks I—II; A1: *Essais* Bks I—II; 3F7ᵛ—8ᵛ: blank; a1: Title (*b*) (verso blank); a2: *Essais* Bk III; z5 (signed Z5): Table of contents for Bk III; z5ᵛ (signed Z5ᵛ): Index to Bk III; 2*A* 8ʳ—ᵛ: blank.

HT: †2   [row of 13 type-orns] AV LECTEVR.
      †5 (signed *5)   [double row of 19 type-orns] TABLE DES PRIN-|CIPALES MATIERES | ET CHOSES PLVS ME-|morables en ceſte pre-|miere partie.|[3 asterisks]
      A1   [headpiece: central vase, 2 birds, volutes] ESSAIS DE MICHEL | DE MONTAIGNE. | Livre Premier.
      V8   [as A1 except] Livre Second. [*variant*: V8 as A1 in Ly]
      a2   [as A1 except] Livre Troisiesme.

RT: Essais De M. De Monta. | Livre Premier [Second] [Troisiesme]. [Essai A1ᵛ; Essai De M. De Monat. 2H3ᵛ; Mont. a2ᵛ; Premier Livre. C3 D4 F8; Livre C5; Secon. Y2; Seocnd. 2D8 2G7 2L4 2O2; Socnd. 3E5; Second. (for Troisiesme.) a8; Premier. (for Second.) once or more in Z 2F—HKNPQR; troisiesme. (for Troisiesme.) once or twice in bceg—nq—sv—y; no RT for sonnets M1ᵛ—7ᵛ]

CW: Page. D8ᵛ donnent,   T8ᵛ autres   2I5ʳ bien   3F2ᵛ re-]cours   18ᵛ combien

Measurements (I4): 33(+2) lines. 139 (145) × 73 mm. 20 lines = 83 mm.

Privilège: None.

Notes: 1. Set from No 4: 1588. The indexes appear for the first time, one for Bks I—II, one for Bk III.

2. On D1 (I 14, p 49) the text reads faultily: 'Ie veux dire mon experience autour de ce subiect l'auarice. Ie veux dire mon experience autour de ce subiect'. The first sentence has been struck out in BN1.

3. On Q5 (p 249) the text jumps from 'produict le second' (I 40, 1588 fol 105ᵛ) to 'sapiens, sibíque imperiosus' (I 42, 1588, fol 108ʳ), thus omitting

I 41 and part of I 42, though they are listed in the table of contents as being on p 230 and p 240 respectively. The same omission occurs in the text of No 6: 1595 Lyons (p 225), but the chapters are omitted from the table of contents.

4. The title of III 1 is changed to *De l'vtilité & de l'honnesteté* in both the table of contents and the text.

Copies:[1] BN1 (Rés. Z 2769); BN2 (Z Payen 14, lacks 3F8); BN3 (16°Z 6530, gathering Z wrongly imposed); BN4 (Rés. Z 2768); Bord; *Eper*; Gren; Ly (tp torn, part of imprint missing); Monp; Nanc 1 (Rés. 10064); Nanc 2 (Rés. 10315); *Stdi*. UK: BL; Cam: Trin (heavily annotated in two contemporary hands); Ox: Bod[2]; RAS; Tay (Bk III only). BELGIUM: Bru. DENMARK: *Cop*. GERMANY: *Aug*; Würz. ITALY: Mil/C; Mod (lacks prelims of Bks I—II, gathering a and t1 of Bk III). NETHERLANDS: *Midd*. USA: Harv; NY/M; Prin; W/Folg. USSR: *Mosc/H*.

---

[1] See also A Salles, 'Les premières éditions', *BSAM*, II, 2 (1937), p 90, for a copy from Montesquieu's library.

[2] This copy was purchased with donations made to the Friends of the Bodleian in memory of Richard Sayce.

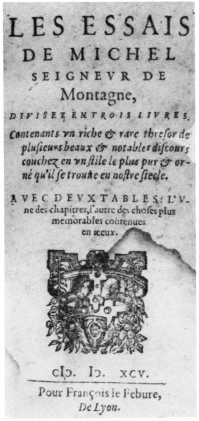

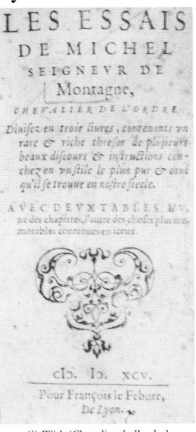

(a) Without 'Chevalier de l'ordre'   (b) With 'Chevalier de l'ordre'
      [120 mm]   [120 mm]

Title-page: The two tps are variants rather than evidence for two issues, and the inserted leaves signed *2 occur irrespective of tp. Tp (*b*) is found only in LL2. It differs from (*a*) in (i) the ornament; (ii) the addition of *Chevalier de l'ordre* beneath *Montagne*; (iii) *Diuisez en trois liures, contenants vn* on one line and in italics; (iv) *rare & riche* for *riche & rare*; (v) *beaux discours & instructions* for *beaux & notables discours*.

Collation: 12°: ¹*¹², **¹², ²*² (signed *2), a—2r¹², 2s² [$6(7) signed, arabic numerals; d4 inverted, missigning i6 as i7, t6 as t9, 2a5 as 2a6, 2c7 as c7, 2h4 as hh4 4, not signing 2p6 2q4 2q6 2r6 (*variants*: not signing a5, missigning e3 as d3, q6 as 6q)]; 508 leaves; pp [ʃ2] 1—211 112 213 210 215—234 213 236—282 383 284—290 29 292—320 32 322 32ç 324—335 235 337—389 90 391—407 *408* 409—472 477 474—601 603 603 904

605—737 720 721 740—760 701 762—770 77 772—839 890—944 94
946—951 1002 953—963 962 963 966—1002 103 1004—1011 1002
[=962] [2].

Contents: [1]*1: Title (verso blank); [1]*2: Table of contents; [1]*4[v]: Index;
**12[v]: blank; [2]*1 (signed *2): *Au lecteur*; [2]*2[v]: Sonnet by Expilly; a1:
Essais; 2s2[r—v]: blank.

HT: [1]*2   [headpiece: tendrils] TABLE DES CHA-|
                      PITRES DV PRE-|mier liure.

      [1]*4[v]   [headpiece: central grotesque head with crescent,
                      2 snails, volutes] TABLE DES PRIN-|CIPALES
                      MATIERES ET | chofes plus memorables conte-
                      |nues aux trois liures du Seigneur | de Montagne.

      [2]*1 (signed *2) [double row of 11 arabesque type-orns] PRE-
                      FACE | de l'Autheur, | AV | LECTEVR BENE-
                      VOLE. (Plate 5)

      [2]*2[v]   [type-orns as [2]*1] SVR LES ESSAIS | du fieur de
                      Montagne. (Plate 5)

      a1   [headpiece: elephant attacking rhinoceros, lion
                      attacking dog, horse kicking dragon] ESSAIS
                      DE MI-|CHEL DE MON-|TAIGNE. | LIVRE
                      PREMIER. | [rule] (Plate 5)

      m10[v]   [headpiece: hounds and rabbits] [as a1 except]
                      LIVRE SECOND. | [rule]

      2h2   [as m10[v] except] LIVRE TROISIESME. | [rule]

RT: ESSAIS DE M. DE MONTA. | LIVRE PREMIER [SECOND] [TROISIESME].
[MONT. a3[v] c1[v] e4[v]; PREMIER LIVRE. a3 b7,9,11 c8,10,11 d8,12 e12 f5,7
g1,6,8 h2 i7 k5,11 l 4,8; PREMIER. (for SECOND.) m12; SECOND LIVRE.
n10 q9 r10 t9 x9 2a8 2c9 2d10 2f11 2g8; SECOMD. p10 r7; SECOD. z4;
SECOND. 2e7 2f12; SECOND. (for TROISIESME.) 2h10 2i9; TROISIESME (no
stop) 2k3 2m1 2n1 2o 6,8 2q10; TROIIESME. 2m12]

CW: Leaf. a12[v] me-]moire,   g12[v] _ _ _o (*sic*)   z12[v] in-]ftrument,   2g12[v]
le fil

Measurements (g4): 35(+2) lines. 116 (124)×55 mm. 20 lines=65 mm.
The type of the two inserted leaves signed *2 is larger, e.g. ([2]*1[v]):
19(+2) lines. 113 (123)×58 mm. 20 lines=120 mm.

Privilège: None.

Notes: 1. The distribution of the gatherings signed to the sixth and to the seventh leaf shows a definite pattern sometimes in runs, sometimes alternating, and suggests two compositors:

$7 signed	$6 signed
ab	c
def	ghikl
mn	op
q	r
f	tvxy
z	2a 2b
2c	2d 2e 2f 2g
2h 2i 2k 2l 2m	2n
2o 2p 2q 2r	

Le Febvre was a genuine bookseller active in Lyons between 1580 and 1607 but he was a Protestant and moved to Geneva about 1590.[1] According to Chaix, Dufour and Moeckli this edition was printed in Geneva.[2]

2. The text was set from No 5: 1593 Lyons, as several common errors show, e.g. the erroneous chapter heading of III 1 and especially the jump from I 40 to I 42 (see No 5, notes 3 and 4). However, there are many more alterations and omissions, probably due to the Genevan censors. The following chapters are completely suppressed: I 29, 35, 54, 55; II 15, 19, 28, 30, 33, 35; III 5. Other chapters are partially omitted. I 28 *De l'amitié*, though it appears in the table of contents, is run together with I 27, and does not have a separate heading in the text (p 160). It is abridged and ends with the quotation '*Quis desiderio* [. . .] *semper amabo*' (p 169). Similarly after the end of II 27 '. . . l'autre vesquit encore depuis' the text runs on without a break to 'Es vies de ces heros . . .' (p 642) which comes from II 29 *De la vertu*. This chapter is also abridged to exclude the story of the man cutting off his testicles and the assassination of Guise. In the text, though not in the table of contents, III 3 *De trois commerces* is rechristened *Du commerce de la vie* and Montaigne's third relationship—with women—is omitted. At 'le registre des productions de telles ames' (III 3, p 758) the text jumps to 'Nous ne regardons guere . . .' from III 4 *De la diversion*, whose title disappears from the text and from the table of contents. III 11 *Des boiteux* becomes III 9 *Des opinions* and most of the references to lameness are cut out. The

[1] Baudrier, *Bibliographie lyonnaise*, V, 351, 355.
[2] *Les livres imprimés à Genève de 1550 à 1600*, p 145.

alterations and omissions are mainly concerned with women, sex and religion, and have been attributed to Simon Goulart by Scaliger.[3]

3. The index in No 6: 1595 Lyons is a conflation of the two indexes in No 5: 1593 Lyons but omitting references to chapters which have been suppressed.

4. The paper of the two inserted leaves signed *2 differs from the rest of the book in having the chain-lines vertical instead of horizontal. Type and ornaments are also different. The leaves are inserted after the tp in LL2 but after the index in BN1, Bod and RAS. The text of Montaigne's *Au lecteur* corresponds to that sent by Mlle de Gournay to Justus Lipsius and to foreign printers which did not receive authorised publication until 1598 (see No 7A†: 1595, note 1, No 8: 1598, note 1 and Plates 3—4). There is no way of knowing when these leaves were inserted[4] but the revised text of *Au lecteur* could have been obtained from those printers who had received Mlle de Gournay's amended copies towards the end of 1595. However, where Mlle de Gournay wrote 'quatre vingtz' the inserted leaves have 'quatre vingts & dix'. The sonnet by Claude d'Expilly, also on the inserted leaves, appears here for the first time (see Plate 5).

5. There are similarities between this edition and No 10: 1602 in the matter of the Expilly sonnet, the index and the erroneous title of III 1, which do not appear in the intervening editions. However, the indexes of 1602 appear to be independent of No 6: 1595 Lyons and the erroneous title of III 1 also occurs in No 5: 1593 Lyons.

Copies: BN1 (Z Payen 17); BN2 (16°Z 6401); Bord (bound in 3 vols); Ly. UK: LL1 (E 955); LL2 (E 958, unique example of tp *b*); Ox:Bod; RAS. AUSTRIA: *Vien/N.* GERMANY: *Det; Ful; Han; Nür;* Tüb; *Ulm.* NETHERLANDS: *Leeuw;* Utr. POLAND: *Wroc/U.* SWITZER-LAND: Gen; *Laus/U; Luz.* USA: Gord; Harv 1 (*Mon 15.95, Grace Norton copy)[5]; Harv 2 (III.1.6, W. Drummond copy); Prin; W/Folg.

---

[3] See A Boase, *The Fortunes of Montaigne*, pp 8—9; M Françon, *Pour une édition critique*, pp 50—3.

[4] See A Salles, 'Encore une petite énigme Montanienne (l'édition 1595 de Lyon)', *BSAM*, II, 2 (1937), pp 86—8.

[5] See M Françon, 'Notes de Miss Grace Norton dans l'exemplaire de l'édition des *Essais* de Montaigne (Lyon, 1595)', *BSAM*, IV, 4 (1965), pp 25—8.

(a) A L'Angelier [275 mm]

Title-page: The two tps differ in the booksellers' devices and imprints. On tp *(b)* the *E* of *EDITION* is displaced.

    (a) Abel L'Angelier.   *(b)* Michel Sonnius.

The text of the title advertises this as a corrected, augmented, and posthumous edition.

LES
ESSAIS
DE MICHEL SEI-
GNEVR DE MONTAIGNE.

EDITION NOVVELLE, TROVVEE APRES
le deceds de l'Autheur, reueuë & augmentée par luy d'vn
tiers plus qu'aux precedentes Impreßions.

A PARIS,
Chez MICHEL SONNIVS, ruë fainct Iaques,
à l'efcu de Bafle.
CIꝐ. IꝐ. XCV.
AVEC PRIVILEGE.

(b) M Sonnius [266 mm]

Collation: 2°: ã⁴ ẽ⁴ ĩ⁴ A—E⁶ F⁶ (±F2.5) G—2V⁶ 2X⁴ 3A—3S⁶ 3T—3V⁴ [$4 signed, roman numerals; *variant*: missigning K3 as 'K iij]; 390 leaves;   pp [*24*] ¹1—86 96 97 89—91 76 93—209 *210 211*—523 *524* ²1—58 56 60—175 178 179 178—231 *232* [*variants*: not numbering 78 (G3ᵛ), misnumbering 228 as 206 (T6ᵛ), 144 as 44 (3M6ᵛ)].

Contents: ã1: Title; ã1ᵛ: *Privilège*; ã2: Long Gournay preface; ĩ3ʳ: Table of contents; ĩ4ᵛ: *Au lecteur*; A1: *Essais* Bk I; S3ᵛ: blank; S4: *Essais* Bk II; 2X4ᵛ: blank; 3A1: *Essais* Bk III; 3V4ᵛ: Errata.

HT: ã2   [headpiece: central winged head, 2 fauns, 2 horses' heads and forelegs] PREFACE SVR LES ESSAIS DE MICHEL | SEIGNEVR DE MONTAIGNE, | Par sa Fille d'Alliance.

   ĩ4ᵛ   [headpiece: central torso, 2 archers, urinating dogs, inits HT] Au lecteur.

   A1   [headpiece as ã2] ESSAIS DE MICHEL | DE MON-TAIGNE. | LIVRE PREMIER.

   S4   [headpiece: 2 heads in cartouches] [as A1 except] Livre second.

   3A1   [as A1 except] LIVRE TROISIESME.

RT: ESSAIS DE MICHEL DE MONTAIGNE. | LIVRE PREMIER [SECOND] [TROISIESME]. [MICHEL MONTAIGNE. 3A3ᵛ, 5ᵛ; MICEL DE MONTAIGNE. 3B1ᵛ (*variant*: MICEL DE MOM-TAIGNE. 3B1ᵛ)]

CW: Leaf. G6ᵛ & au [& auquel   O6ᵛ guider; [guider: V6ᵛ doctri-]ne, c'est 2D6ᵛ au-]thorité 2K6ᵛ transformant 2R5ʳ toutes [the only CW on a recto] 3G4ᵛ presumen [presument 3N6ᵛ part; &   3V1ᵛ ny à [ny a

Measurements (K2): 44(+2) lines. 257 (267) × 149 mm. 20 lines = 116 mm.

Privilège: To Abel L'Angelier for 10 years to publish *Les Essais de Michel Seigneur de Montagne, reueuz & augmentez de plus du tiers par le mesme Autheur*. Paris, 15 October 1594, signed RAMBOVILLET.

Notes: 1. Set from a transcription of No 4†: 1588 The Bordeaux Copy sent by Montaigne's widow to Mlle de Gournay in Paris. Chapter I 14 of the Bordeaux Copy, *Que le goust des biens et des maux depend en bonne partie de*

l'opinion que nous en avons, becomes I 40 in this edition, and the numbers of the intervening chapters are consequently reduced by one. It is not clear whether this displacement was in accordance with Montaigne's wishes, transmitted via the transcription sent to Mlle de Gournay, or whether it was the result of an error in the process of printing. La Boétie's sonnets, which are struck out in the Bordeaux Copy, are omitted here.

2. The edition was divided between L'Angelier and Sonnius, with L'Angelier playing the leading part. The printer was Léger Delas. The printing of Bk III is of inferior quality. Its signatures and pagination are independent, starting at 3A1 and p 1 respectively. Yet it was not produced in a different workshop, since many of the initials of Bk III can be found in the first two books, and in some copies the same paper has been used from gathering 2L to the end of the volume. Therefore it seems that two sets of compositors and two presses were employed in the same workshop, printing Bk III more or less simultaneously with Bks I and II. About fifty press-corrections have been discovered by Dr Sayce.[1]

3. The Errata exists in two states which occur indifferently in the L'Angelier and Sonnius copies. The first state is slightly commoner than the second, the proportion being approximately 5 to 4. The second state has three extra corrections and three variants in the existing corrections. The heading: 'Fautes à corriger en l'Impression de quelques Exemplaires' implies that the errors had already been corrected in most copies, though only two of the corrections listed in the Errata are found among the press-variants listed by Dr Sayce (*Ammurath, la diuersité*).

4. It is clear that exceptional care was taken to ensure the accuracy of this edition. This was no doubt partly due to the vigilance of the printer, but especially to the zeal of Mlle de Gournay. Probably working on the sheets before binding, she corrected by hand about twenty further errors and these ink-corrections are found in almost all copies. Since Mlle de Gournay explains and lists these ink-corrections at the end of her preface (ĩ2ᵛ), we may assume that the last page of the preface was printed after this first series of ink-corrections. For the second series of ink-corrections, see No 7A†: 1595.

5. Montaigne's *Au lecteur*, corrected by the author, was not available when printing started. Mlle de Gournay explained this later when she

---

[1] For a full discussion of the printing, press-corrections, ink-corrections, cancels and reset sheets of this edition, see R A Sayce, 'L'édition des *Essais* de Montaigne de 1595', *BHR*, 36 (1974), pp 115—41.

was at the Château de Montaigne and was able to supply the corrected text to printers who might produce new editions of the *Essais*: 'Cette preface recorrigée de la derniere main de l'autheur ayant este esgarée en la premier impression depuis sa mort, a naguere esté retrouuée' (see Plate 3). Montaigne's *Au lecteur* is lacking in the Sonnius copies but it was made good in nearly all the L'Angelier ones (31 out of 33 examined by Dr Sayce). Presumably the sheet ĩı.4, on which was already printed part of the Gournay preface and the table of contents, was passed again through the press to receive Montaigne's *Au lecteur* on the blank page (ĩ4ᵛ). However, the text of this *Au lecteur* is inaccurate for it corresponds neither to the 1588 text nor to the Bordeaux Copy version, and it was later corrected by Mlle de Gournay during her stay at the Château de Montaigne, though not from the Bordeaux Copy (see No. 7A†: 1595).

6. Another omission rectified concerns a MS addition at the end of *De la coustume* (I 23 in the Bordeaux Copy, I 22 in No 7A: 1595). This passage ('Car qui se mesle . . . *Chrysippum sequor*') was omitted in printing but restored by means of the cancel sheet F2.5. The omitted passage was inserted on p 63, where it occupies 24 lines, and the rest of the text on pp 63—64 was recomposed to occupy less space.[2] The other half of the sheet, pp 69—70, was also reset and this resulted in new errors one of which, *presenter* for *representer*, was later corrected in ink by Mlle de Gournay. Copies with the cancel (all L'Angelier) are rare—only BN1, BN3, Ant 1 and SZ (for this last see No 7B)—which suggests that the omission was noticed at a late stage.

Copies (all L'Angelier, except where Sonnius is indicated): BN1 (Rés. Z 357); BN2 (Rés.gr.Z 238); BN3 (Z Payen 15, marginal notes); BN4 (Z Payen 16, Sonnius); BN5 (Fol. Z 1580); Ars; Cass; Sorb; *Agen* (Sonnius); Avig; Bes; Bord; *Carp*; Châm (Sonnius); Chan/C; *Chan/F*; Dij; Gren; Ly; *Monb*; *Monta*; Poi.   UK: BL; Carl; *Cole*; Ed/N (Sonnius); Ex (Sonnius); Mers; Ox: Bod (Sonnius); Mert; Wad.   BELGIUM: Ant 1 (R 405, see No. 7A†); Bru (Sonnius).   DENMARK: *Thor*.   USA: Chap (Sonnius); Chic/U; Gord (Sonnius); NY/P; Prin; Virg/U; W/Cong; W/Folg; Yale (Sonnius).

---

[2] See A Salles, 'Le fameux carton de la page 63 (édition de 1595)', *BSAM*, II, 7 (1939), p 101.

FULLY CORRECTED IN INK BY MLLE DE GOURNAY

[289 mm]

The differences between Nos 7A and 7A†:1595 lie in further ink-corrections made by Mlle de Gournay in her efforts to make the posthumous text of the *Essais* as accurate as possible. The principal copy exhibiting these corrections is Ant 1, but the copy several times described, which once belonged to Montesquieu, appears to have the same characteristics,[1] and so too does SZ, for which see No 7B: 1595. What follows here is a description of Ant 1.

Title-page: The three lines *Edition . . . impressions* are deleted. Beneath is added *Viresq; acquirit eundo* in Mlle de Gournay's hand. At the foot of the page *Leonor de Môtaigne* has been written and crossed out.

Collation: As No 7A: 1595 except that ã2—ĩ2 are removed leaving stubs. The cancellans F2.5 is present.

Contents: As No 7A: 1595 except that the long preface (ã2—ĩ2ᵛ) is replaced by a short MS preface by Mlle de Gournay (but not in her hand) attached to the stub of ĩ2.[2] The Errata (3V4ᵛ) is deleted by ink strokes, but not all misprints have been corrected in the text.

HT: As No 7A: 1595 but lacking ã2.

RT, *CW*, *Measurements*, *Privilège*: As No 7A: 1595

Notes: 1. In addition to the modifications to the title and preface already described, there are MS corrections to *Au lecteur* and to the text—not only the twenty or so corrections which Mlle de Gournay made to most copies while she was in Paris (see No 7A: 1595, note 4) but also about fifty new corrections. These corrections were made by Mlle de Gournay during her stay at the Château de Montaigne as the guest of Montaigne's widow. Two letters dated 2 May and 15 November 1595, sent by Mlle de Gournay to Justus Lipsius attest her presence at the château and her efforts to improve the accuracy of her edition of the *Essais*. With the letter of 15 November she sent Justus Lipsius 'trois exemplaires des *Essais* que i'ay faict imprimer [. . .] ayant corrigé ces exemplaires de ma main propre (avec un soin extrême) sur quelques fautes eschappées en l'impression aprez l'Errata, et sur celles de l'Errata mesme, de peur que

---

[1] See A Salles, 'Le Montaigne de Montesquieu', *BBB*, 1930, pp 315—20; 'Le Montaigne de Montesquieu', *BSAM*, II, 3 (1938), pp 24—5; *ibid.*, II, 6 (1939), p 84, with reproduction of title-page; R A Sayce, 'L'édition des *Essais* de 1595', *BHR*, 36 (1974), p 133; *Catalogue Drouot Rive Gauche: Livres rares et précieux composant la bibliothèque d'un amateur*, 10 December 1976, No 25, with reproduction of Mlle de Gournay's note concerning the mislaid *Au lecteur*.

[2] For a discussion of Ant 1 and reproduction of Mlle de Gournay's short MS preface, see A Abel, 'Juste Lipse et Marie de Gournay: autour de *l'exemplaire d'Anvers* des *Essais* de Montaigne', *BHR*, 35 (1973), pp 117—29.

les imprimeurs ne negligeassent de se servir de luy'. One of these copies was for Justus Lipsius, the others for him to send to printers in Basel and Strasbourg. She says that she has already sent similarly corrected copies to Plantin and 'à toutes les fameuses impressions de l'Europe'. Ant 1 is almost certainly the copy she sent to Plantin since it appears in a seventeenth-century inventory of the Plantin printing-house library.

2. From the letters to Justus Lipsius it seems clear that Mlle de Gournay brought with her, or had sent from Paris, several copies of the 1595 folio edition to continue the work of correcting the text while at the Château de Montaigne. One of these copies she seems to have presented to Leonor de Montaigne and then requested it back to send with corrections to Plantin. This would explain why Leonor's name is crossed out on the tp. But what was the source of her corrections? She may have consulted the Bordeaux Copy, but if she did, she did not attempt to correct the numerous divergences which exist between the Bordeaux Copy and the 1595 edition. Indeed, in some places she modified the 1595 text where it agreed with the Bordeaux Copy. It seems therefore more likely that she continued to work from the transcription of the Bordeaux Copy, which Mme de Montaigne had originally sent to Paris to serve as the basis for the 1595 edition, and which Mlle de Gournay had perhaps brought with her to the château to continue the task of correction. Herein lies the importance of Ant 1, SZ and the Montesquieu copy, for they represent what Mlle de Gournay, working at the Château de Montaigne as the guest of Montaigne's widow, believed to be the most accurate and authentic posthumous text of the *Essais*.[3]

3. In three places the corrected text of *Au lecteur* in Ant 1 (Plate 3) differs from the Bordeaux Copy. It seems therefore that Mlle de Gournay was not following the Bordeaux Copy but the missing page of the

[3] For a discussion of the problems raised by the Bordeaux Copy and the edition of 1595, see R Dezeimeris, *Recherches sur la recension du texte posthume des Essais*, 1866; J Zeitlin, 'The relation of the text of 1595 to that of the Bordeaux Copy' in his translation of the *Essays*, 1934—36 (appendix to vol I); A Salles, 'Le duel entre l'édition de 1595 et le manuscrit de Bordeaux', *BSAM*, II, 4 (1938), pp 29—32 and *ibid.*, II, 5 (1939), pp 24—6; P Michel, 'Le problème des éditions', *BSAM*, III, 1 (1957), pp 16—19; P Bonnet, 'Le texte des *Essais*', *BSAM*, IV, 7 (1966), pp 70—81; R Trinquet, 'Le cinquantenaire de l'édition Armaingaud', *BSAM*, V, 13 (1975), pp 37—42; D Maskell, 'Quel est le dernier état authentique des *Essais* de Montaigne?', *BHR*, 40 (1978), pp 85—103, and 'Montaigne correcteur de l'exemplaire de Bordeaux', *BSAM*, V, 25—6 (1978), pp 57—71.

transcription which had now turned up. The epigraph *Viresque acquirit eundo* on the tp could have come from the Bordeaux Copy but it too may have come from the transcription, since the tp is in the same gathering ã as the mislaid *Au lecteur*, and was perhaps mislaid and found in the same way.

Copies: Ant 1 (R 405); SZ (see No 7B: 1595).

7B: RE-ISSUE OF 1595
WITH RESET SHEETS

LES
ESSAIS DE
MICHEL SEIGNEVR
DE MONTAIGNE.

EDITION NOVVELLE, TROVVEE APRES
le deceds de l'Autheur, reneuë et augmentee par luy d'vn
tiers plus qu'aux precedentes Jmpreßions.

A   PARIS,
Chez ABEL l'ANGELIER, au premier pilier
de la grand' ſalle du Palais.

CIƆ. IƆ. XCV.
AVEC PRIVILEGE.

[283 mm]

Title-page: The text of the title is the same as that of No 7A: 1595 (*a*) except for the disposition of the line-endings and certain typefaces. In addition No 7B has a different device, it has *grand' ſalle* instead of *grandè ſalle* and has the rule above the date instead of below it. The only consistent feature of this issue is the tp. It is impossible to describe the ideal copy because of the widely varying numbers of reset sheets to be found in different copies. What follows is the description of Kings, which has the largest number of reset sheets.

Collation: 2°: ã^4 ($\pm$ã1, $-$ã2.3,4) ĩ^4 ($-$ĩ 1,2) A^6 B^6 ($\pm$B1.6) C—K^6 L^6 ($\pm$L1.6) M—R^6 S^6 ($\pm$S3.4) T—2G^6 2H^6 ($\pm$2H1.6, 3.4) 2I^6 2K^6 ($\pm$2K3.4) 2L^6 ($\pm$2L3.4) 2M^6 ($\pm$M2.5) 2N^6 2O^6 ($\pm$2O1.6) 2P^6 ($\pm$2P3.4) 2Q—2S^6 2T^6 ($\pm$T1.6) 2V^6—2X^4 3A—3B^6 3C^6 ($\pm$3C3.4) 3D^6 ($\pm$3D3.4) 3E—3F^6 3G^6 ($\pm$3G2.5) 3H^6 ($\pm$3H2.5) 3I^6 ($\pm$3I2.5, 3.4) 3K^6 3L^6 ($\pm$3L3.4) 3M—3P^6 3Q^6 ($\pm$3Q1.6) 3R—3S^6 3T^4 ($\pm$3T2.3) 3V^4 ($\pm$) [$4 ($-$2L4, 3C4, 3I4) signed, roman numerals; missigning 2K3 as KK iij (for Kk iij), 2K4 as KK iiij (for Kk iiij), 3C3 as C3, 3D3 as 2D3, 3L4 as 3L3]; 386 leaves; pp [*6*] [1]1—86 96 97 89—91 76 93—209 *210 211*—364 *365 366 367 368* (2H3.4) 369—388 388 389 390 341 (2K3.4) 393—523 *524* [2]1—28 111 112 113 114 (3C3.4) 33—58 56 60—102 105 (3I4) 104—114 *115* 116—124 *125 126 127 128* (3L3.4) 129—175 178 179 178—231 *232*].

Contents: As No 7A: 1595 except that the verso of the tp is blank (omitting the *privilège*), the long Gournay preface is deleted (ã2—ĩ2^v) and 3V4^v is blank (omitting the Errata).

HT: As No 7A: 1595 except S4 [headpiece: central female head, 2 putti] [. . .]

RT: As No 7A: 1595 but with the following on reset sheets: MONTAGNE. L6^v 2H1^v, 6^v 2M5^v 3Q1^v; MONTAIGNE (no stop) 2L3^v, 4^v; MIC HEL DE MONTAIGME. 3I5^v; TROSIESME. 3L3.

CW: As No 7A: 1595 except for reset sheets.

Measurements (2H3): 44($+$2) lines. 259 (270) $\times$ 152 mm. 20 lines $=$ 118 mm. This provides a basis for comparison with No 7A: 1595 for size of type, but many of the reset pages have one or two lines more or less than the corresponding pages in No 7A.

Privilège: None.

Notes: 1. Although this issue bears the date 1595, the printer's device on the tp does not appear on other L'Angelier editions before 1601. The copy-text for the reset sheets is the 1602 edition, as is shown by certain errors common to this issue and No 10: 1602 but not occurring earlier.[1] It seems that L'Angelier, seven years after publishing the 1595 folio edition, found himself with a number of imperfect copies, perhaps those unsold by Sonnius. Where necessary he replaced missing or spoiled pages with reset sheets and made a new tp either to cancel that of Sonnius or to replace his own if it were missing. Despite the lapse of time he retained the date 1595, doubtless because he was offering what was still for the most part the folio edition of 1595.

2. Kings has 22 reset sheets (88 pages), the greatest number. The copy described by J Mégret as sold at the J D sale in Paris on 6 and 7 December 1961 has four reset sheets (L1.6, S3.4, 2L3.4, 3Q1.6). SZ has three reset sheets (L1.6, S3.4, 3Q1.6). Orl has two (L1.6, 3Q1.6) and the rest—Inst, Vers, Ant 2, Harv—have only one (2L3.4). A copy sold at the Salle Silvestre on 2 December 1867 and described by Payen with a tracing of the tp in a manuscript note in No 7A: 1595 BN4 is clearly of this issue, but Payen gives no details of reset sheets which might serve to identify it. All these copies have tp No 7B, but Bes, which has tp No 7A(*a*), has one reset sheet (2L3.4) and may therefore also be associated with this re-issue.

3. The long Gournay preface, which is lacking in Kings, is present in all other copies, and all have Montaigne's *Au lecteur*. All of them except SZ have sheet F2.5 uncancelled—in other words they omit the passage 'Car qui se mesle . . . *Chrysippum sequor*' (see No 7A: 1595 note 6). SZ is a particularly interesting and important copy since it has not only the cancel at F2.5, but also most of Mlle de Gournay's ink-corrections of both the first and second series, as well as further corrections by her.[2]

Copies: Inst; Orl; Vers.   UK: Cam: Kings.   BELGIUM: Ant 2 (BH 3052).   USA: Harv; SZ.

---

[1] See R A Sayce, 'L'édition des *Essais* de 1595', *BHR*, 36 (1974), p 139.

[2] See R A Sayce, 'L'édition des *Essais* de 1595', *BHR*, 36 (1974), pp 133—7. This copy is described in the Sotheby catalogue of 5 October 1971, No 307. It was bought by Zeitlin and Ver Brugge of Los Angeles, but has been examined by Dr Sayce, and is referred to by him as Sotheby/Zeitlin.

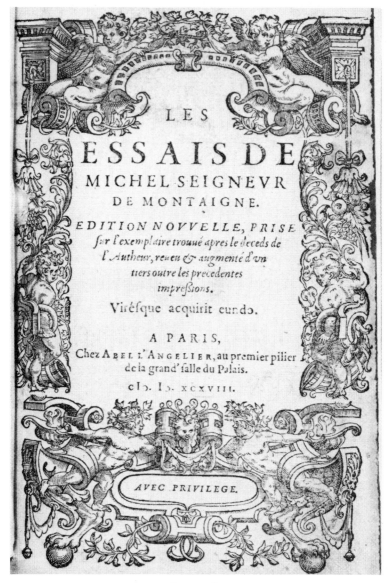

[174 mm]

Title-page: The date is faulty (X after C). The monogram beneath
AVEC PRIVILEGE is IDG (probably Jars de Gournay). The
border is in four pieces.

Collation: 8°: ã⁴ A—4C⁸ 4D—4E⁴ [$4 signed, roman numerals; missigning K2 as ᴋ ij (for K ij)]; 588 leaves; pp [*8*] 1—202 103 204—232 243 234—539 540 [inside HL] 541—829 840 831—987 886 989—1116 1017 1118—1152 115 1154—1161 162 1163—1165 [*3*] [*variants*: misnumbering 485 as 405, 514 as 4, 595 as 585, 614 as 914, 662 as 6 or as 648, not numbering 832, 833, misnumbering 834 as 844].

Contents: ã1: Title (verso blank); ã2: Table of contents; ã4: Short Gournay preface; ã4ᵛ:*Au lecteur*; A1: *Essais*; 4E3ᵛ:*Privilège*; 4E4ʳ⁻ᵛ: blank.

HT: ã4	[headpiece: central head, 2 reclining putti, fruit] PRE-FACE SVR LES ESSAIS | ᴅᴇ Mɪᴄʜᴇʟ Sᴇɪɢɴᴇᴠʀ | de Montaigne, | PAR SA FILLE D'ALLIANCE.
ã4ᵛ	[headpiece: palms, foliage, fruit] AV LECTEVR.
A1	[headpiece=ã4] ESSAIS DE MICHEL | DE MON-TAIGNE. | LIVRE PREMIER.
On X1	[as A1 except] LIVRE SECOND.
On 3E5ᵛ	[headpiece=ã4ᵛ] [as A1 except] LIVRE TROI-SIESME.

RT: Essaɪs ᴅᴇ Mɪᴄʜᴇʟ ᴅᴇ Mᴏɴᴛᴀɪɢɴᴇ. \| Lɪᴠʀᴇ ᴘʀᴇᴍɪᴇʀ [sᴇᴄᴏɴᴅ] [ᴛʀᴏɪsɪᴇsᴍᴇ]. [Lɪᴠʀᴇ sᴇᴄᴏɴᴅ. recto RT) 2L6ᵛ; ʟɪᴠʀᴇ A3; sᴇᴄᴏɴᴅ (for ᴛʀᴏɪsɪᴇsᴍᴇ.) 3E6,8 3F1,3]

CW: Quire. F8ᵛ prefter S8ᵛ Et vn, 2D8ᵛ nous 2Q8ᵛ ce qu'il 3L8ᵛ parts. 4A8ᵛ n'auroit

Measurements (2Q4): 37(+2) lines. 148 (162) × 88 mm. 20 lines = 83 mm.

Privilège: As No 7A: 1595 but new setting.

Notes: 1. Set from a copy of No 7A: 1595 with MS corrections similar to those of No 7A†. No 8: 1598 thus prints the following for the first time: (i) *Virésque acquirit eundo* on the tp; (ii) a short preface (ã4ʳ) in which Mlle de Gournay retracts her long preface of 1595; (iii) about three-quarters of the MS corrections to the text found in No 7A†(Ant 1). In addition the revised text of Montaigne's *Au lecteur*, which had appeared in some copies of 1595 Lyons (see No 6, note 4), now received its first authorised printing, together with a note explaining its absence from 1595 (see

Plates 3—5). The passage 'Car qui se mesle . . . *Chrysippum sequor*' on the cancellans F2.5 of 1595 is also included on F8 in 1598 (see No 7A, note 6).

2. The two following passages from No 7A:1595, pp 62—3, are omitted in No 8: 1598 F6ᵛ, p 94: (i) after *entreprises*: 'Et nous aduient ce que Thucydides dit des guerres ciuiles de son temps, qu''; (ii) after *tres-dangereux*: 'Adeò nihil motum ex antiquo probabile est'. These omissions are found in all editions which derive from 1598.[1]

3. On ã3ᵛ there are errors of alignment between the numbers and titles of chapters, and on line 5 TAALE (for TABLE).

4. There is overlapping between the editions of 1598, 1600 and 1602 (Nos 8—10). BN4 and BN5 have tp, prelims and last gathering of 1598 with the text of 1600. There is a note on this by Payen on the fly-leaf of BN5 and a less accurate one in BN4. Rom/N has tp and prelims of 1598, text of 1598 or 1600 and indexes from 1602. See also No 9, note 4.

Copies: BN1 (Z Payen 18); BN2 (Z Payen 19); BN3 (Z Payen 20–21); BN4 (Z Payen 22, see note 4); BN5 (Rés. Z 2770, see note 4); BN6 (16°Z 6526, Armaingaud copy); *Bord*; *Foix*; *Laf*; *Monb*.   UK: BL; Cam: Em; Gla 1 (PQ 1641); Gla 2 (Mu 51 g 1); Ox: Ball; Bod.   ITALY: Pad/U; Rom/N (see note 4).   USA: Harv; Hunt; Ill; Prin.

9: 1600

Title-page: The border is the same as No 8: 1598. The letterpress has been very carefully reset, though this is not immediately obvious since the type is the same. However, the alignment is different in several places and the date is changed to M.D C.

Collation: 8°: ã⁴ A—4C⁸ 4D—4E⁴ [$4 signed, roman numerals; missigning 2K1,2,3 as Kᴋ, Kᴋ ij, Kᴋ iij (for Kk), 3K1,4 as Kᴋᴋ, Kᴋᴋ iiij (for Kkk)]; 588 leaves; pp [*8*] 1—28 27 30—44 41 46—150 151 (digits tilted to right) 152—182 153 184—202 103 204—206 277 208—235 136 237—358 379 360—380 183 382—434 345 436—552 153 554—629 930 631—661 648 663—685 986 687—771 778 773—784 751 786—792 743 794—813 184 815—907 608 909—973 674 975—1038 1036 1040—1097 1068 1099—1102 1003 1104—1108 1106 1110—1165 [*3*] [*variants*: misnumbering 485 as 405].

---

[1] See P Bonnet, 'Le texte des *Essais*', *BSAM*, IV, 7 (1966), pp 72—3.

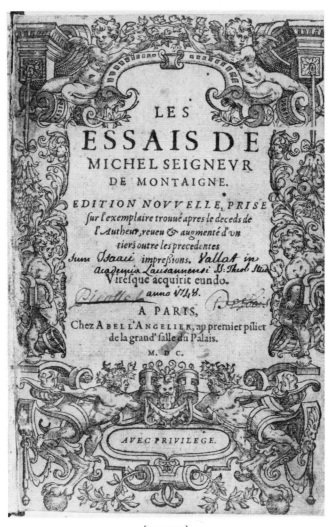

[174 mm]

Contents: As No: 8 1598.

HT: ã4   [headpiece: central vase, foliage, 2 birds] PREFACE
                 SVR LES ESSAIS | DE MICHEL SEIGNEVR | de
                 Montaigne, | PAR SA FILLE D'ALLIANCE.

     ã4ᵛ   [headpiece: lion's head in central square, 2 semi-
                 human figures, serpent, snail] AV LECTEVR.

A1   [headpiece: flower in central roundel, 2 putti, 2 grotesque monsters] ESSAIS DE MICHEL | DE MONTAIGNE. | LIVRE PREMIER.

On X1   [headpiece=ã4ᵛ] [as A1 except] LIVRE SECOND.

On 3E5ᵛ   [headpiece: central head, volutes, 2 snakes] [as A1 except] LIVRE TROISIESME.

RT: Essais de Michel de Montaigne. | Livre premier [second] [troisiesme]. [Montagne. 2Y5ᵛ 3B1ᵛ 3E4ᵛ; second. (for troisiesme.) 3E6 3E8]

CW: Selected CWs as 1598 except S8ᵛ Et vn (no comma)

Measurements (2H2): 37(+2) lines. 153 (160) × 88 mm. 20 lines = 81 mm.

Privilège: As No 7A: 1595 and No 8: 1598 but new setting (Plate 6).

Notes: 1. A very close line-by-line resetting of No 8: 1598 with which it shares some pagination errors (103 for 203, and the variants 648 for 662, 405 for 485). The majority of the 1598 pagination errors are corrected in 1600, but new ones are introduced. Further distinguishing features are the headpieces and most initials. The error in 1598 ã3ᵛ TAALE for TABLE is corrected. See also No 10, note 1 for textual and typographical differences which distinguish 1598 from both 1600 and No 10: 1602.

2. In the text but not in the table of contents III 1 is given the erroneous title *De l'vtilité & de l'honnesteté* which occurs in No 5: 1593 Lyons and No 6: 1595 Lyons.

3. Most copies lack 4E4 but it is present and blank in Tro and BL.

4. There is overlapping between the editions of 1600 and 1602. Péri has tp, prelims and text of 1600 with indexes and *privilège* from 1602. See also No 8, note 4.

Copies: BN1 (Z Payen 23); BN2 (Z Payen 24); *Avr*; *Colm*; *Louv* (lacks tp and 4E3,4); Ly (bound in 3 vols); Monp (V Alfieri copy); Péri; Tro; Vers (tp remounted, but good uncut copy). UK: BL; Cam: Trin; Ox: RAS; Sthi; *Shef*. POLAND: *Wroc/U*. USA: Chic/N; Harv. USSR: *Len/S*.

[139 mm]

Title-page: The engraving is considerably smaller than the type-page. The text of the title is the same as in No 8: 1598 and No 9: 1600 but with *Enrichis de deux Tables curieusement exactes et elabourées* added after *impressions*.

Collation: 8°: ã⁴ A—4C⁸ 4D⁴ 4E⁴(±4E2.3) 4F—4I⁸ 4K⁶ [$4 signed, roman numerals; missigning 4K2 as 3K2 (*variants*: missigning F2 as F)]; 626 leaves; pp [*8*] 1—266 367 268—376 337 378—578 576 580—646 547 648—838 83 840—1165 [*79*] [*variants*: misnumbering 229 as 129, 236 as 136, 290 as 90, 561 as 56, 1093 as 109].

Contents: ã1: Title (verso blank); ã2: Table of contents; ã4: Short Gournay preface; ã4ᵛ: *Au lecteur*; A1: *Essais*; 4E3ᵛ: *Privilège*; 4E4: Sonnet by Expilly (verso blank); 4F1: Index of subjects; 4H8: Index of proper names; 4K4ᵛ: Index to life; 4K6ʳ⁻ᵛ: blank.

HT: ã4   [headpiece: bacchic procession] PREFACE SVR
              LES ESSAIS | DE MICHEL SEIGNEVR | de Mon-
              taigne, | PAR SA FILLE D'ALLIANCE.

ã4ᵛ   [headpiece: central head, volutes, 2 snakes, inits IG
              in volutes above snakes] AV LECTEVR.

Aɪ   [headpiece: central cock, 2 fish-eating herons]
              ESSAIS DE MICHEL | DE MONTAIGNE. |
              LIVRE PREMIER.

On Xɪ   [as Aɪ except] LIVRE SECOND.

On 3E5ᵛ   [headpiece: central head, volutes, 2 snakes, inits IG
              in volutes above snakes] [as Aɪ except] DE MON-
              TAIGNE, | LIVRE TROISIESME.

4Fɪ   [headpiece: flowers] LES PAGES DV SIEVR | DE
              MONTAIGNE. | Où font contenuës les plus rares
              remarques de fon liure, à | fçauoir les exemples des
              vertus & des vices, les plus gra- | ues fentences,
              fimilitudes & comparaifons, auec vn re- | cueil des
              loix anciennes des peuples & nations. | *Plus la vie de
              l'Autheur par remarques principales & precifes | fur fon
              propre liure, le tout en forme de lieux | communs.*

RT: ESSAIS DE MICHEL DE MONTAIGNE. | LIVRE PREMIER [SECOND]
[TROISIESME]. [MONTAIGNE (no stop) 2Nɪᵛ 3N3ᵛ 3Qɪᵛ; MONTAIGNE. once
in 2RSTX 4BCE; MICHEL DE MONTAIGNE. once or twice in 3BCEFHIL-
MORSXZ 4A; SCOND 2T6]

CW: Quire. Selected CWs as No 8: 1598 and No 9: 1600 except S8ᵛ Et vn
(no comma) 4F8ᵛ Eftran- [Eftrangers 4G8ᵛ Phyfionomie 4H8ᵛ
Antiochus 4I8ᵛ Pierre

Measurements (P2): 37(+2) lines. 152 (160) × 89 mm. 20 lines = 82 mm.

Privilège: Cancellandum as Nos 7A, 8 and 9, 1595, 1598 and 1600, but
different setting. The cancellans changes the title, the date and the
signature, and draws attention to the indexes: *Les Essais du Seigneur de
Montaigne, reueuz, corrigez & augmentez de deux tables & de la vie de
l'Autheur, outre les Impressions cy deuant faictes.* Paris, 1 April 1602, signed
RENOVARD (Plate 6).

Notes: 1. This edition is very close to No 8: 1598 and No 9: 1600, but it is set from 1600 as certain readings common to 1600 and 1602 but not found in 1598 show:

				1598	1600, 1602
I	6	B3ᵛ	(p 22, lines 14–15)	Bertheuille	Berthelemy, Barthelemy
I	40	P5ᵛ	(p 234, line 9)	& luy promettoit	& leur promettoit
II	6	2A1	(p 369, line 14)	ſKeletos	ĸeletos, Keletos
III	1	3E5ᵛ	(p 810)	De l'vtile & de l'honneste	De l'vtilité & de l'honnesteté
III	13	4D4ᵛ	(p 1160, line 35)	cõpenſer	cõpêſer
			(p 1160, line 36)	Cõbien	Cõbiẽ

The headpieces on ã4ᵛ and 3E5ᵛ are very close to 1600 3E5ᵛ but the initials IG are added in 1602. The main novelty of 1602, however, are the indexes which do not occur in 1598 or 1600.

2. The cancellans 4E2.3 supplies the text of a new *privilège* drawing attention to the indexes (Plate 6). This has resulted in some minor variants in the resetting of the end of Bk III (4E2ʳ—3ʳ), e.g. on p 1165 the cancellans adds a stop after TROISIESME and substitutes ESSAIS for ESSAIS in line 13.

3. There are affinities between this edition and No 6: 1595 Lyons. They alone contain Expilly's sonnet, though with minor orthographical variants. Both have indexes, though those of 1602 are different and more thorough than those of 1595 Lyons.

4. In the re-issue of 1595 by L'Angelier the missing or spoiled pages were reset from this edition (see No 7B, note 1).

5. Ly lacks a tp but seems to be a copy of this edition with the final gathering from 1600. For the overlapping between 1598, 1600 and 1602, see No 8, note 4 and No 9, note 4.

Copies (4E2.3 cancelled unless otherwise stated): BN1 (Z Payen 25); BN2 (Z Payen 26, portrait inserted); BN3 (Z Payen 27, note on the two *privilèges* by Payen on flyleaf); BN4 (Z Payen 28, facsimiles or remounting of gathering ã and A1,2); BN5 (Z Payen 29, tp remounted on ã4; ã2.3 after 4E4); BN6 (Z Payen 30); Bar (lacks tp, 4E2.3 uncancelled but cancellans after 4K3); Bord; Ly (see note 5); *Nant*; Orl; *Rhei*; Stdi. UK: BL; Ed/NB; Ox: RAS (4E2.3 uncancelled but cancellans after 4E1). BELGIUM: Ant (4E2.3 uncancelled but cancellans after 4K3). GERMANY: *Mai*. HUNGARY: *Bud/N*. ITALY: Lucc (tp lacks date,

4E2.3 uncancelled).   SWITZERLAND: *Frib*; Gen; *Laus/P*.   USA: Harv; Prin; W/Cong.

11: 1602 Leiden A

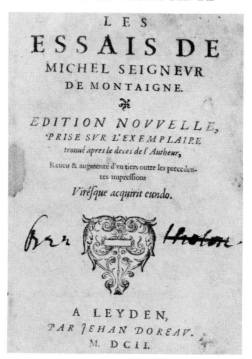

LES
ESSAIS DE
MICHEL SEIGNEVR
DE MONTAIGNE.

EDITION NOVVELLE,
PRISE SVR L'EXEMPLAIRE
trouué apres le deces de l'Autheur,
Reueu & augmenté d'vn tiers outre les preceden-
tes impressions
Virésque acquirit eundo.

A LEYDEN,
PAR JEHAN DOREAV.
M. DCII.

[134 mm]

Title-page: Text of title as No 8: 1598.

Collation: 8°: ã⁴ A—3S⁸ 3T⁴ [$4 signed, roman numerals; missigning 2C4 as 2C3, 2M2 as M2 (*variants*: missigning 2E2 as E2)];   520 leaves; pp [*8*] 1—390 381 392—403 405 405—645 466 647—655 356 657—740 727 742—743 743 743 746—747 747 749—751 718 753—780 481 782—882 887 884—902 803 904—1031 [*1*].

Contents: ã1: Title (verso blank); ã2: Short Gournay preface; ã2ᵛ: *Au lecteur*; ã3: Table of contents; A1: *Essais*; 3T4ᵛ: blank.

HT: ã2   [headpiece: central head with crescent, volutes] *PRE-FACE SVR LES* | Essais de Michel Sei-|*gneur de* *Montaigne,* | *PAR SA FILLE D'ALLIANCE.*

ã2ᵛ   [headpiece: central animal head, 2 cornucopiae] *AV* *LECTEUR.*

A1   [headpiece: central torso, grotesque animals, volutes] ESSAIS DE MICHEL | DE MONTAIGNE. | LIVRE PREMIER.

S6   [as A1 except] LIVRE SECOND.

2Y6ᵛ   [headpiece as A1 with slight variations] [as A1 except] LIVRE TROISIESME.

RT: Essais de Michel de Montaigne. | Livre premier [second] [troisiesme].[Essais Michel de Montaigne. 2P2ᵛ; Essais ee Michel de Montaigee. 2Z7ᵛ; ee (for de) 3B7ᵛ; Montaigne (no stop) 2I1ᵛ; livre (and whole RT to left) M8; Livre. Premierr. F1; premier (no stop) M7; prmier. N3; premir. C7 D4 E6; Lirve 2P3 2Q6; troisiesmes. 3B3; troisieisme. 3D1]

CW: Leaf. F8ᵛ ayans S8ᵛ mai-]fons 2D8ᵛ au-]tre re- 2O8ᵛ miennes, 2Q8ᵛ aux 3L8ᵛ entre 3S6ᵛ me-]moire, 3S7ᵛ vefcu? 3T1ᵛ iouyffance,

Measurements (M4): 41(+2) lines. 136 (143) × 74 mm. 20 lines=66 mm.

Privilège: None.

Notes: 1. Set from No 8: 1598 rather than No 9: 1600 or No 10: 1602 since it returns to some readings of 1598, e.g. Bertheuille (B2ᵛ), & luy promettoit (N7), *ſKeletos* (X3), *De l'vtile & de l'honneste* (2Y6ᵛ), where both 1600 and 1602 Paris differ (see No 10, note 1).

2. The catch-words listed clearly distinguish this edition from Nos 8, 9 and 10, 1598, 1600 and 1602. They are the same as those of No 12: 1602 Leiden B but there are slight variations.

3. This edition may have been printed in Geneva as suggested by Dezeimeris in a MS note in his copy of No 19: [1617] Envers reproduced by P Bonnet.[1]

---

[1] 'Une édition in-8°', *BSAM*, IV, 4 (1965), pp 29—31.

Copies: BN1 (Z Payen 31); BN2 (Z Payen 33); BN3 (16° Z 6359); BN4 (Z 19572); *Inst*; *Chamb*.   UK: BL; LU; Cam: *Trin*; Ox: AS; Bod; RAS. BELGIUM: Bru.   DENMARK: *Cop*.   GERMANY: *Cob*; *Reg*; Wolf. ITALY: Bol/A; Pad/C; Rom/C.   SPAIN: *Madr*.   SWITZERLAND: *Luz*; *Zür*.   USA: W/Folg.

12: 1602 Leiden B

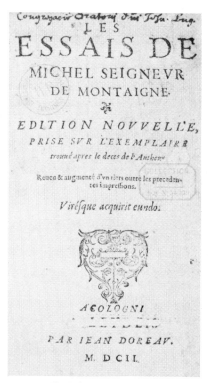

(*a*) Leiden [143 mm]   (*b*) Cologny [143 mm]

Title-page: The two tps are very close to No 11: 1602 Leiden A, but differ as follows: (i) *IEAN* for *JEHAN*; (ii) stop after *impressions*; (iii) no swash caps in *PRISE*, *EXEMPLAIRE*, *PAR*, *DOREAV*. In addition some copies have the imprint altered from Leiden to Cologny in roman or italic caps.

(*a*) Leiden.   (*b*) Cologny (BN2).

Collation: 8°: ã⁴ a—d⁸ A—3S⁸ 3T⁴ [\$4 signed, roman numerals; missigning 2K1 as Kᴋ (for Kk), 2K4 as Kᴋ iiij, 3K4 as Kᴋᴋ iiij (*variant*: 3M4 unsigned)]; 552 leaves; pp [72] 1—20 12 22—132 135 134—155 136 157—164 365 166—219 20 221—336 331 338—342 345 344—354 35 356—359 60 361—510 115 512—623 614 625—633 934 635—640 941 642—673 974 675—697 968 699—712 613 714—725 926 727—744 845 746—877 879 878 880—1011 012 1013—1029 1130 1031 [1] [*variant*: misnumbering 90 as 0].

Contents: ã1: Title (verso blank); ã2: Short Gournay preface; ã2ᵛ: *Au lecteur*; ã3: Table of contents; a1: Index of subjects; d6: Index to life; d7ᵛ—8ᵛ: blank; A1: *Essais*; 3T4ᵛ: blank.

HT: ã2	[headpiece: central head, volutes, 2 snakes] *PREFACE SVR LES* | Eꜱꜱᴀɪꜱ ᴅᴇ Mɪᴄʜᴇʟ Sᴇɪ-|*gneur de Montaigne,* | *PAR SA FILLE D'ALLIANCE.*	
ã2ᵛ	[headpiece: central lion's head, tendrils] *AV LECTEVR.*	
a1	[headpiece=ã2] LES PAGES DV SIEVR | ᴅᴇ Mᴏɴ-ᴛᴀɪɢɴᴇ, | [. . .] (see note 3)	
A1	[headpiece=ã2] ESSAIS DE MICHEL | DE MON-TAIGNE. | LIVRE PREMIER.	
S6	[as A1 except] LIVRE SECOND.	
2Y6ᵛ	[as A1 except] LIVRE TROISIESME,	

RT: Eꜱꜱᴀɪꜱ ᴅᴇ Mɪᴄʜᴇʟ ᴅᴇ Mᴏɴᴛᴀɪɢɴᴇ. \| Lɪᴠʀᴇ Pʀᴇᴍɪᴇʀ [Sᴇᴄᴏɴᴅ] [ᴛʀᴏɪꜱɪᴇꜱᴍᴇ]. [ᴍɪᴄʜᴇʟ ᴅᴇ ᴍᴏɴᴛᴀɪɢɴᴇ. B3ᵛ; ᴍᴏɴᴛᴀɪɢɴᴇ. 3A8ᵛ 3C5ᵛ 3G4ᵛ 3I1ᵛ 3O2ᵛ; ᴘʀᴇᴍɪᴇʀ. OPR(—R3); Pʀᴇᴍɪᴇʀ. (for Sᴇᴄᴏɴᴅ.) S7 T3; ꜱᴇᴄᴏɴᴅ. once or more in XZ 2B—FHKMO—QS—Y; Tʀᴏɪꜱɪᴇᴍᴇ. 2Z1,4,6—8 3BFK1,4—8 3DHM1,4,6—8 3O7; Tʀᴏɪꜱɪᴇꜱᴍᴇ. 2Z2,3 3BD—FH—M2,3 and once or more in 3ACGNO—T; ᴛʀᴏɪꜱɪᴇᴍᴇ. 2Z5 3DHM5 3O1; Tʀᴏɪꜱᴇꜱᴍᴇ. 3I7 (*variant*: Mᴏɴᴛᴀɪɢ 3S1ᵛ)]

CW: Leaf. As No 11: 1602 Leiden A on F8ᵛ S8ᵛ 2D8ᵛ 2Q8ᵛ 3L8ᵛ; 2O8ᵛ miennes (no comma) 3S6ᵛ me-]moi- 3S7ᵛ vefcu (no question mark) 3T1ᵛ iouiffance (no comma) c8ᵛ Serment

Measurements: (E2): 41(+2) lines. 138 (145) × 74 mm. 20 lines=68 mm.

Privilège: None.

Notes: 1. A line-by-line reprint of No 11: 1602 Leiden A with indexes of subjects and life set from No 10: 1602. In some cases the page references in the 1602 Leiden B index of subjects refer incorrectly to the pages of 1602 Paris, e.g.

Rubric in the index of 1602 Paris	*Page reference in the index of 1602 Paris*	*Page reference in the index of 1602 Leiden B*	*Correct page reference to the text of 1602 Leiden B*
Allemans yures se ressouuiennent de leurs affaires.	330	330	291
ne trient le vin qu'ils boiuent	332	332	292

Most copies have the indexes at the beginning, but BN3 and Gren 1 have them at the end after 3T4.

2. The headpiece on No 12: 1602 Leiden B ã2 is very close to that on No 10: 1602 ã4ᵛ and 3E5ᵛ but lacks the initials IG.

3. On a1 the heading of the index follows that of No 10: 1602 (4F1) except for changes of alignment and *precieuſes* for *preciſes*.

4. The substitution of Cologni for Leyden on some tps suggests that this edition may have been printed in Geneva.

Copies: (with Leyden on tp except where Cologni is indicated): BN1 (Z Payen 32); BN2 (Z Payen 34, Cologni); BN3 (Z 19573); Bord; Dij; Gren 1 (S 1922, Cologni); Gren 2 (P 1558, Cologni, tp torn); *Stra* (tp torn); Vers. UK: Ox: Ori. GERMANY: *Brem*. POLAND: *Poz*. USA: Harv; Prin; W/Cong.

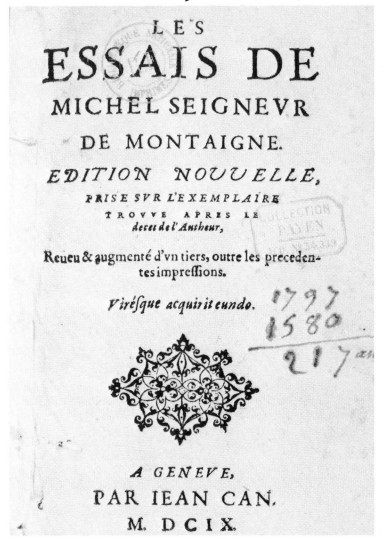

LE'S
ESSAIS DE
MICHEL SEIGNEVR
DE MONTAIGNE.
EDITION NOUUELLE,
PRISE SVR L'EXEMPLAIRE
TROVVE APRES LE
deces de l'Autheur,

Reueu & augmenté d'vn tiers, outre les precedentes impreſſions.

Viréſque acquirit eundo.

A GENEVE,
PAR IEAN CAN.
M. DCIX.

[140 mm]

The cancel title-page is similar to the Leiden tps of 1602 and 1609 (see Nos 11, 12 and 15) but the rest is as No 12: 1602 Leiden B of which it therefore seems to be a re-issue. The new Geneva imprint argues in favour of 1602 Leiden B having been printed in Geneva.

Copy: BN (Z Payen 48).

12B: 1616 Geneva

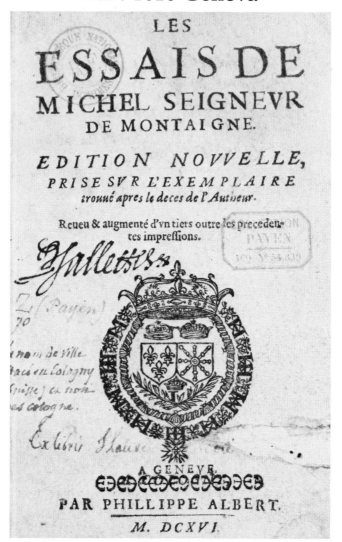

[135 mm]

The cancel title-page is the same as No 17: 1616 Cologny (*a*), but is overprinted A GENEVE. The rest is as No 12: 1602 Leiden B. This combination again confirms the links between 1602 Leiden B and Geneva.

Copies: BN (Z Payen 70); Avig.

[139 mm]

Title-page: The engraving is the same as No 10: 1602, except that 2 is changed to 4 in the date.

Collation: 8°:ã⁴ A—₃S⁸ ₃T⁴ a—d⁸ [$4 (—₃T4) signed, roman numerals; missigning T₁ as Tj, V₁ as Vj, X₁ as Xj, Y₁ as Yj, Z₁ as Zj, 2F₃ as Ff iij, 2H₃ as H₃, 3C₁ as Cec]; 552 leaves; pp [*8*] 1—126 117 128—157 258 159—193 198 195—489 460 491—645 466 647—712 613 714—741 247 743—780 751 782—820 8ᴢ1 822—837 83d 836 840—845 849 847—878 798 880—883 834 885—925 928 927—961 96ᴢ 163 964—991 692 993—1031 [*65*].

Contents: As No 12: 1602 Leiden B except that the indexes a1ʳ—d7ʳ are placed after ₃T4ᵛ, which carries the *privilège* instead of being blank.

HT: ã2	[double row of 12 arabesque type-orns] PREFACE SVR LES ESSAIS | ᴅᴇ Mɪᴄʜᴇʟ sᴇɪɢɴᴇᴠʀ | de Montaigne. | *PAR SA FILLE D'ALLIⲒANCE,*
A1	[headpiece: central torso, grotesque animals, volutes] ESSAIS DE MICHEL | DE MONTAIGNE. | LIVRE PREMIER.
S6	[headpiece: central grotesque head, 2 cornucopiae, inits MV] [as A1 except] LIVRE SECOND.
2Y6ᵛ	[as A1 except] LIVRE TROISIESME.
a1	[headpiece: owl, 2 dogs, volutes, inits LC (or LO?)] LES PAGES DV SIEVR | ᴅᴇ Mᴏɴᴛᴀɪɢɴᴇ.

RT: Essᴀɪs ᴅᴇ Mɪᴄʜᴇʟ ᴅᴇ Mᴏɴᴛᴀɪɢɴᴇ. \| Lɪᴠʀᴇ ᴘʀᴇᴍɪᴇʀ [sᴇᴄᴏɴᴅ] [ᴛʀᴏɪsɪᴇsᴍᴇ]. [ᴍɪᴄʜᴇʟ ᴅᴇ ᴍᴏɴᴛᴀɪɢɴᴇ. ₃T2ᵛ, 3ᵛ; Mɪʜᴇʟ ₃E7ᵛ ₃F1ᵛ; Mɪᴄʜᴇʟ ᴅᴅ 2S₃ᵛ 2T1ᵛ; Mᴏɴᴛᴀɪɢɴᴇ, PQRS (—S₅); Mᴏɴᴛᴀɪɢɴᴇ (no stop) K4ᵛ, 6ᵛ and once in LMOT 2LPR; ʟɪᴠʀᴇ once or more in I—M 2GHM; ᴘʀᴇᴍɪᴇʀ. A2; ᴘʀᴇᴍɪᴇʀ (no stop) once or more in ABH—MN; sᴇᴄᴏᴅᴅ. T7; sᴇᴄᴏɴᴅ. (for ᴛʀᴏɪsɪᴇsᴍᴇ.) 2Y7, 8; Tʀᴏɪsɪᴇᴍᴇ. 2Z1; ᴛʀᴏɪsɪᴇsᴍꟼ. ₃R6; ᴛʀᴏɪsɪᴇsᴍᴇ, ₃L6 ₃P7; ᴛʀᴏɪsɪᴇᴍᴇ. once or more in 2Z ₃Q—S; Tʀᴏɪsɪᴇsᴍᴇ. once or more in ₃A—DRS] [*variants*: Lɪᴠɪᴇ ᴘʀᴍɪᴇʀ. B6]

CW: Leaf A—H, T—₃P; quire I—S, ₃Q—₃T; as Nos 11 and 12: 1602 Leiden A and B on F8ᵛ S8ᵛ 2Q8ᵛ ₃L8ᵛ; no CW on ₃S6ᵛ, 7ᵛ ₃T1ᵛ; 2D8ᵛ au-]tre re 2O8ᵛ miennes, c8ᵛ serment

Measurements (M4): 41 (+2) lines. 137 (145) × 72 mm. 20 lines = 67 mm.

Privilège: To Abel L'Angelier for 10 years. Paris, 1 April 1602, signed RENOVARD (Plate 6).

Notes: 1. This edition is for the most part a close line-by-line reprint of the text of 1602 Leiden A or B. It agrees with No 12: 1602 Leiden B against No 11: 1602 Leiden A on a number of errors (e.g. the pagination error 613 for 713) and also in the tapered setting at the end of Bk I. But it agrees with 1602 Leiden A against 1602 Leiden B on other points (e.g. the pagination error 466 for 646).

2. However, there are many curious features which link this edition with No 10: 1602. The engraved tp of 1604 is identical with 1602 Paris, L'Angelier, except for the difference in date which has been clumsily altered in some copies. The *privilège* reproduces the substance of the cancellans 4E3ᵛ in 1602 Paris, though the wording is slightly different (Plate 6). On a1 the heading of the index in 1604 returns to the reading *precises* of 1602 Paris instead of *precieuses* in 1602 Leiden B.

3. Yet there is almost overwhelming evidence that this edition came from the same printer as No 11: 1602 Leiden A. The headpieces on A1 and 2Y6ᵛ are identical with that on 2Y6ᵛ in 1602 Leiden A, though they are slightly different from the similar ones on A1 and S6 in 1602 Leiden A. In both editions 33 out of the 104 initials are the same. Since 1602 Leiden A and B may have been printed in Geneva (see No 11, note 3 and No 12, note 4), it would therefore follow that 1604 was also printed there, and the signatures Tj, Vj, Xj and Zj are also a slight argument in favour of this. But if this edition was printed in Geneva where did the L'Angelier tps, which seem genuine, come from? If on the other hand 1604 is a genuine L'Angelier edition, what is its connection with the printer of 1602 Leiden A and perhaps with Geneva? It is difficult to offer a satisfactory solution to these problems.

Copies: BN1 (Z 19575); BN2 (Z Payen 35); Ars; Stge (prelims restored, lacks *Au lecteur* ã2ᵛ); Bes (tp date corrected, portrait inserted signed Rais del. Le Coeur); Bord; Brg 1 (M 889, lacks tp); Brg 2 (112554, tp may be a cancel); *Cout*; Gren 1 (P 255); Gren 2 (J 2423); Ly (tp date corrected); Monp (lacks all after 2M4); *Touls*; Tro (tp remounted, lacks d5—8); *Verd*. UK: BL (3 vols, M L Schiff—G P Best copy); Cam: Kings; *Leeds*; Ox: Bod (marginal notes identify some characters); RAS (tp may be a cancel, date corrected).   AUSTRIA: *Graz/U*.   HUNGARY: *Bud/M*; *Bud/N*.   USA: Harv; Prin.   USSR: *Mosc/L*.

14: 1608

(*a*) M Nivelle [149 mm]

Title-page: An engraving signed on the plinths 'Emundus Charpy fecit'.[1]
The only differences between the five tps are the booksellers' imprints:

    (*a*) Michel Nivelle (BN1, Tro, RAS, Ham).

    (*b*) Jean Petit-pas (BN2,9, Vend 2, BL, LU, Rom/V, Len/S).

    (*c*) Claude Rigaud (BN6,7, Bud/U, Lucc, Parm, Mosc/H).

    (*d*) Veuve Dominique Salis (BN4,5, Chan/F, Ill).

    (*e*) Charles Sevestre (BN3, Stge, Senl, Vend 1).

The design of the tp with its pediment, columns and plinths is similar to
No 10: 1602 but includes three allegorical figures and is more ornate.
The text of the title is also similar to 1602 but it omits *prise sur
l'Exemplaire trouué apres le deceds de l'Autheur* and adds *enrichie d'annotations
en marge*.

---

[1] For reference to other engravings by Charpy, see Duportal, *Catalogue*, No 31 (1603),
No 228 (1611).

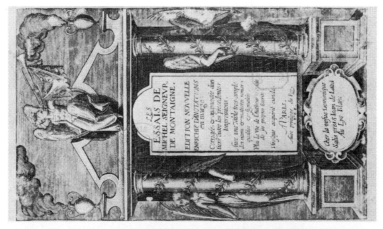

(d) Veuve D Salis [149 mm]

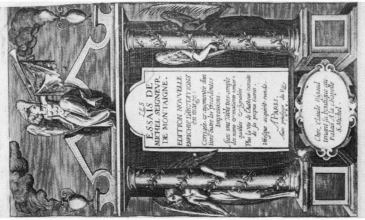

(c) C Rigaud [149 mm]

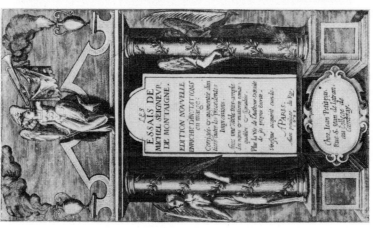

(b) J Petit-pas [149 mm]

(*e*) C Sevestre [149 mm]

Collation: 8°: ã⁸ A—₃I⁸ ₃K⁸ (±₃K₁.8) ₃L—₃Y⁸ 4A—4B⁸ 4C² [$4 signed, roman numerals; missigning 2T4 as Tr iiij (*variants*: missigning 2R2 as 2Q2)];   570 leaves;   pp [*16*] 1—295 196 297—351 325 353—373 74 375—460 361 462—566 597 568—580 581, 582—604 607—738 779—911 612 913—1007 10C8 1009—1129 [=1087] [*37*] [*variants*: misnumbering 352 as 52 or 523, 869 as 698, 937 as 936].[2]

Contents: ã1: Title (verso blank); ã2: *Au lecteur*; ã2ᵛ: Short Gournay preface; ã3: Table of contents; ã4ᵛ: Life; ã8: blank; ã8ᵛ: Portrait by Thomas de Leu; A1: *Essais*; 3Y8ᵛ: blank; 4A1: Index; 4C2ᵛ: End of index, *Privilège*.

HT: ã2   [headpiece: central head with crescent, volutes, 2 winged figures] *AV LECTEVR*.

---

[2] The usefulness of the pagination jumps 604 607 and 738 779 in determining derivation from this edition has been pointed out by P Bonnet, 'L'édition de 1608 des *Essais* de Montaigne et sa pagination réelle', *BSAM*, III, 27 (1963), pp 47—9.

ã2ᵛ [headpiece: central head, volutes, 2 snakes, inits CR] PREFACE SVR LES | ESSAIS DE MICHEL | Seigneur de Montaigne, | PAR SA FILLE D'ALLIANCE. (Plate 9)

ã4ᵛ [headpiece: central horned head, fruit, 2 torch-bearing putti, inits DC] SOMMAIRE | DISCOVRS SVR LA VIE | DE MICHEL, SEIGNEVR | de Montaigne, extraict de | ſes propres eſcrits.

A1 [headpiece: central goat's head, 2 birds, 2 cornucopiae, inits FM] ESSAIS | DE MICHEL | DE MONTAIGNE, | LIVRE PREMIER.

T7 [as A1 except] LIVRE SECOND.

3B3 [as A1 except] LIVRE TROISIESME.

4A1 [headpiece=ã2] TABLE | DES MATIERES | ET NOMS PLVS MEMO- | RABLES CONTENVS AVX | Eſſais de Michel ſieur de | Montagne.

RT: ESSAIS DE MICHEL DE MONTAIGNE. | LIVRE PREMIER [SECOND] [TROISIESME]. [ESSAIS DE MICHEL DE MOTAIGNE. 3I8ᵛ; MICHEL DE MONTAIGNE, once in 3K—PRTXY, 3V3ᵛ, 5ᵛ; MICHEL DE MONTAIGNE. once in CEFHKMNPRTXZ 2BDFHKMOQSVY 3BDFHILNQRT; MONTAIGNE, once or more in 2S—Z 3A—Y; MONTAIGNE (no stop) Z7ᵛ 3S4ᵛ; MONTIGNE. 2D5ᵛ 2F6ᵛ; LIVRE once in 2HLNPRSVYZ 3BCE—IN; TROSIESME. 313] [*variants*: ESSAIS DE MICHEL DE MOTAIGNE. 3G7ᵛ 3K8ᵛ; MONTAIGINE. H2ᵛ; TROSIESME. 3M7; ROISIESME. 3M7 3K8]

CW: Quire. I8ᵛ MET-]tray- T8ᵛ merueille, 2I8ᵛ craignons 2X8ᵛ train 3I8ᵛ forts 3K8ᵛ (cancelland) merueil-] leuſe 3K8ᵛ (cancellans) qu'el-]les 3T8ᵛ contem- 4A8ᵛ coulpe 4B8ᵛ Trahiſon

Measurements (2A1): 42(+2) lines. 143(148) × 68 mm. 20 lines=68 mm. Width with sidenotes 82 mm.

Privilège: For 7 years to Charles Sevestre, Michel Nivelle and Claude Rigaud. Paris, 23 May 1608, signed BERGERON (see note 4 below and Plate 10).

Notes: 1. Set from No 9: 1600. Although 1600 and No 10: 1602 are very close, No 14: 1608 shares certain features with 1600 which are not present in 1602. For example, 1608 returns to readings of 1600 where there are errors in 1602:

	1600	*1602*	*1608*	
2P6 line 16, 17	dix fens	fix fens	dix fens	2N2 line 13
3N3 lines 34—5	à mefpris	à mefme prix	à mefpris	3I4 line 24
4C8 line 32	comte	contre	compte	3Y2 line 19

Elsewhere an accumulation of small details shows 1608 agreeing with 1600 against 1602. E.g. 1600, 1602 (O6^r, p 219), 1608 (N7$^{r—v}$, pp 205—6):

Line number in 1600 and 1602	*1600 and 1608*	*1602*
2	vn'affection	vne affectiõ
3	ayfément	aifément
11	Ce ne l'eft	ce ne l'eft
22—3	mefmes	mefme
30	fouz	fous
35—6	d'vtenfiles	d'vftenfiles

2. Although the text of No 14: 1608 derives from No 9: 1600, the index derives from No 10: 1602, and is a conflation of the indexes of subjects and of proper names first printed in that year. The 1602 index to Montaigne's life has been used as the basis for the *Sommaire discours sur la vie de Michel, Seigneur de Montaigne* which here appears for the first time. 1608 is the first edition with sidenotes giving summaries. These two novelties, the life and the summaries, are mentioned on the title-page and in the *privilège*; they were later strongly criticised by Mlle de Gournay in her prefaces of 1617 and 1625. The portrait signed 'Thomas de Leu fecit' with the quatrain attributed to Malherbe also appears for the first time[3] (Plate 7).

3. The cancellans 3K1.8 corrects the text on p 938. The cancellandum 3K8^v, though correctly numbered p 938, in fact carries a duplicate text of p 939 beginning: '[qu'el]les ne font?', and ending: 'merueil-[leufe]'. The cancellans restores the correct text to p 938 whilst at the same time correcting certain errors on 3K8^r, and there is also a slight change of alignment at the end of this page (Plate 8). 3K1$^{r—v}$ (pp 923—4) has also been reset with some corrections, e.g. 3K1^r (line 21—22): d'vn (d'vne) fi longue captiuité; 3K1^v (sidenote): *Or des Indiens ammoncelez* (*amõcelé*). In most cases 3K1.8 has been replaced by a cancellans fold (BN4,5,6, Tro, BL, LU, Parm). In BN9 the cancellans has been inserted but the

---

[3] See E Labadie, *Les Essais de Montaigne*, 1916, p 27.

cancelled fold is bound in at the end. Elsewhere the two leaves have been inserted separately on stubs (BN1). Uncancelled copies are rare (RAS). In Dur, which despite its 1636 tp, is a copy of 1608, the erroneous text on p 938 has been crossed out in ink and the correct text supplied in MS on an inserted leaf.

4. The index and *privilège*, 4A—4C, pose difficult problems. BN3 and BN7, with 1608 tps, contain gatherings 4A and 4B of the index belonging to 1611. Moreover, these two copies together with BN4 show three settings of the final gathering of the index, which also contains the *privilège* (4C2^v, Plate 10). The three settings of the *privilège* are distributed as follows:

(a) Sevestre/Nivelle/Rigaud *privilège* 1608: BN1, 4, 5, 9, Tro, BL, LU, RAS, Ham, Lucc, Parm, Rom/V.

(b) Sevestre/Petit-pas *privilège* 1608: BN3 1611: BN4, Chan/C, Chau.

(c) Rigault/Nivelle *privilège* 1608: BN7 1611: BN2, 3, BL, Trin, Jes, Wolf.

From this it appears that *privilège* (a) belongs to 1608 and *privilège* (c) belongs to 1611. *Privilège* (b) is typographically closer to (a) than to (c) yet seems to be found mainly in the 1611 edition. It must be stressed, however, that the index has only been fully collated in six copies of 1608 (BN3, 4, 7, BL, LU, RAS) and two of 1611 (BL, Jes). Of these, BN3 and BN7, despite their 1608 tps, should perhaps be assigned to 1611, since they exhibit other features of 1611 in addition to the index and *privilège*, e.g. *Aduis* (for *Preface*) ã2^v; sources of quotations in sidenotes; the correct text on 3K8^v. The whole matter must therefore be treated with caution, and the overlapping between 1608 and 1611 requires fuller investigation.

Copies: BN1 (Z Payen 36); BN2 (Z Payen 37—39, heavily sophisticated); BN3 (Z Payen 44—46, lacks portrait); BN4 (Z Payen 42, portrait misplaced); BN5 (Z Payen 43, lacks portrait, MS notes); BN6 (Z Payen 40, lacks portrait and all after 3Y8); BN7 (Z Payen 41, prelims mixed up, lacks portrait); BN8 (16°Z 6413, lacks tp and portrait); BN9 (8°Z Don 597 (3), contains 3K1.8 cancellandum and cancellans); *Hist*; Stge; Bar (lacks tp, prelims and gathering 4C); *Chan/F*; *Senl*; Tro; *Vend 1* (175); *Vend 2* (176). UK: BL; LU; Dur (tp of 1636); Ox: RAS. GERMANY: Ham. HUNGARY: *Bud/U*. ITALY: Lucc; Parm; Rom/V. SWITZERLAND: *Laus/P*. USA: Harv 1 (*MON 16.08P); Harv 2 (*MON 16.08.5); Ill; W/Folg. USSR: *Len/S*; *Mosc/H*.

15: 1609 Leiden

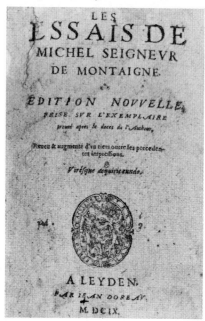

[144 mm]

Title-page: A close resetting of No 12: 1602 Leiden B (*a*). The main differences are: (i) in 1609 three asterisks replace the tendril ornament below line 4 in 1602 Leiden B; (ii) the printer's device in 1609 shows three smiths and an anvil; (iii) 1609 has *cA* for *A* in *EXEMPLcAIRE*, *cAutheur* and *PcAR IEcAN DOREcAV*; (iv) the date.

Collation: 8°: ã⁴ a—d⁸ A—3S⁸ 3T⁴ [$4 signed, roman numerals; missigning 2K1—4 with small caps instead of lower case (*variants*: missigning 2Q1 as Q)]; 552 leaves; pp [72] 1—9 0 11—161 *162* 163 164 164 166—174 375 176—194 295 196—213 84 215—234 33 236 237 38 239—261 562 263—296 397 298—336 331 338—356 573 358—362 36 364 365 266 367—391 9ẓ 393—398 999 400—427 82* 429—539 440 541—547 48 549—555 56 557—595 696 597—623 614 625 626 267 628—640 941 642—659 600 661 630 663—698 996 700—702 107 704—712 613 714—725 926 727—782 785 784—827 818 829—866 86 868—877 879 878 880—903 604 905—953 654 955 956 959 958—960 917 962—987 788 989—1016 9017 1018—1029 1130 1031 [*1*] [*variants*: misnumbering 228 as 28, 264 as 164, 330 as 30, 374 as 74, 696 (for 596) as 698, 716 inside HL].

Contents: As No 12: 1602 Leiden B.

HT: ã2   [headpiece: central lion's head, stylised vine and grapes]
            PREFACE SVR LES | Essais de Michel Sei-|*gneur de
            Montaigne,* | *PAR SA FILLE D'ALLIANCE.*

ã2ᵛ   [headpiece: 2 central birds' heads, volutes] *AV LEC-
            TEVR.*

a1   [headpiece: arabesque orns] LES PAGES DV SEIG-
            NEVR | de Montaigne.

A1   [headpiece: central head, volutes, 2 snakes] ESSAIS DE
            MICHEL | DE MONTAIGNE. | LIVRE PREMIER.

S6   [headpiece=a1] [as A1 except] LIVRE SECOND.

2Y6ᵛ   [headpiece=ã2ᵛ] ESSAIS DE MICHEL | de Mon-
            taigne. | LIVRE TROISIESME,

RT: Essais de Michel de Montaigne. | Livre Premier [Second]
[Troisieme]. [Assais 3B1ᵛ; deMichel 3H6ᵛ 3L4ᵛ 3O1ᵛ; ichel
Z2ᵛ; michel once or more in BCEFKMQV 2ABEHKOPRVYZ
3ABGKLOPQ; deMontaigne. 2O3ᵛ; Montaigne (no stop)
Y2ᵛ 3P1ᵛ; Montaigme. 2O1ᵛ, 2ᵛ; Montaig me. 2P3ᵛ; montaigne.
once or more in B—GKM—OQR—VYZ 2ABDGHK—MORTY
3A—DFHKLNOQ; livre once in BCEM—OTYZ 2ABDGLMOR
3D, K4,6 Y4,5; second. 2A1,2 2B7,8 2C1,5,7,8; Second (no stop)
2O5; troisieme. 3A1,4,5,7,8; troisiesme. once or more in 2Y 3ABD—
FHIMRS; Troisiesme. once or more in 2Z 3A—T]

CW: Leaf. As No 12: 1602 Leiden B on F8ᵛ S8ᵛ 2D8ᵛ 2O8ᵛ 2Q8ᵛ 3L8ᵛ;
S5ᵛ ES- [ESSAIS

Measurements (E2): 41 (+2) lines. 138 (145) × 77 mm. 20 lines = 67 mm.

Privilège: None.

Notes: 1. A close resetting of No 12: 1602 Leiden B. Collation, contents
and most catch-words are the same and, in addition, the following errors
in pagination are common to this edition and 1602 Leiden B, but are not
found in No 11: 1602 Leiden A: misnumbering 337 as 331, 624 as 614,
641 as 941, 713 as 613, 726 as 926, 878 as 879, 879 as 878, 1030 as 1130.

2. The same printer probably printed No 12: 1602 Leiden B and this edition, since the same ornamented initials are found on ã2(L), ã3(P), ã4(D), A7ᵛ(V), the same headpiece at the start of Bk I (A1), and the same tapered setting and tailpiece at the end of Bk I (S5ᵛ).

3. For a copy bearing the imprint Jean Can, Geneva, 1609 on the tp, see No 12A.

Copies: BN1 (Z 19574); BN2 (Z Payen 49); BN3 (16°Z 6361); BN4 (Z Payen 50, Bk I only); Vers.   UK: Ox: Tay.   DENMARK: *Cop.*   EIRE: Dub/T.   GERMANY: *Aug.*   POLAND: *Wroc/O.*   USA: Prin.

16: 1611

(*a*) F Gueffier [149 mm]

(*b*) M Nivelle [149 mm]

Title-page: The same engraved plate has been used as in No 14: 1608, but
08 has been scratched out and 11 substituted in 1611 (*b*)—(*d*). In 1611(*a*),
however, 1608 still appears in the central cartouche but 1611 is added to
the imprint in the oval cartouche. The only differences between the five
tps are the booksellers' imprints. Those of Nivelle, Petit-pas, Rigaud
and Sevestre are as in 1608, see No 14 (*a*), (*b*), (*c*), (*e*). There is one
newcomer, F Gueffier.

    (*a*) François Gueffier (BN1, Chau)

    (*b*) Michel Nivelle (BN2,3, Trin, Jes, Stut, Wolf, Vat).

    (*c*) Jean Petit-pas (BN4, Cath, Ill).

    (*d*) Claude Rigaud (Chan/C, BL).

    (*e*) Charles Sevestre (Abbv, Mich).

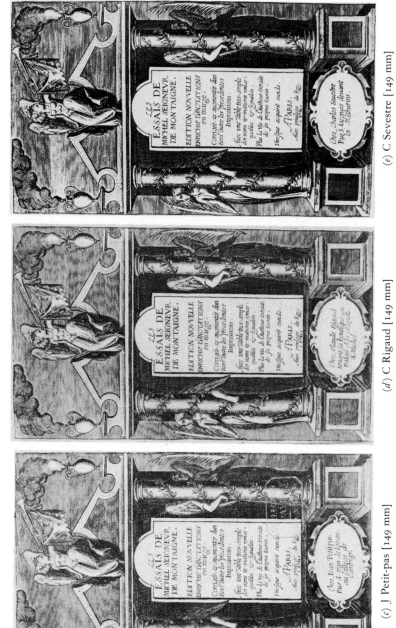

(c) J Petit-pas [149 mm]   (d) C Rigaud [149 mm]   (e) C Sevestre [149 mm]

Collation: 8°: ã⁸ A—₃Y⁸ 4A—4B⁸ 4C² [\$4 signed, roman numerals; missigning ã4 as ã iiil, I4 as I₃, M4 as M ii:j, ₃B1 as Bbb (for BBb), ₃I2 as 2I₃, ₃M4 as MMɯ iiij, ₃O2 as 2O2]; 570 leaves; pp [*16*] 1—15 16 [inside HL] 17—75 34 77—86 58 [inside HL] 88—203 304 205—251 252 253—287 828 289—340 431 342—396 367 398—438 436 440—472 44 474—493 794 495—496 797 498—593 5æ4 595—605 608—738 779—789 791 791 892 793 791 795—839 404 841—893 898 895—920 121 922—926 979 928—932 913 934—944 645. 946—950 195 952—1033 1014 1035—1057 1068 1059—1129 [=1087] [*37*].

Contents: As No 14: 1608.

HT: ã2   [headpiece: central head with crescent, volutes, 2 winged figures] *AV LECTEVR*.

    ã2ᵛ   [headpiece: central head, volutes, 2 snakes, inits CR] ADVIS SVR LES ESSAIS | DE MICHEL SEIGNEVR | de Montaigne, | PAR SA FILLE D'ALLIANCE. (Plate 9)

    ã4ᵛ   [as No 14: 1608]

    A1   [headpiece: central goat's head, 2 birds, 2 cornucopiae, inits FM] ESSAIS | DE MICHEL | DE MONTAIGNE, | LIVRE PREMIER.

    T7   [headpiece=ã2ᵛ] [as A1 except] LIVRE SECOND.

    ₃B₃   [as A1 except] LIVRE TROISIESME.

    4A1   [headpiece=ã2] TABLE | DES MATIERES | ET NOMS PLVS MEMO-|RABLES CONTENVS AVX | Eſſais de Michel ſieur de | Montagne.

RT: ESSAIS DE MICHEL DE MONTAIGNE, | LIVRE PREMIER [SECOND] [TROISIESME]. [ESSIAS 2A1ᵛ; ESAISS P₃ᵛ; ESSAIS DEMICHEL F5ᵛ H5ᵛ; MICEHEL C₃ᵛ; MICHEL once in ACIMNPQSVXZ 2BDEGLO; MICHEL DE MONₑIIGNE, B5ᵛ; MONTAIGNE (no comma) N₃ᵛ 2K1ᵛ 2Z8ᵛ ₃B8ᵛ ₃E6ᵛ ₃F1ᵛ ₃O7ᵛ; MONTAIGNE. 2L8ᵛ 2Z5ᵛ ₃N7ᵛ; MONTAGNE (no comma) ₃O3ᵛ; MONTAIG, ₃X₃ᵛ; MONTAIGNE, once in 2MNP—Y ₃ACEGHKMO; LI RE VSECOND. 2I7; PREMIER (no stop) B1 D1 G5 H1; PREMIER. (for SECOND.) Y1; SECNOD. 2T1; SECOND, V₃ Y8 Z8 2A2; SEEOND. X7 Z4; SEOND. 2B6; SECOND. 2L4 2N₃,₅,₈ 2O2—4 2P₃—4,7; TOISIESME. ₃D₃ ₃F8; TROISIESME (no stop) ₃D8 ₃E2 ₃I4]

CW: Quire. I8ᵛ co-]gnoiſſoit T8ᵛ merueille, 2I8ᵛ craignons 2X8ᵛ train ₃I8ᵛ forts ₃K8ᵛ qu'el-]les ₃T8ᵛ contem- 4A8ᵛ coulpe 4B8ᵛ Trahiſon

Measurements (E2): 42 (+2) lines. 142 (149) × 70 mm. 20 lines = 68 mm. Width with sidenotes 82 mm.

Privilège: There are two states both substantially the same as 1608 except for the names of the booksellers. For 7 years to *either* Charles Sevestre and Jean Petit-pas (BN4, Chan/C, Chau) *or* Claude Rigault and Michel Nivelle (BN2, 3, BL, Trin, Jes, Wolf). Paris, 23 May 1608, signed BERGERON. (See note 2 below and Plate 10)

Notes: 1. A close resetting of the prelims and text of No 14: 1608 but adding as sidenotes the sources of the quotations which appear in 1611 for the first time. The same printer printed 1608 and 1611 as the headpieces and some initials show (e.g. C on A4, D on E6). The distinguishing features of 1611 are the errors in signing and pagination, the running-titles with a comma after MONTAIGNE, and the following points:

	1608	*1611*
ã2	*AV LECTEVR.*	*AV LECTEVR.*
ã2ᵛ	PREFACE SVR LES	ADVIS SVR LES
I8ᵛ catch-word	met-]tray-	co-]gnoiſſoit
T7 headpiece	central goat's head	central human head
3Y8 line 18	iouyr loyallement	loyallement iouyr

Some words are omitted in the 1611 *Advis* (Plate 9).

BL and LU are clearly distinguished throughout, but other copies show some overlap between the editions (e.g. 1608 BN3 and BN7). The close connection between 1608 and 1611 is characterised by the Gueffier tp which carries both dates.

2. The two states of the *privilège* (Plate 10) are found in conjunction with the following imprints:

> Sevestre/Petit-pas *privilège*
> > with Gueffier imprint: Chau
> > with Petit-pas imprint: BN4
> > with Rigaud imprint: Chan/C
>
> Rigault/Nivelle *privilège*
> > with Nivelle imprint: BN2,3, Trin, Jes
> > with Rigaud imprint: BL

For these *privilèges* in copies with 1608 tp see No 14, note 4.

Copies: BN1 (Z Payen 59); BN2 (Z Payen 60, lacks portrait); BN3 (16° Z 6397); BN4 (Z Payen 61, portrait misplaced); *Cath*; *Inst*; *Abbv*; *Auch*; Chan/C; Chau (lacks portrait).   UK: BL; Cam: Trin; Ox: Jes. GERMANY: *Stut*; Wolf (lacks portrait).   ITALY: Vat.   USA: *Harv*; *Ill*; *Mich*; *Yale*.

17: 1616 Cologny/Geneva

(*a*) Arms of France and Navarre *A COLOGNY*, PAR PHILLIPPE ALBERT. [144 mm]

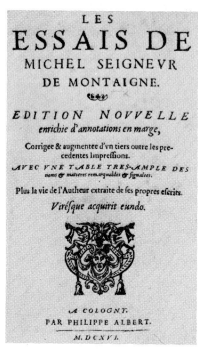

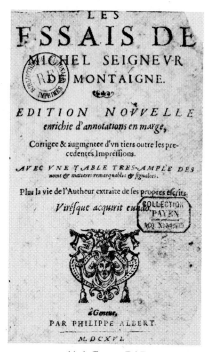

(b) *A COLOGNY*. PAR
PHILIPPE ALBERT. [144 mm]

(c) *à Geneue*, PAR
PHILIPPE ALBERT. [144 mm]

Title-page: Tp (*a*) is distinguished from the other seven by the arms of France and Navarre surrounded by the collars of the Order of St Michael and the Order of the Saint-Esprit, and also by PHILLIPPE for PHILIPPE. The orn on the other tps is a central head with basket of fruit flanked by two horn-blowing figures. They fall into two groups: 'PAR PHILIPPE ALBERT' (*b*), (*c*); 'De l'Imprimerie de Philippe Albert' (*d*)—(*h*). The wording of tp (*a*) closely resembles that of Nos 11 or 12, 1602 Leiden A or B; that of the others is the same as No 16: 1611. The place is variously given as Cologny or Geneva in different type-faces or no place is given. Tps (*f*)–(*h*) are not reproduced here.

   (*a*) Arms of France and Navarre, *A COLOGNY*, PAR PHIL-
        LIPPE ALBERT (BN2, Gen 1, Vien/N, Len/S). For this tp
        overprinted A GENEVE, see No 12B.

   (*b*) *A COLOGNY*. PAR PHILIPPE ALBERT (BN1,3, Stra, BL,
        Rom/C).

   (*c*) *à Geneue*, PAR PHILIPPE ALBERT (BN5).

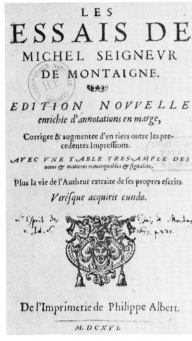

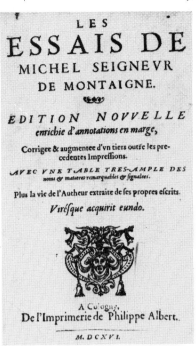

(d) No place, De l'Imprimerie
de Philippe Albert. [147 mm]

(e) A Cologny. De l'Imprimerie
de Philippe Albert. [147 mm]

(d) No place, De l'Imprimerie de Philippe Albert (BN6,7, Monb, Stj, Dill, Rom, Bresc, Gen 2, Scha).

(e) A Cologny. De l'Imprimerie de Philippe Albert (Wars/N).

(f) *A Geneue*, De l'Imprimerie de Philippe Albert (Carp).

(g) A GENEVE, De l'Imprimerie de Philippe Albert (BN4).

(h) *A GENEVE*, De l'Imprimerie de Philippe Albert (Gött).

Collation: 8°: ã⁸ A—4A⁸ 4B² [$4 signed, roman numerals; missigning 3B3 as Bbb iij (for BBb)]; 570 leaves; pp [*16*] 1—75 34 77—154 157 156—188 289 190—215 116 217—254 225 256—340 431 342—542 5 3 544—574 5 5 576—605 608—738 779—791 892 793—946 847 948—1100 1001 1102—1129 [=1087] [*37*].

Contents: ã1: Title (verso blank); ã2: *Au lecteur*; ã3ᵛ: Short Gournay preface; ã4: Table of contents; ã5ᵛ: Life; A1: *Essais*; 3Y8ᵛ: blank; 3Z1: Index.

HT: ã2　　[headpiece: central torso, grotesque animals, volutes] *AV*
　　　　　　LECTEVR.

ã3ᵛ　　[double row of 8 type-orns] AVIS SVR LES ESSAIS | DE
　　　　　MICHEL SEIGNEVR | de Montaigne, | PAR SA FILLE
　　　　　D'ALLIANCE.

ã5ᵛ　　[headpiece: central salamander, 2 seated figures pouring
　　　　　water] SOMMAIRE | DISCOVRS SVR LA VIE | DE MICHEL,
　　　　　SEIGNEVR | de Montaigne, extrait de | ſes propres eſcrits.

A1　　[headpiece=ã5ᵛ] ESSAIS | DE MICHEL | DE MON-
　　　　　TAIGNE, | LIVRE PREMIER.

T7　　[as A1 except] LIVRE SECOND.

3B3　　[as A1 except] LIVRE TROISIESME.

3Z1　　[headpiece=ã2] TABLE | DES MATIERES | ET NOMS
　　　　　PLVS MEMO- | RABLES CONTENVS AVX | Eſſais de
　　　　　Michel ſieur de | Montaigne.

RT: ESSAIS DE MICHEL DE MONTAIGNE, | LIVRE PREMIER [SECOND]
[TROISIESME]. [ESSAISDE 2L3ᵛ; MONTAIGNE (no comma) 2I7ᵛ; SECOND.
(for TROISIESME.) 3B5,7]

CW: Quire. On T8ᵛ 2I8ᵛ 2X8ᵛ 3I8ᵛ 3T8ᵛ as No 16: 1611; ã3ᵛ TABLE
ã8ᵛ ESSAIS I8ᵛ co-]noiſſoit 3Z8ᵛ coulpe 4A8ᵛ Trahiſon

Measurements (E2): 42(+2) lines. 141(148)×69 mm. 20 lines=68 mm.
Width with sidenotes 81 mm.

Privilège: None.

Note: Very close to 1608 and 1611, but set from No 16: 1611 as the
pagination jump 605 608 and the CW on I8ᵛ show. The *Avis* with the
omitted words (ã3ᵛ), and the sources of quotations in the sidenotes, also
link it with 1611 rather than 1608.

Copies: BN1 (Z Payen 62); BN2 (Z Payen 63, tp a cancel); BN3 (Z Payen
64—66, bound in 3 vols); BN4 (Z Payen 67); BN5 (Z Payen 68—69);
BN6 (Z Payen 71); BN7 (16° Z 6528); *Carp*; Monb; *Nant*; Stra. UK:
BL; Ed/N; Ox: Stj. AUSTRIA: *Vien/N*. GERMANY: *Dill*; Gött;
Pom. ITALY: Bresc; Rom/C. POLAND: *Wars/N*. SWITZER-
LAND: Gen 1 (Sm 1042, bound in 3 vols); Gen 2 (Hf 3372, bound in 3
vols); Scha; *Stga*; *Zür*. USA: *Temp*. USSR: *Len/N*; *Len/S*; *Mosc/L*.

(*a*) T Daré [149 mm]

Title-page: The engraved border and title are a close copy of No 14 or No 16, except that the *Ɛ* of *Ɛxtraite* is damaged in its upper curve, and the *Ɛ* of *Ɛscrits* has become *e*. *Avec privilege du Roy* is omitted and Charpy's signature is missing from the plinths. *A Paris* is changed to *A Rouen* and the date 1617 is transferred to the oval cartouche. The four tps differ only in the booksellers' imprints:

 (*a*) Thomas Daré (CCC, Wolf).
 (*b*) Jean Osmont (BN1, Vers, Tay, Rom/A).
 (*c*) Manassez de Preaulx (Mich, W/Folg).
 (*d*) Robert Valentin (BN2,3, RAS, Hunt).

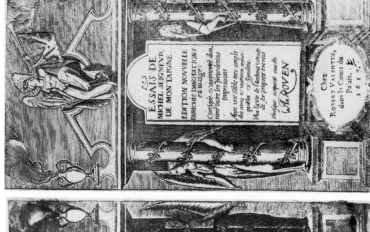

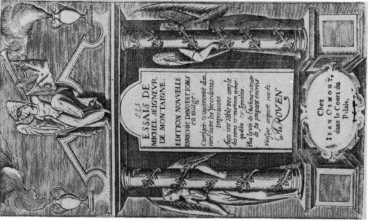

(b) J Osmont [149 mm]

(c) M de Preaulx [149 mm]

(d) R Valentin [149 mm]

Collation: 8°: ã⁸ A—3Y⁸ 4A—4B⁸ 4C² [\$4 signed, ã, A—3A, 3I—3Q arabic numerals, 3B—3H, 3R—4B roman numerals; missigning 3T4 as 3T3, 3V3 as 3T3 (*variant*: missigning 3N4 as NNn)]; 570 leaves; pp [*16*] 1—497 488 499—520 512 522—607 610—678 663 680—738 779—799 770 801—836 873 838—856 875 858—925 629 927—1049 1048 1051—1084 1083 1086—1129 [=1087] [*37*] [*variants*: misnumbering 607 610 611 612 613 as 607 608 611 812 613].

Contents: ã1: Title (verso blank); ã2: *Au lecteur*; ã2ᵛ: Short Gournay preface; ã3: Table of contents; ã4ᵛ: Life; ã8: blank; ã8ᵛ: Portrait after Leu; A1: *Essais*; 3Y8ᵛ: blank; 4A1: Index; 4C2ᵛ: End of index, *achevé d'imprimer*.

HT: ã2   [headpiece: 2 dogs' heads, volutes] *AV LECTEVR*.
        ã2ᵛ   [double row of 9 arabesque type-orns] ADVIS SVR LES ESSAIS | DE MICHEL SEIGNEVR | de Montaigne, | PAR SA FILLE D'ALLIANCE.
        ã4ᵛ   [headpiece=ã2] SOMMAIRE | DISCOVRS SVR LA VIE | DE MICHEL, SEIGNEVR | de Montaigne, extraict de | ſes propres eſcrits.
        A1   [headpiece=ã2] ESSAIS | DE MICHEL | DE MONTAIGNE, | LIVRE PREMIER.
        T7   [as A1 except] LIVRE SECOND.
        3B3   [headpiece: 2 grotesque figures, 2 dolphins' heads] [as A1 except] LIVRE TROISIESME.
        4A1   [headpiece: central Indian's head, 2 nude figures] TABLE | DES MATIERES | ET NOMS PLVS MEMO- |RABLES CONTENVS AVX | Eſſais de Michel ſieur de | Montaigne.

RT: A—3A, 3C–3R, ESSAIS DE MICHEL DE MONTAIGNE, | LIVRE PREMIER [SECOND] [TROISIESME]. [LIVRRE V5; LIRVE 2S7; TROISIEME. 3C5] 3B, 3S—3Y, *Eſſais de Michel de Montaigne, | Liure ſecond* [*troiſieſme*]. [*Eſaie* 3B6ᵛ; *Montaigne,* 3S1ᵛ 3V4ᵛ 3Y3ᵛ; *Nichel* 3S4ᵛ 3T3ᵛ; *Meicheld Montagne* (no comma) 3S6ᵛ; *Montaigne* (no comma) 3T6ᵛ]

CW: Quire. C8ᵛ rolle S8ᵛ *Des* 2I8ᵛ craignons 3A8ᵛ aſſeurer 3R8ᵛ en-]gendre 4A8ᵛ coulpe 4B8ᵛ Trahiſon

Measurements (F2): 42 (+2) lines. 143 (149) × 66 mm. 20 lines=68 mm.

Width with sidenotes 81 mm. (3S3): 42 (+2) lines. 147 (153) × 69 mm. 20 lines = 69 mm. Width with sidenotes 83 mm.

Privilège: None. *Achevé d'imprimer*: Nicolas L'Oyselet, 2 January 1617.

Notes: 1. A paginal resetting of No 16: 1611. It is of course very close to No 14: 1608 as well, but the following characteristics shared by 1611 and 1617 Rouen differentiate both from 1608: (i) swash *R* in *AV LECTEVR* (ã2); (ii) ADVIS instead of PREFACE (ã2ᵛ); (iii) comma in verso RT instead of stop; (iv) sources of quotations in sidenotes where 1608 has only summaries.

2. The portrait is a poor copy of 1611 and lacks Leu's signature. The words of the quatrain are the same as those in 1608 and 1611 and do not have the variants of No 20: 1617 Paris (Plate 7).

3. Six gatherings, 3B 3S—3Y, corresponding to the beginning and end of Bk III, have different type and different headline, and are perhaps the work of a separate printer. These gatherings also have roman instead of arabic numerals in the signatures, but gatherings 3C—3H 3R, also with roman numerals, do not have the different headline.

Copies: BN1 (Z Payen 77); BN2 (Z Payen 78); BN3 (Z Payen 79, lacks portrait, Bk I only); Gren (lacks tp); *Lons* (lacks tp); Vers. UK: Ox: CCC; RAS; Tay. GERMANY: Wolf. ITALY: Rom/A. USA: *Harv*; Hunt; Ill; *Mich*; W/Folg; *Yale*. USSR: *Len/N*.

19: [1617] Envers

Title-page: The engraved border and title appear to come from the same plate as No 18: 1617 Rouen with which it shares the particularities in *Extraite* and *escrits*. However, *A Rouen* is deleted in the central cartouche and the imprint in the oval cartouche reads A ENVERS CHEZ ABRAHAM MAIRE.

[149 mm]

Collation: 8°: π² ã⁴ A—3Y⁸ 4A—4B⁸ 4C² [$4 (−F2, P4) signed, roman numerals; missigning E3 as C3, P3 as P4]; 568 leaves; pp [*12*] 1—88 585 90—130 331 132—144 155 146—147 184 149—220 173 222—238 235 240—266 297 268—282 832 284—295 196 297—302 253 304—327 238 329—337 318 339—342 357 344—356 375 358—360 261 362—421 224 423—426 423 428—433 414 435—451 425 453—562 593 564—566 597 568—602 903 604 607—650 951 952 653—681 632 683—692 963 694—698 696 700 710 702—723 728 729 726—729 710 731—737 378 779—787 787 789—793 792 795—821 122 823—824 925 826—868 698 870—962 993 964—1027 1208 1029—1060 1065 1062—1088 1098 1090—1094 109 1096—1098 1990 1100—1112 1115 1114—1129 [= 1087] [*37*] [*variants*: misnumbering 157 as 77, 160 as 62, 579 as 576, 953 as 95, 1023 as ∠50].

Contents: π1: Title (verso blank); π2: blank; π2ᵛ: Portrait; ã1: Table of contents; ã2ᵛ: Life; A1: *Essais*; 3Y8ᵛ: blank; 4A1: Index.

HT: ã2ᵛ   [row of 11 arabesque type-orns] *SOMMᴄAIRE* | *DIS-COVRS SVR Lᴄᴀ* | VIE DE MICHEL, SEIGNEVR DE | *ᴄMontaigne, extraict de ſes propres eſcrits.*

      A1   [double row of 12 arabesque type-orns] ESSAIS | DE MICHEL | DE MONTAIGNE, | LIVRE PREMIER.

      T7   [double row of 9 arabesque type-orns with different orn at end of each row] [as A1 except] LIVRE SECOND.

      3B3   [as T7 except] LIVRE TROISIESME. (However, DE MONTAIGNE is in larger and bolder capitals than on T7 and A1)

      4A1   [row of 14 arabesque type-orns] TABLE | DES MATIERES | ET NOMS PLVS MEMO-|RABLES CONTENVS AVX | Eſſais de Michel Sieur de | Montaigne.

RT: A–3K 3M—3Y *Eſſais de ᴄMichel de ᴄMontaigne,* | *Liure premier* [*ſecond*] [*troiſiéme*]. [*Eſſais* S4ᵛ Z6ᵛ; *deᴄMichel* P6ᵛ 2B3ᵛ 2D5ᵛ; *Mcihel* 3QR4ᵛ 3ST6ᵛ; *deMontagne,* 2XY7ᵛ 2Z8ᵛ 3Q7ᵛ; *Montaigne.* C8ᵛ D6ᵛ E6ᵛ; ᴍontaigne, one or twice in A—EKLNOQTY 2V—2Z 3Q—3V; *Montaigne,* once or twice in B—ELNOQTY 2V—2Z 3DE 3Q—3Y; *ᴄMontaigne.* once or twice in ABSZ 3FK; *Liure* once or more in A—EKLNOQTY 2V—2Z 3Q—3V; *prmier.* I5; *premier* (no stop) S8; *ſecond.* (for *premier.*) I6 R1; *premier.* (for *ſecond.*) 2C6 2E6 2L2 2T2; *troiſiéme.* (for *ſecond.*) 3B1, 2; *troiſieſme.* once or more in 3B—3K 3M—3P 3VXY] 3L Essais de Michel de Montaigne, | Livre troisieme. [Momtaigne 3L3ᵛ]

CW: Quire. C8ᵛ rolle   I8ᵛ Met-] tray   2I8ᵛ craignons   3A8ᵛ aſſeurer 3K8ᵛ qu'el-] les   3R8ᵛ en-] gendre

Measurements (F3): 42 (+2) lines. 143 (150) × 69 mm. 20 lines = 68 mm. Width with sidenotes 83 mm.

    (3S3): 42 (+2) lines. 143 (150) × 72 mm. 20 lines = 68 mm. Width with sidenotes 85 mm.

    (3L2): 42 (+2) lines. 140 (148) × 68 mm. 20 lines = 66 mm. Width with sidenotes 83 mm.

Privilège: None.

Notes: 1. The derivation of this edition is hard to establish satisfactorily. In many respects it agrees with No 14: 1608 against the two intervening editions Nos 16 and 18, 1611 and 1617 Rouen, principally in the absence of sources in the sidenotes (except in gathering 3L) and also as follows:

References to [1617] Envers	1608, [1617] Envers	1611, 1617 Rouen
Table of contents, I 13	l'entree des Roys	l'entreueuë des Roys
last line of 'Life'	magnifique sepulture	honnorable sepulture
P5 line 9	Syracusain	Syracusien
3Y8 line 18	iouyr loyallement	loyallement iouyr
4B7ᵛ last line	Saturnius	Saturninus
4C2 last line	Virginité plus aspres	Virginité plus aspre

In gathering 3L, which has different headlines and type from the rest, the first page carries the text of p 939, which was the text erroneously printed on p 938 in 1608 and which necessitated the cancel 3K8 (see No 14, note 3). However, [1617] Envers agrees with 1611 and 1617 Rouen against 1608 in some typographical details, e.g.

	1608	1611, 1617 Rouen, [1617] Envers
A1 sidenote	*offen-|cez.*	*of-|fencez.*
line 8	quelquesfois	quelquefois
last line begins	de l'Epire	l'Epire
sidenote	*mité de cou-|rage*	*mité de | courage*

On balance the derivation of [1617] Envers from 1608 seems most likely but the use of other editions cannot be excluded.

2. The place of printing is also uncertain. In Bord the *achevé d'imprimer* of Nicolas L'Oyselet of Rouen is present, dated 2 January 1617, and this, together with the similarities of typography between [1617] Envers and No 18: 1617 Rouen might suggest Rouen as the place of printing. But since the *achevé* is lacking in all other copies examined, the evidence of Bord is not conclusive. This may therefore be a pirated edition printed in Antwerp as the imprint suggests.[1]

3. On the basis of the RT variants, the gatherings fall into two main groups: (i) F—IMPRSVXZ 2A—2T 3A are mainly regular apart from isolated aberrations; (ii) A—EKLNOQTY 2V—2Z 3Q—3Y have [*Mcihel*] [*deMontagne,*] [*Montaigne.*] [ᴍᴏntaigne,] [*Montaigne,*] [*Liure*] once or more. Within the second group 3BC 3F—3K 3M—3P 3VXY are

---

[1] See P Bonnet, 'Une édition in -8° des *Essais* publiée sans date au XVIIᵉ siècle', *BSAM*, IV, 4 (1965), pp 29—31.

distinguished by the presence of [*troifiefme.*] whilst 3L is alone in having roman for italic.

4. In BN1 and Bord, π^2 is folded round gathering ã so that the portrait faces the first page of the text. In BN2 gathering ã is at the end of vol i.

5. This edition lacks Montaigne's *Au lecteur* and the preface by Mlle de Gournay.

Copies: BN1 (Z Payen 51—54, bound in 4 vols); BN2 (Z Payen 55—57, bound in 3 vols); BN3 (Z Payen 58, lacks tp, portrait, ã2,3 and 2X4,5); Ars; Bord (contains *achevé*, see note 2); Chau (lacks portrait); Ren (tp remounted, lacks portrait).   UK: BL (GP Best copy with typed note at end referring to peculiarities of Bord); Aber.   BELGIUM: Ant; Bru; Ghe.   USA: *Harv*; Prin.

20: 1617

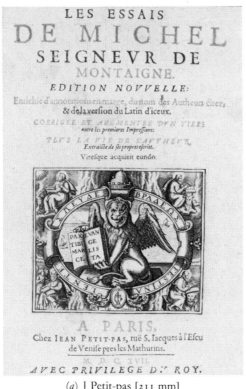

(*a*) J Petit-pas [211 mm]

LES ESSAIS
DE MICHEL
SEIGNEVR DE
MONTAIGNE.

EDITION NOVVELLE:

Enrichie d'annotations en marge, du nom des Autheurs citez,
& de la version du Latin diceux.

CORIGEE ET AVGMENTEE D'VN TIERS
outre les premiers Impressions:

PLVS LA VIE DE L'AVTHEVR,
Extraicte de ses propres escrits.

Vireíque acquirit eundo.

A PARIS,
Chez FRANÇOIS GVEFFIER, rüe S. Iean de
Latran deuant le College Royal.
M. D. C. XVII.
AVEC PRIVILEGE DV ROY,

(c) F Gueffier [212 mm]

LES ESSAIS
DE MICHEL
SEIGNEVR DE
MONTAIGNE.

EDITION NOVVELLE:

Enrichie d'annotations en marge, du nom des Autheurs citez,
& de la version du Latin diceux.

CORIGEE ET AVGMENTEE D'VN TIERS
outre les premiers Impressions:

PLVS LA VIE DE L'AVTHEVR,
Extraicte de sa propre escrits.

Vireíque acquirit eundo.

A PARIS,
Pour CLAVDE RIGAVD, Libraire
demeurant à Lyon.
M. D. C. XVII.
AVEC PRIVILEGE DV ROY.

(b) C Rigaud [211 mm]

LES ESSAIS
DE MICHEL
SEIGNEVR DE
MONTAIGNE.

EDITION NOVVELLE:
Enrichie d'annotations en marge, du nom des Autheurs citez,
& de la verfion du Latin d'iceux.

CORRIGEE ET AVGMENTEE D'VN TIERS
outre les premieres Impreffions:

PLVS LA VIE DE L'AVTHEVR.
Extraicte de fes propres efcrits.

. Vireíque acquirit eundo.

A PARIS,
Chez CHARLES SEVESTRE, en l'Iſle du Palais aux
trois Perruques, deuant le cheual de bronze.
M. D. C. XVII.
AVEC PRIVILEGE DV ROY.

(*e*) C Sevestre [212 mm]

LES ESSAIS
DE MICHEL
SEIGNEVR DE
MONTAIGNE.

EDITION NOVVELLE:
Enrichie d'annotations en marge, du nom des Autheurs citez,
& de la verfion du Latin d'iceux.

CORRIGEE ET AVGMENTEE D'VN TIERS
outre les premieres Impreffions:

PLVS LA VIE DE L'AVTHEVR.
Extraicte de fes propres efcrits.

Vireíque acquirit eundo.

A PARIS,
Chez MICHEL NIVELLE, ruë S. Iacques
aux Signes.
M. D. C. XVII.
AVEC PRIVILEGE DV ROY.

(*d*) M Nivelle [212 mm]

Title-page: On all five tps, the wording of the title is the same. It is substantially that of No 16: 1611 but adds *du nom des Autheurs citez, & de la version du Latin d'iceux*, drawing attention to the translations of Montaigne's quotations which appear for the first time. Tp (*a*) Petit-pas and (*b*) Rigaud have distinctive devices. Tps (*c*), (*d*), (*e*) have the same device, which is also found on ĩ2ᵛ and 2X4 of No 7A: 1595. Lines 2, 4, 6, 8, 10, A PARIS, and the date are in red.

> (*a*) Jean Petit-pas, winged lion device, signed 'I. de Courbes f.' (BN4,6, Bord 2, Chau, Sens, BL).
> (*b*) Claude Rigaud, water-spraying device, signed 'Halbeck f.' (BN5, Carc, Lan, Nîm, Heid).
> (*c*) François Gueffier (BN1,2, Cass, Châm, Tro, Mich, Mosc/L).
> (*d*) Michel Nivelle (BN3,7, Bord 1, AS, Bod, Wolf).
> (*e*) Charles Sevestre (Ami, Metz, Poi, Val, Ill).
> (*f*) Veuve Dominique Salis (no copy seen but mentioned by Tchemerzine, viii, 420).

Collation: 4°: ã⁴ ẽ⁴ ĩ⁴ A—3X⁸ 3Y⁴ *A—E⁴* a—c⁴ [$4 (+M5−N4) signed, roman numerals; missigning 2K4 as Kκ iiij (for Kk iiij) (*variants*: missigning G3 as F3, 3C3 as 3C2)]; 584 leaves; pp [*24*] *1* 2—122 121 124—159 161 161—235 239 237—347 347 349—382 387 384—465 467 467—742 343 744—750 725 752—857 878—899 890—910 912 912—925 929 927—958 961—967 969 969—987 *988* 989—1067 1468 1069—1072 1061 1074—1089 [=1077] [*67*] [*variant*: misnumbering 1074 as 1072].

Contents: ã1: Title (verso blank); ã2: Printers' preface; ã2ᵛ: Life; ã4ᵛ: Long Gournay preface, revised; ĩ3: End of preface, Table of contents; ĩ4: *Au lecteur*; ĩ4ᵛ: Portrait; A1: *Essais*; 3P8ᵛ: blank; 3Q1: Gournay's introduction to translations; 3Q2ᵛ: Translations of quotations; 3Y3: End of translations, Errata. 3Y3ᵛ: Montaigne's epitaph; 3Y4ʳ⁻ᵛ: blank; *A*1: Index of subjects; *E*4ᵛ: blank; a1: Index of proper names; c3ᵛ: End of index of proper names, Index of life; c4ᵛ: *Privilège*.

HT: ã2   [headpiece: central head, 2 dolphins' heads, 2 cornucopiae, inits HT, 24 × 115 mm] LES IMPRIMEVRS | AV LECTEVR.

ã2ᵛ   [rule] VIE DE MICHEL | SEIGNEVR DE MON-TAIGNE, | tiree prefque entierement de fes | Oeuures tres-conformes | à la verité.

ã4^v [headpiece: central winged head, volutes, flanked by 2 pairs of arabesque type-orns with rules above and below] PREFACE SVR LES ESSAIS | DE MICHEL, SEIG-NEVR | de Montaigne. | *Par ſa fille d'alliance.*

ĩ4 [headpiece=ã2] Au lecteur.

A1 [headpiece: central head, 2 dolphins' heads, 2 cornuco-piae, no inits, 27 × 102 mm] ESSAIS DE MICHEL | DE MONTAGNE. | LIVRE PREMIER.

R6^v [headpiece: central head, 2 snakes, volutes, 2 grotesque faces] ESSAIS | DE MICHEL DE | MONTAIGNE. | LIVRE SECOND.

2V2^v [headpiece: owl, phoenix, eagle, 2 winged insects, volutes] [as R6^v except] LIVRE TROISIESME.

3Q1 [headpiece=2V2^v] AV LECTEVR.

*A*1 [double row of 20 arabesque type-orns] LES PAGES DV SIEVR | DE MONTAIGNE.

a1 [headpiece=ã4^v but type-orns are entirely enclosed in rules] Table Exacte, | Des noms propres ou appelatifs, d'hommes, de peuples, d'a-|nimaux, de villes, de pays, de montagnes, de fleuues, d'iſles, | & autres choſes particulieres, contenuës en ce liure.

RT: *Eſſais de Michel de Montaigne* | *Liure Premier* [*Second*] [*troiſieſme*]. [The variations are exceptionally complex and are best summarised as follows. Firstly, some aberrations: *ds* (for *de*) A8^v; *Liur8* L8; *Premier* N4 O4 P2,5 Q1 R6; *Second* (for *troiſieſme*) 2V3,5 2X6. *Libre* I6 is corrected in some copies. Variations occurring frequently and without apparent pattern are *Eſſais* for *Eſſais* and a stop after *Montaigne*. Swash caps for *Michel* and *Montaigne* are also frequent in gatherings A—K. *Montagne* or *Montagne* (with or without stop) is also found on many pages of A—K and the pages in these gatherings which do have *Montaigne* usually have *Eſsais* as well: A5^v B3^v C6^v D6^v E4^v F6^v G4^v, 7^v H1^v I1^v K8^v. *Eſsais* also occurs on L3^v but not thereafter. A smaller setting occurs on some pages of gathering M. In the earlier gatherings are found the variations *premier* (with stop) on C7,8 D4 E1,5 F3,8 G1,2,5 H8 I2,8 M1,2 and *premier* (no stop) on M8.

In Bk III two compositors can be distinguished. One, in 2V4—8 2X 3G 3H 3O and 3P, combines *Troiſieſme* (or *Troiſieſme*) with the original verso RTs. The other, in 2Y, 2Z 3A—3F 3I—3N, combines *Eſſais* (or *Eſſais*) *de Michel de Montaigne* (or *Montaigne*), with *Liure troiſieſme*. The constant feature of the latter is the comma in the verso RT and the lower-case *t* on the recto.]

CW: Quire. ã4ᵛ hon-]neſte ẽ4ᵛ euſt E8ᵛ foibleſſe, R8ᵛ Clytus, 2A8ᵛ priſes, 2O8ᵛ contre 3F8ᵛ des 3O8ᵛ appetit *A*4ᵛ Conſeruation *B*4ᵛ Foy *C*4ᵛ Mots *D*4ᵛ 97. quel a4ᵛ Eryngium. b4ᵛ 762.

Measurements (P2): 40 (+2) lines. 189 (200) × 111 mm. 20 lines = 96 mm. Width with sidenotes 127 mm.

Privilège: To the Damoiselle de Gournay for 10 years to publish *le liure des Essais de Michel Seigneur de Montaigne, reueu, corrigé & augmenté, tant des Autheurs Latins en marge, que de la version de tous les passages Latins*. Paris, 28 November 1614, signed RENOVART. Ceded to François Gueffier, Jean Petit-pas, Charles Sevestre, Michel Nivelle, Claude Rigault, 28 November 1614, signed Gournay. *Achevé d'imprimer*: 8 May 1617.

Notes: 1. Set from No 8: 1598, which 1617 follows against No 7A: 1595 in many places, especially in the omission of the Thucydides sentence and of the quotation *Adeô nihil motum* in I 22 (see No 8, note 2). The sidenotes of this edition differ from those of No 16: 1611 and No 18: 1617 Rouen.

2. The printers' preface announces the novelty of this edition, namely that translations are given of the Latin quotations, and also that a revised version of Mlle de Gournay's long preface precedes the *Essais* despite her protests that it is unworthy to do so. The sources of Montaigne's quotations are also, the printers say, mainly the work of Mlle de Gournay, but include those that one of their friends had added to their previous edition (No 16: 1611). Another friend is responsible for the 'sommaires ou notes de la marge'. They apologise for the misprints but blame the war (ã2).

3. The Gournay preface to the *Essais* is that of 1595 heavily revised. She has suppressed the militant feminism and most of the personal, self-glorifying remarks. She has added the refutation of more objections, especially those of Baudius. She publicises her disagreements with the printers, disapproving strongly of the introductory life of Montaigne, the marginal summaries and the indexes. She admits partial responsibility for giving the sources of the quotations, adding that she has been helped by MM Bergeron, Martinière, Machard and Bignon (ĩ2ᵛ).

4. In her introduction to the translations Mlle de Gournay shows that she has thought in a serious and scholarly fashion about problems of translating Montaigne's quotations. She has undertaken the work with reluctance yielding only to pressure from the printers (3Q1).

5. A paste-down cancel slip is probably an example of Mlle de Gournay's scrupulous care in the translations: 'de souffrir & louer les actions de leur maistre' replaces 'de louër autant des actions de leur maistre, qu'ils en souffrent'. It is found on 3R5 in Ami, Bord 1 and 2, Châm, Etam, Tro, BL, AS, Wolf and relates to the quotation *Maximum hoc regni* in I 42.

6. Most copies have the index of proper names at the beginning between Mlle de Gournay's preface and the text of the *Essais*. These copies also usually have at the foot of 3Y3 a list of twelve errors to be corrected in the translations. However, in all copies with the Nivelle imprint, the index of proper names is placed at the end after the index of subjects, and the Errata for the translations is transferred to the top of 3Y4, which is otherwise blank. The first of these changes is logical, the second less so. Only Tro has the Errata for the translations at the bottom of 3Y3 and the index of proper names at the end after the index of subjects. This order has been adopted as that of the ideal copy, but there are many variations. BN7 (Nivelle) has the Errata on 3Y4, followed by the index of proper names; BL (Petit-pas) has the Errata on 3Y3, with 3Y4 blank, followed by the index of proper names; Avig (imprint lacking) has the Errata on 3Y4, but the index of proper names precedes the text of the *Essais*.

7. The portrait by Thomas de Leu is very close to that of 1608, but there are small differences and also changes in the quatrain (Plate 7).

Copies:[1] BN1 (Z Payen 72, lacks 3Y4 and gatherings *A—E*); BN2 (Z Payen 73); BN3 (Z Payen 74, lacks portrait); BN4 (Z Payen 75); BN5 (Z Payen 76, gatherings *A—E* after ĩ4); BN6 (8°Z 33612); BN7 (Z 3984); *Ars*; Cass; *Cath*; Ami; *Auch*; Avig (tp torn, device and imprint missing); Bord 1 (S 1239 Rés); Bord 2 (MF 3694); *Carc*; Châm; Chau; Etam (lacks tp and ã4); *Lan*; *Metz*; *Monp/U*; *Nîm*; Poi; *Sens*; Tro; *Val*. UK: BL (GP Best copy); Ox: AS; Bod. GERMANY: *Heid*; Wolf. SWITZER-LAND: *Zof*. USA: *Harv*; Ill; *Mich*; Prin. USSR: *Mosc/L*.

---

[1] See also A Salles, 'Mon exemplaire Petitpas 1617', *BSAM*, II, 5 (1939), p 38.

(*a*) T Daré [149 mm]

Title-page: The engraved border and title appear to come from the same plate as No 18: 1617 Rouen. The five tps differ only in the booksellers' imprints:

    (*a*) Thomas Daré (BN1)
    (*b*) Veuve Thomas Daré (BN2,3).
    (*c*) Jean Osmont (BN4,5, Clark, Harv 2).
    (*d*) Adrian Ouyn (Bod, Harv 3).
    (*e*) Robert Valentin (BN6, Pra/S, Harv 1, W/Folg).
    (*f*) Pierre Daré (Maz, see note 3).

(c) J Osmont [149 mm]

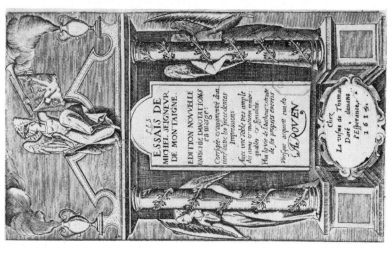

(b) Veuve T Daré [149 mm]

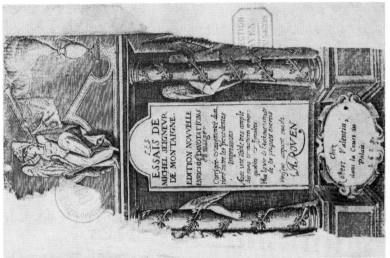

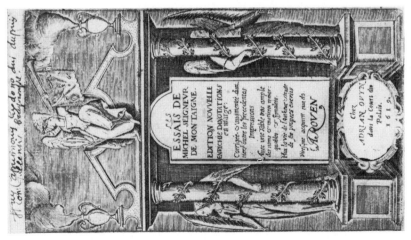

(d) A Ouyn [149 mm]

(e) R Valentin [149 mm]

(*f*) P Daré [149 mm]

Collation: 8°: ã⁸ A–4A⁸ [$4 signed, arabic numerals]; 568 leaves; pp [*16*] 1—608 611—738 779—836 873 838—932 953 934—1129 [=1087] [*33*].

Contents: ã1: Title (verso blank); ã2:*Au lecteur*; ã2ᵛ:Short Gournay preface; ã3: Table of contents; ã4ᵛ: Life; ã8: blank; ã8ᵛ: Portrait after Leu; A1: *Essais*; 3Y8ᵛ: blank; 3Z1: Index of subjects.

HT: ã2   [headpiece: 2 dogs' heads, volutes] *AV LECTEVR*.

     ã2ᵛ   [double row of 9 arabesque type-orns] ADVIS SVR LES ESSAIS | DE MICHEL SEIGNEVR | de Montaigne, | PAR SA FILLE D'ALLIANCE.

     ã4ᵛ   [headpiece=ã2] SOMMAIRE | DISCOVRS SVR LA VIE | DE MICHEL, SEIGNEVR | de Montaigne, extraict de | ſes propres eſcrits.

A1   [headpiece=ã2] ESSAIS | DE MICHEL | DE MON-
TAIGNE, | LIVRE PREMIER.

T7   [headpiece=ã2] [as A1 except] DE MONTAIGNE. |
LIVRE SECOND.

3B3   [as T7 except] LIVRE TROISIESME.

3Z1   [double row of 11 arabesque type-orns] TABLE | DES
MATIERES, ET NOMS | PLVS MEMORABLES
CONTENVS | aux Eſſais de Michel ſieur de Montaigne.

RT: Essais de Michel de Montaigne, | Livre premier [second]
[troisiesme]. [Montaigne. A1ᵛ; Montaigne (no comma) H6ᵛ; montaigne, 3Y6ᵛ; preimer. K6]

CW: Quire. C8ᵛ rolle S8ᵛ *Des* 2I8ᵛ craignons 3A8ᵛ aſſeurer 3R8ᵛ
en-]gendre

Measurements (F3): 42 (+2) lines. 145 (151) × 70 mm. 20 lines=69 mm.
Width with sidenotes 85 mm.

Privilège: None.

Notes: 1. A paginal resetting of No 18: 1617 Rouen, with which it shares
one pagination error (873 for 837) as well as the usual jump (738 779).
The main difference is in the signing of the index, which in 1617 Rouen
starts on 4A1, and in this edition on 3Z1. The alignment of the HT for
the index also differs. In the table of contents on ã3 1617 Rouen ends
with I 29 *Qu'il faut sobrement se mesler de iuger des ordonnances diuines* and this
edition with *Des Canibales. c. 30.* The difference of one line continues
throughout the prelims.[1]

2. The signing, pagination and running-titles are remarkably free from
error.

3. Maz is the only copy with the imprint of Pierre Daré. It has the prelims
of this edition, though the portrait is on ã8 instead of ã8ᵛ, but the rest is
as No 22: [1619] Rouen B as far as 4B5 its last leaf.

Copies: BN1 (Z Payen 85); BN2 (Z Payen 86, lacks portrait); BN3 (Z
Payen 87, Bk I only); BN4 (Z Payen 88); BN5 (16°Z 6360); BN6 (Z

[1] See P Bonnet, 'Sur un exemplaire des *Essais* portant l'adresse d'un libraire de Rouen
et le millésime 1619', *BSAM*, IV, 8 (1966), pp 13—14, for a discussion of this edition in
relation to others of the same family.

Payen 89); Maz (see note 3).   UK: Ox: Bod.   CZECHOSLOVAKIA: *Pra/S*.   ROMANIA: *Buc*.   USA: Clark; Harv 1 (*61—1098); Harv 2 (Mon.16.19*, has 3B3 and most of Bk III from No 18: 1617 Rouen); Harv 3 (Mon.16.20*, Bk III and index from No 22: [1619] Rouen B); *Prin*; *W/Folg*.

21A: 1620 Rouen

[149 mm]

Title-page: As No 21 except for the imprint of Manassez de Preaulx and the date 1620. Apart from the tp the rest of the copy is as 1619 Rouen A, of which it therefore seems to be a re-issue.

Copies: BN (Z Payen 90); Bord; Ren/U (tp and portrait detached). ITALY: Vat (tp remounted followed by portrait).

(*a*) N Angot [145 mm]

Title-page: The engraved border is quite different from No 21: 1619 Rouen A. The upper third is occupied by a bust of Montaigne above which two winged figures are holding a laurel wreath. On each side of the central cartouche there are two columns instead of one. The words of the title are the same as in 1619 Rouen A, but with several variations of lettering and alignment, in particular SEIGNEVr and *eumdo* for SEIGNEVR and *eundo*. Moreover, A ROVEN is transferred from the central panel to the cartouche beneath. The engraving is signed 'T. [or I] Honeruogt fecit' on the right hand plinth. There is no date. The tps differ only in the booksellers' imprints, with two states for J Besongne.

(*a*) Nicolas Angot (BN1, Châm 1, RAS).
(*b*) Jean Berthelin (BN2, Chan/F, Ren/U, Wolf, Wars/N, Chap, Eut).
(*c*) Jacques Besongne (besongue) (BN3).
(*d*) Jacques Besongne (besongne) (Colm, BL, Kings).

(a) J Besongne (besongne) [145 mm]

(c) J Besongne (besongue) [145 mm]

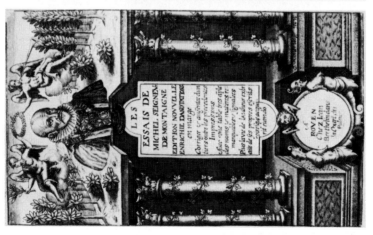

(b) J Berthelin [145 mm]

Collation: 8°: [engraved tp+] ã⁶ A—3Y⁸ 4A—4B⁸ 4C² [\$4 signed, arabic numerals (except 4A—4B roman); missigning ã3 as ã4, 2K as Kᴋ, 3K1,2 as Kᴋᴋ, Kᴋᴋ2, 3K3,4 as KKᴋ3,4, 3M4 as MMm 4, 3N3,4 as NNn 3,4, 3P3 as PPp3, 3V2,4 as VVv2,4, 3Y3 as Yyy iij (*variants*: missigning 3P3 as PPp)]; 568 leaves; pp [*12*] 1—268 169 270—288 389 290—608 611—713 696 715—716 71 718—738 779—1129 [=1087] [*37*].

Contents: [Engraved title] ã1: *Au lecteur*; ã1ᵛ: Short Gournay preface; ã2: Table of contents; ã3ᵛ (signed ã4): Life; A1: *Essais*; 3Y8ᵛ: blank; 4A1: Index; 4C2ᵛ: End of index, *achevé d'imprimer*.

HT: ã1   [double row of 8 arabesque type-orns] *AV LECTEVR.*

    ã1ᵛ   [type-orns=ã1] ADVIS SVR LES ESSAIS | DE MICHEL SEIGNEVR | de Montaigne, | PAR SA FILLE D'ALLIANCE.

    ã3ᵛ   (signed ã4) [type-orns=ã1] SOMMAIRE | DISCOVRS SVR LA VIE | DE MICHEL, SEIGNEVR | de Montaigne, extraict de | fes propres efcrits.

    A1   [headpiece: central grotesque head, 2 torch-bearing putti, fruit] ESSAIS | DE MICHEL | DE MONTAIGNE, | LIVRE PREMIER.

    T7   [type-orns similar to ã1 but turned] [as A1 except] LIVRE SECOND.

    3B3   [as T7 except] LIVRE TROISIESME.

    4A1   [double row of 9 arabesque type-orns] TABLE | DES MATIERES | ET NOMS PLVS MEMORA-|BLES CONTENVS AVX | Effais de Michel Sieur de | Montaigne.

RT: ESSAIS DE MICHEL DE MONTAIGNE, | LIVRE PREMIER [SECOND] [TROISIESME]. [MONTAIGME, T3ᵛ X4ᵛ; MONTAIGNE (no comma) A7ᵛ; DEMONTAIGNE, Q3ᵛ; MONTAIGN 2E4ᵛ; MONTAIGNE. 2X8ᵛ; LIVERE 2L1; PREMIER. A3—5 M6; SECOND. (for PREMIER.) A7; PREMIER: M5, 2H5; SECOND. 2X(−2X2) 2Y (−2Y5); TROISIESME (no stop) 3C1; TROISIESNE. 3D1 3E2 3G3]

CW: Quire. C8ᵛ rolle S8ᵛ *Des* 2I8ᵛ craignons 3A8ᵛ affeurer 3R8ᵛ en-]gendre 4A8ᵛ coulpe 4B8ᵛ Trahifon.

Measurements (F3): 42 (+2) lines. 143 (150)×71 mm. 20 lines=68 mm. Width with sidenotes 83 mm.

Privilège: None. *Achevé d'imprimer*: 31 August 1619, IEAN DVRAND.

Notes: 1. This edition[1] may be quickly distinguished from No 18: 1617 Rouen and No 21: 1619 Rouen A by (i) the undated tp signed by Honervogt instead of Charpy (though this undated Honervogt tp is also found on copies of No 24: 1627 Rouen); (ii) the lack of a portrait facing the text; (iii) the *achevé d'imprimer* of Jean Durand; (iv) the large caps in the recto RT LIVRE PREMIER [SECOND] [TROISIESME] where the other two editions have small caps for PREMIER, SECOND and TROISIESME.

2. This edition is closer to No 18: 1617 Rouen than to No 21: 1619 Rouen A on the following points: (i) the index begins on 4A1 instead of 3Z1; (ii) the signature numeration is arabic, except for 4A—4B in roman, whereas 1619 Rouen A is arabic throughout; (iii) the setting of the index HT on 4A1; (iv) the presence of an *achevé d'imprimer*. These similarities unfortunately occur only in the index but they suggest that 1619 Rouen A and No 22: [1619] Rouen B derive independently from 1617 Rouen. In any case these three editions all differ from No 19: [1617] Envers which has roman numerals in all the signatures, italic RTs (except for 3L) and lacks *Au lecteur* and the Gournay preface.

3. For the text of this edition with tp and prelims of 1619 Rouen A, see No. 21, note 3 (Maz).

Copies: BN1 (Z Payen 80, tp remounted); BN2 (Z Payen 81—83, tp repaired, bound in 3 vols); BN3 (Z Payen 84, tp remounted); Bord; Châm 1 (AF 17243); Châm 2 (Gt 9920, lacks tp and ã1); *Chan/F*; *Colm*; *Evr*; Ren/U (gathering ã misplaced after A8, gathering 3D inside out); *Sal*. UK: BL; Cam: Em; Kings; Trin; Ox: RAS. AUSTRIA: *Vien/N*. BELGIUM: Ant. GERMANY: *Eut*; Wolf (top of tp cut out, gathering 2G inside out). HUNGARY: *Bud/U*. NETHERLANDS: *Leid*. POLAND: *Tor*; *Wars/N*. USA: Chap.

---

[1] See P Bonnet, 'Sur un exemplaire des *Essais* appartenant à une édition non datée du XVIIe siècle [à l'adresse de: Rouen, J. Berthelin]', *BSAM*, IV, 9 (1967), pp 46—8.

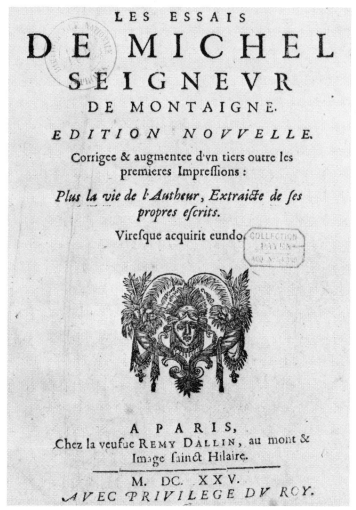

LES ESSAIS
DE MICHEL
SEIGNEVR
DE MONTAIGNE.

EDITION NOVVELLE.

Corrigee & augmentee d'vn tiers outre les
premieres Impreſſions :

*Plus la vie de l'Autheur, Extraicte de ſes
propres eſcrits.*

Vireſque acquirit eundo.

A PARIS,
Chez la veufue REMY DALLIN, au mont &
Image ſainct Hilaire.

M. DC. XXV.
AVEC PRIVILEGE DV ROY.

(*a*) Veuve R Dallin; Red Indian device [195 mm]

Title-page: The fourteen tps differ in the booksellers' imprints and in the
ornaments or devices, of which there are four. There are two devices for
veuve Remy Dallin (*a*) and (*b*), one for Targa (*c*), and one for Bertault
(*d*). The Red Indian device (*a*) is found with all other imprints. There are
swash caps in *AVEC PRIVILEGE* in all except (*b*) and (*j*). The text
of the title is as in No 20: 1617, but omitting *Enrichie d'annotations en
marge, du nom des Autheurs citez, & de la version du Latin d'iceux.*

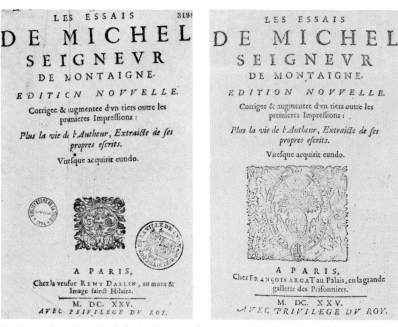

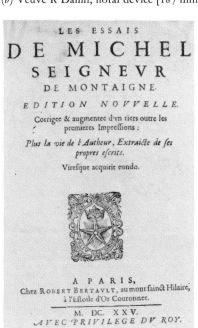

(b) Veuve R Dallin; floral device [187 mm]

(c) F Targa (misspelt) [195 mm]

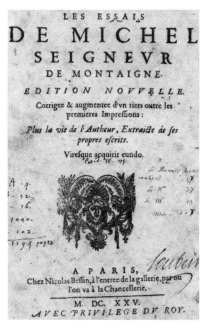

(d) R Bertault [195 mm]

(e) N Bessin [195 mm]

(*f*) R Boutonné [195 mm]

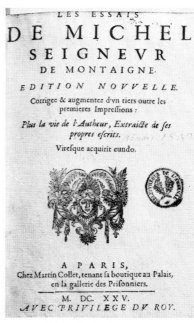

(*g*) M Collet [195 mm]

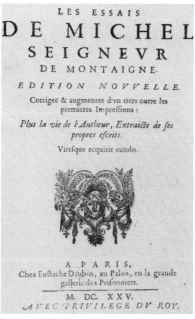

(*h*) E Daubin [195 mm]

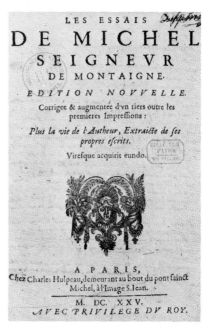

(*i*) C Hulpeau [195 mm]

LES ESSAIS
DE MICHEL
SEIGNEVR
DE MONTAIGNE.
EDITION NOVVELLE.
Corrigee & augmentee d'vn tiers outre les
premieres Impreſſions :
Plus la vie de l'Autheur, Extraicte de ſes
propres eſcrits.
Vireſque acquirit eundo.

A PARIS,
Chez THOMAS DE LA RVELLE, au Palais,
ſur les degrez de la ſaincte Chappelle.
M. DC. XXV.
AVEC PRIVILEGE DV ROY.

(j) T de La Ruelle [195 mm]

LES ESSAIS
DE MICHEL
SEIGNEVR
DE MONTAIGNE.
EDITION NOVVELLE.
Corrigee & augmentee d'vn tiers outre les
premieres Impreſſions :
Plus la vie de l'Autheur, Extraicte de ſes
propres eſcrits.
Vireſque acquirit eundo.

A PARIS,
Chez Guillaume Loyſon, au Palais en la gallerie
des Priſonniers.
M. DC. XXV.
AVEC PRIVILEGE DV ROY.

(k) G Loyson [195 mm]

LES ESSAIS
DE MICHEL
SEIGNEVR
DE MONTAIGNE.
EDITION NOVVELLE.
Corrigee & augmentee d'vn tiers outre les
premieres Impreſſions :
Plus la vie de l'Autheur, Extraicte de ſes
propres eſcrits.
Vireſque acquirit eundo.

A PARIS,
Chez Gilles & Anthoine Robinot, Marchant Libraire, au
Palais, en la Gallerie, en allant à la Chancellerie.
M. DC. XXV.
AVEC PRIVILEGE DV ROY.

(l) G and A Robinot [195 mm]

LES ESSAIS
DE MICHEL
SEIGNEVR
DE MONTAIGNE.
EDITION NOVVELLE.
Corrigee & augmentee d'vn tiers outre les
premieres Impreſſions :
Plus la vie de l'Autheur, Extraicte de ſes
propres eſcrits.
Vireſque acquirit eundo.

A PARIS,
Chez Pierre Rocolet, au Palais en la gallerie
des Priſonniere.
M. DC. XXV.
AVEC PRIVILEGE DV ROY.

(m) P Rocolet [195 mm]

(*n*) E Saucié [195 mm]

(*a*) Veuve Remy Dallin, Red Indian device (BN2, Bourges, Nio, USC).

(*b*) Veuve Remy Dallin, floral device, smaller type for imprint than (*a*) (Cass, Bord, Ly, Eton, Harv 2).

(*c*) François Targa (misspelt ARGAT), sun and head device (Chic/U, Prin).

(*d*) Robert Bertault, crown and star device (BN1, Tro, BL, Mun).

(*e*) Nicolas Bessin (Coul, Mn).

(*f*) Rolet Boutonné (BN8, Dub/W).

(*g*) Martin Collet (Ars).

(*h*) Eustache Daubin (Rhei, Dub/T, Wars/M).

(*i*) Charles Hulpeau (BN3, Kings).

(*j*) Thomas de La Ruelle (Ohio).

(*k*) Guillaume Loyson (BN4, BN5, Old, Mosc/H).

(*l*) Gilles and Anthoine Robinot (BN6, BN10, Chât, Pra/M, Pad/C, Harv 1, Len/S).

(*m*) Pierre Rocolet (BN7).

(*n*) Estienne Saucié (BN9, Avig, Frei).

Collation: 4°: ã⁴ ẽ² ũ² ¶—7¶² *⁴ A—F⁸ G—6H⁴ 6I⁴ (−6I4) a—n⁴ [$3 (4) (−LS2, 2MRV3, 4E2, 5B2, 6F3) signed, roman numerals; missigning K1 as k, L1 as ʟ, V3 as *V* iij, 2E1 as *E*e, 2G4 as *G*g iiij, 2Q2—4 as *Q*q ij, *Q*q iiij, *Q*q iiij, 3P1 as ppP, 4K1 as Kĸĸk, 4K2 as Kĸĸk ij, 5I3 as 5I2, 5K2 as Kĸĸĸk ij, 5M4 as 4M4, 5N2 as 4N2, 5O3 as 4O3, d3 as D iij, ĸ1—3 as ĸ, ĸ ij, ĸ iij (*variants*: missigning B3 as B4, not signing S1, missigning T2 as ij or ijT, X1 as *X*, 2H3 as hH iij, missigning 3A2 as 2A2, not signing 3A3, missigning 3D2 as 3D, 4L3 as 4L2 or not signed)]; 597 leaves; pp [*52*] 1—97 89 99—115 115 117—129 120—121 212 123—125 125 127—144 133 146—151 512 153—160 191 162—194 165 199 197—202 203 [inside HL] 204—205 106 207—221 222 [inside HL] 223—234 23 236—267 *268* 269 240 271—282 823 284—308 209 310—361 392 363—375 ç76 377—393 349 395—517 517 519—525 508 527—555 557 557—574 579—628 929 630—631 263 633—637 637 638 640—651 252 653—678 676 980 681—682 673 684—703 407 705—731 237 733—769 780 771 782 773—775 786 777—778 789 780—781 792 793 784—785 796 787—809 819 809—838 849 840 851—868 896 870—871 882 873—1007 0108 1006 1010—1031 1030 1033—1039 [= 1037] [*1*] 1—16 57 18—30 29 23 33—67 58 69—77 67 68 80—87 86—95 90 ∠6 98—101 [= 103] [*1*] [*variants*: misnumbering 38 as 83, 95 as 59, 443 as 43, 771 as 781, 774 as 784, 775 as 748, 778 as 788].

Contents: ã1: Title (verso blank); ã2: Printers' preface; ã3: Life; ẽ2ᵛ: blank; ũ1: Long Gournay preface, revised; 7¶2ᵛ: Errata for Gournay preface; *1: Table of contents; *3ᵛ: blank; *4: *Au lecteur*; A1: *Essais* Bk I; 2F3ᵛ: blank; 2F4: *Essais* Bks II—III; 6I3ᵛ: blank; a1: Gournay's introduction to translations; a2ᵛ: Translations of quotations; n4ᵛ: blank.

HT: ã2   [double row of 17 arabesque type-orns] LES IMPRI-MEVRS | AV LECTEVR.

     ã3   [headpiece: 2 reclining figures, volutes, animals] VIE DE MICHEL | SEIGNEVR DE MONTAIGNE, | tiree preſque entierement de ſes | Oeuures tres-conformes | à la verité.

     ũ1   [type-orns=ã2] PREFACE SVR | LES ESSAIS DE | MICHEL, SEIGNEVR | DE MONTAIGNE. | *Par ſa fille d'alliance.*

     *1   [headpiece: central shield with 3 fleurs-de-lis, 2 male nudes, volutes, dogs, rabbits] TABLE DES | CHA-PITRES DV | premier Liure.

*4   [headpiece=ã3] L'AVTHEVR, | au Lecteur.
A1   [headpiece: 4 seated gods and goddesses] ESSAIS DE
            MICHEL | DE MONTAGNE. | LIVRE PREMIER.
            [*variant*: headpiece as ã3, then as A1]
2F4   [headpiece=ã3] ESSAIS DE MICHEL | DE MON-
            TAIGNE. | Livre second. [*variant*: ESSAIS D EMI-
            CHEL]
4P1   [headpiece=ã3] LES ESSAIS | DE MICHEL | SEIG-
            NEVR | DE MONTAIGNE. | LIVRE TROISIESME.
a1   [double row of 9 (or 18) type-orns] AV LECTEVR.

RT: *Eſſais de Michel de Montagne.* | *Liure Premier* [*Second*] [*Troiſieſme*].
[The variations are extremely complex and are best summarised as
follows. Firstly, some aberrations: *Eſais* G1ᵛ; *Eſsais* 2S3ᵛ 2V4ᵛ 3B3ᵛ;
Mantange (no stop) 4T3ᵛ; *Liure Preremier.* F4. Variations occurring
frequently and without apparent pattern are the omission of the stops;
swash caps or large or small roman caps for any of the italic caps;
Montaigne with or without stop for *Montange*; *ſecond* for *Second*]

CW: Quire with irregularities. D6ᵛ poids   X4ᵛ merueil-   2V4ᵛ Il faut
con-   3I4ᵛ croire   4Y4ᵛ Rome,   6D4ᵛ bouche,

Measurements (O2): 40(+2) lines. 189(201) × 107 mm. 20 lines=94 mm.
No sidenotes.
     (A2, state A): 40(+2) lines. 195(201) × 112 mm. 20 lines=97 mm.
Width with sidenotes 128 mm. (See note 4)
     (A2, state B): 40 (+2) lines. 193(201) × 115 mm. 20 lines=96 mm. No
sidenotes.
     (E3): 40(+2) lines. 190(201) × 111 mm. 20 lines=95 mm. Width with
sidenotes 128 mm.

Privilège: *Avec Privilege du Roy* on tp but there is no *privilège* in any copy
seen.

Notes: 1. Set from No 20: 1617 this edition reproduces substantially the
same printers' preface as in that year. They continue to announce the
marginal summaries, although these are absent after gathering F, and in
some copies do not appear in gathering A, nor on some pages of
gathering B. The printers continue to blame the war for the misprints
(ã2ʳ⁻ᵛ).

2. There are variations in the order of the prelims. Gathering ∗ is placed after ẽ2 in BN8, Avig, Bord, Ly, Nio, Tro, Mn, Dub/W. Gatherings a—n are placed before gathering A in BN3, BN4 but are missing in BN7.

3. Montaigne's *Au lecteur* is found on both ∗4 in the prelims and on 6I4 at the end of the *Essais* with slight differences between the two versions:

		Leaf ∗4	Leaf 6I4
Recto	line 3	*tree,*	*tree;*
	line 10	*perdu,*	*perdu;*
	line 15	*paré:*	*paré;*
Verso	line 6	*ſuiet*	*ſubiect*

Clearly the correct place for *Au lecteur* is in the prelims. Why then does it occur on 6I4? It is not easy to account for all the facts, but perhaps at an early stage there was no gathering ∗ and *Au lecteur* was printed on 6I4 to be transferred to the prelims. This has been done in BN2 and BN3, which have 6I4 in the prelims and no gathering ∗ (though BN2 does have ∗1—3 bound in at the end, probably from another copy). Gathering ∗ is also lacking in Sorb but this copy lacks 6I4 as well. The printers may later have decided to add gathering ∗ containing the table of contents on ∗1—3 and *Au lecteur* on ∗4. This would render the *Au lecteur* on 6I4 superfluous, and it should have been discarded. This has been done in 10 copies which have *Au lecteur* on ∗4 and in which 6I4 is deleted (e.g. BN1, Bord, Mn, Harv 2), but in 18 others *Au lecteur* is present on both ∗4 and 6I4 (e.g. BN4, BL, Chic/U). This tangled situation has led to confusion in other copies. In Nio ∗4 has been substituted for 6I4 at the end. Tro lacks 6I4 but ∗4 is placed before ∗1. In Kings both ∗4 and 6I4 have been deleted.

4. Even harder to elucidate is the problem of gatherings A—F. They differ from the rest of the book in that they are quartos in eights (instead of quartos alone from gathering G onwards) and in most copies they have sidenotes not found in the bulk of the work. But in a few copies (BN2, 3, Sorb, Bourges, Nio) gathering A and the inner sheet of gathering B exist in another state, without sidenotes, and with a number of changes in the text. The text without sidenotes is much less correct than that with sidenotes. Moreover there are variant states even for the text with sidenotes, e.g. B2^v vagu champ (vague champs), sidenote *enir* (*tenir*). It is difficult to offer an explanation for all this. What is certain is that Mlle de Gournay disapproved of the sidenotes and that mention of them was dropped from the title of the work, though not from the printers' preface (see note 1).

5. The only Errata is for Mlle de Gournay's preface, though the 'Erreurs à corriger en cette Preface' are mostly revisions, not corrections of misprints. After the Errata, Mlle de Gournay adds a note in which she deplores the misprints in the body of the work, and touchingly expresses the hope that she may have the *Essais* printed once more—correctly— before she dies (7¶2^v).

6. At the end of her preface she adds an important statement, which appears here for the first time, concerning changes to the text which have been forced upon her by the printers: 'Leur mesme priere expresse, m'a contrainte de changer en ce Liure trois mots à travers champ & de ranger la syntaxe d'autant de clauses: ces mots sans nulle consequence, comme aduerbes ou particules, qui sembloient vn peu vieux: & ces clauses sans aucune mutation de sens, mais seulement pour leur oster certaine durté ou obscurité, qui sembloit naistre de quelque erreur de tant de diuerses impressions qui s'en sont faictes. Ie ne suis pas si inconsiderée ou si sacrilege, que de toucher en plus forts termes que ceux-là, ny a mot ny a phrase d'vn si precieux ouurage: basty d'alieurs [*sic*] de telle sorte, que les mots & la matiere sont consubstantiels'. The text has indeed been modernised, perhaps rather more than this statement implies. Mlle de Gournay also admits to modifying the passage in praise of her at the end of II 17: 'En ce seul point ay-je esté hardie, de retrancher quelque chose d'vn passage qui me regarde: à l'exemple de celuy qui mit sa belle maison par terre, affin d'y mettre auec elle l'enuye qu'on luy en portoit. Ioinct que ie veux dementir maintenant & pour l'aduenir, si Dieu prolonge mes années, ceux qui croient; que si ce Liure me loüoit moins, ie le cherirois & seruirois moins aussi' (7¶1^v—2^r). The passage in question has indeed been modified.

Copies:[1] BN1 (Z Payen 91); BN2 (Z Payen 92, tp remounted, *1—3 bound in at end, probably from another copy); BN3 (Z Payen 93, tp remounted); BN4 (Z Payen 94); BN5 (Z Payen 95); BN6 (Z Payen 96); BN7 (Z Payen 97, lacks gatherings a—n); BN8 (Z Payen 98); BN9 (Z Payen 99); BN10 (4°Z 361); BN11 (Z Payen 100, a—n only, with Gournay signature); *Ars*; Cass; Sorb (tp remounted); Avig; Bord; *Bourges*; *Chât*; *Coul*; Ly; Nio; *Rhei*; Tro.　UK: BL (GP Best copy); Cam: Kings; Eton; Ox: Mn.　CZECHOSLOVAKIA: *Pra/M*.　DEN-MARK: *Cop*.　EIRE: Dub/T; Dub/W.　GERMANY: *Frei*; *Mun*; *Old*. ITALY: Pad/C.　POLAND: *Kat*; *Wars/M*.　SPAIN: *Madr*.　SWIT-

---

[1] See also A Masson, 'Un exemplaire curieux des *Essais*', *BSAM*, II, 6 (1939), p 80.

ZERLAND: *Bas.*   USA: Chic/U (lacks all after k2); Harv 1 (Mon 16.25*); Harv 2 (Mon 16.25.3*); *Ohio*; *Prin*; USC; *Yale.*   USSR: *Len/S Mosc/H.*

23A: 1626

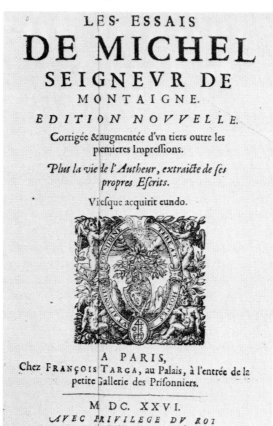

[195 mm]

Title-page: As No 23 (*c*), 1625, but ARGAT corrected to TARGA with a new address and the date changed to 1626. The tp is clearly a cancel and the rest is as No. 23. *Au lecteur* is found on both leaves *4 and 6I4. There are sidenotes in gatherings A—F.

Copy: Harv.

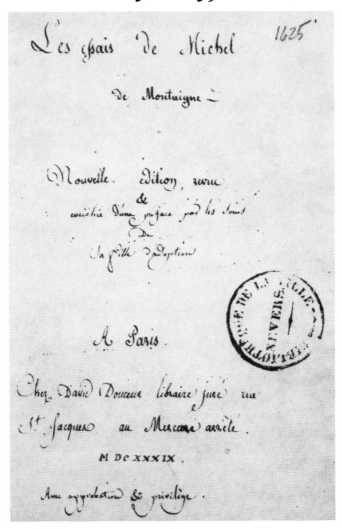

[150 mm]

Title-page: Supplied in MS it differs from all others in the imprint of David Douceur and in the words *enrichie d'une preface par les soins de sa fille d'adoption* and *Avec approbation & privilège*. The rest is as No 23, except that gathering * comes after ẽ2. *Au lecteur* is found on *4, and 6I4 is deleted. There are sidenotes in gatherings A—F.

Copy: Nev.

24: 1627 Rouen

(*a*) J Cailloüé [149 mm]

Title-page: Six of the nine tps have the same copy of the Charpy engraving as No 18: 1617 Rouen and No 21: 1619 Rouen A, and differ only in the booksellers' imprints (*a*) to (*f*). The Honervogt engraving of No 22: [1619] Rouen B is found here with Berthelin's imprint (*g*) or with a blank oval cartouche (*h*), both without date. Besongne's imprint is found on a blank leaf (*i*).

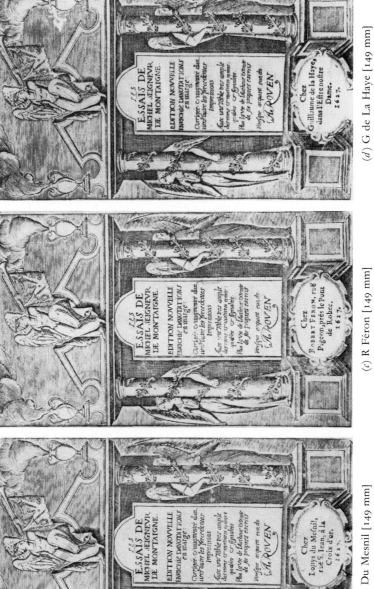

(d) G de La Haye [149 mm]

(c) R Féron [149 mm]

(b) L Du Mesnil [149 mm]

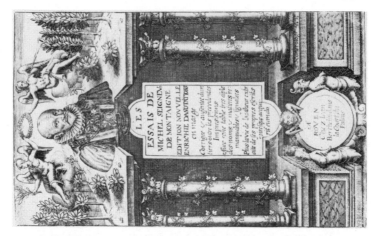

(g) J Berthelin; no date [145 mm]

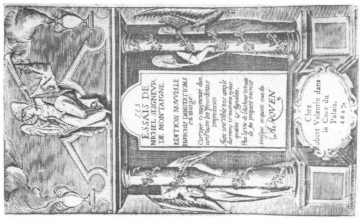

(f) R Valentin [149 mm]

(e) P de La Motte [149 mm]

(*b*) Blank cartouche [145 mm]

(*i*) J Besongne;
no engraved frame [131 mm]

(*a*) Jacques Cailloüé (BN1, BN2, Düss, Wars/U, Chic/U).

(*b*) Louis Du Mesnil (BN3, BN4, Bord, Lucc).

(*c*) Robert Féron (BN5, Bar, Coln).

(*d*) Guillaume de La Haye (Epin, Ven).

(*e*) Pierre de La Motte (BN6, Avig, Pau, Det, Mosc/G).

(*f*) Robert Valentin (BN7, BN8, LU, Gla, Wup).

(*g*) Jean Berthelin, Honervogt frame, no date (BN9, Châm, BL, CUL, Bod, Wroc/U).

(*h*) Honervogt frame with oval cartouche blank (BN11).

(*i*) No engraved frame, *Chez Iacques Besongne, dãs la Cour du Palais. 1627* (BN11).

Collation: 8°: ã⁸ A—4A⁸ [$4 signed, arabic numerals; missigning 2S4 as
S4, 3K3 as 3K2, 3L4 as Ill4 (*variant*: signing 2X4 with damaged
characters)];   568 leaves;   pp [*16*] 1—63 34 65—72 71 74—142 145
144—205 208 207—224 125 226—317 218 319—346 634 348—434 433
436—488 189 490—518 419 520—522 503 524—608 611—650 51
652—738 779—836 873 838—891 692 893—929 630 931 932 953
934—941 642 943—1042 104 1044—1067 1098 1069—1078 1097
1080—1108 1119 1110—1129 [= 1087] [*33*] [*variants*: 1078 1067 1080].

Contents: ã1: Title (verso blank); ã2: *Au lecteur*; ã2ᵛ: Short Gournay
preface; ã3: Table of contents; ã4ᵛ: Life; ã8: blank; ã8ᵛ: Portrait after
Leu; A1: *Essais*; 3Y8ᵛ: blank; 3Z1: Index.

HT: ã2	[double row of 12 arabesque type-orns] *AV LEC-TEVR*.	
ã2ᵛ	[type-orns = ã2] ADVIS SVR LES ESSAIS | DE MICHEL SEIGNEVR | de Montaigne, | PAR SA FILLE D'AL-LIANCE.	
ã4ᵛ	[headpiece: central seated putto, plants, fruit, 2 flying birds] SOMMAIRE | DISCOVRS SVR LA VIE | DE MICHEL, SEIGNEVR | de Montaigne, extraict de | ſes propres eſcrits.	
A1	[headpiece: central cock, 2 fish-eating herons, inits RF] ESSAIS | DE MICHEL | DE MONTAIGNE, | LIVRE PREMIER. [*variant*: headpiece = ã4ᵛ, then same text as A1, but different setting].	
T7	[as A1 except] LIVRE SECOND.	
3B3	[as A1 except] LIVRE TROISIESME.	
3Z1	[double row of 12 arabesque type-orns, the twelfth pair differing from the rest] TABLE | DES MATIERES, ET NOMS | PLVS MEMORABLES CONTENVS | aux Eſſais de Michel ſieur de Montaigne. [*variant*: Montaigne,]	

RT: ESSAIS DE MICHEL DE MONTAIGNE, | LIVRE PREMIER [SECOND]
[TROISIESME]. [MICHELDE 3R4ᵛ; LIVREE 3QS1; PREMIER. (for SECOND.)
T8; SECOND (no stop) 3B2] [*variants*: MICHELDE A6ᵛ; TRIOISESME. 3G2
3I1]

CW: Quire. As Nos 21 and 22: 1619 Rouen A and B on C8ᵛ S8ᵛ 2I8ᵛ 3A8ᵛ
3R8ᵛ; 3Z8ᵛ Mariages

Measurements (F3): 41(+2) lines. 139 (146)×70 mm. 20 lines=68 mm. Width with sidenotes 85 mm.

Privilège: None.

Notes: 1. A paginal resetting of No 21: 1619 Rouen A with which it shares two pagination errors (873 for 837, 953 for 933). There are striking misprints in the table of contents.[1]

2. The outer forme of gathering A exists in two states differentiated chiefly by the headpiece (see HT) but also by minor typographical variants, e.g. A1, line 8 Edoüard (Edouard), line 18 armee (armée).

3. The Honervogt tp is always a cancel with horizontal chain-lines, and copies with this tp usually lack the portrait.

4. BN11 has two tps. The Besongne imprint on the otherwise blank page (*i*) is too wide for the blank oval cartouche in the Honervogt engraving (*h*), but it would fit the oval cartouche in the Charpy engraving, e.g. tp (*a*). The leaf bearing the Besongne imprint is conjugate with ã8, which, however, is blank and lacks the portrait. The Honervogt tp seems to be inserted. Gathering Y is displaced before gathering X. Otherwise BN11 is a standard copy.

5. This edition, with the tp of J. Cailloüé, was probably the one read by the censors when the *Essais* were placed on the Index of prohibited books in 1676.[2]

Copies: BN1 (Z 19576); BN2 (Z Payen 103); BN3 (Z 19578); BN4 (Z Payen 104); BN5 (Z Payen 105, variant setting of outer forme of A); BN6 (Z Payen 106); BN7 (Z 19577, lacks 4A8); BN8 (Z Payen 107, date on tp changed to 1697, a second tp (Féron) pasted in); BN9 (Z Payen 101); BN10 (Z Payen 108, Bk III only ending at 3Y8, MS tp and contents, 'Bourdeaus 1580'); BN11 (Z Payen 102, see note 4); Avig (tp remounted); Bar (tp remounted, bound in 3 vols); Bord; Châm; *Epin*; *Pau*. UK: BL (527.h.1, catalogued as [1641?]); LU (lacks prelims); Cam: CUL; Gla; Ox: Bod (Douce M268, wrongly catalogued as [1619]). GERMANY: *Coln*; *Det*; *Düss*; *Wup*. ITALY: Lucc; Ven. POLAND: *Wars/U*; *Wroc/U*. SWITZERLAND: *Bas*. USA: Chic/U; *Harv*; *Prin*; *Yale*. USSR: *Mosc/G*.

[1] P Bonnet, 'L'édition des *Essais* de 1627', *BSAM*, IV, 8 (1966), pp 15—16.
[2] R Bernoulli, 'La mise à l'Index des *Essais* de Montaigne', *BSAM*, IV, 8 (1966), pp 4—10. See also, P Bonnet, 'Les *Essais* à l'Index', *ibid*, pp 11—12.

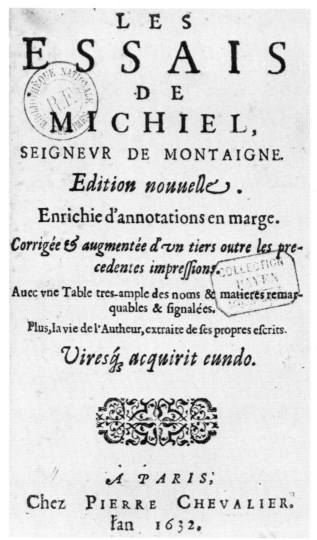

[131 mm]

Title-page: The words of the title are as in No 24: 1627 Rouen, but with MICHIEL for MICHEL and the new imprint of Pierre Chevalier, Paris, 1632. In the only copy known the tp is inserted, the prelims are missing and some leaves are made up in MS. Otherwise it is as No 24.

Copy: BN (Z Payen 109).

First issue

(*a*) Engraved title and portrait; T Du Bray and P Rocolet [331 mm]

First
issue

(c) Printed title; P Rocolet [309 mm]

(b) Printed title; no name [309 mm]

Second issue

LES ESSAIS DE MICHEL, SEIGNEVR DE MONTAIGNE.

EDITION NOVVELLE.

EXACTEMENT CORRIGEE SELON LE VRAY EXEMPLAIRE.

ENRICHIE A LA MARGE DV NOM DES AVTHEVRS CITEZ, ET DE LA VERSION DE LEVRS PASSAGES, mise à la fin de chasque Chapitre.

Auecque la vie de l'Autheur.

Plus deux Tables : l'vne des Chapitres, & l'autre des principales Matieres.

A PARIS,

Chez IEAN CAMVSAT, ruë Sainct Iacques, à la Toyson d'or.

M.DC.XXXV.

AVEC PRIVILEGE DV ROY.

(e) Printed title; J Camusat [300 mm]

(d) Engraved title and portrait; J Camusat [331 mm]

FIRST ISSUE

Title-page: The engraved tp is found with printed tp (*b*) in BN4, 6, Maz and with printed tp (*c*) in Sorb, Chap. Tp (*b*) is alone in Ars 2, Gren, and tp (*c*) alone in BN7. The printed tps (*b*) and (*c*) seem to be variant states in which the ornament of (*b*) is replaced by the device of (*c*) causing over-crowding in the lower half. Tp (*b*) has lines 2, 4, 6, 8, 10, 13, A PARIS, and AVEC PRIVILEGE DV ROY in red (BN6, Gren); tp (*c*) has lines 2, 4, 6, 8, 10, 13, A PARIS, PIERRE ROCOLET and the date in red (BN7). The words *Exactement corrigee selon le vray exemplaire* appear for the first time (see note 1).

   (*a*) Engraved title, portrait, imprint of Du Bray and Rocolet.[1]
   (*b*) Printed title with head and snakes orn and no name of bookseller (BN4,6, Ars 2, Maz, Gren).
   (*c*) Pierre Rocolet, printed title with ship and fleur-de-lis device, inits PR (BN7, Sorb, Chap).

Collation: 2°: [engraved tp+] ¶—3¶⁶ ã² A—4E⁶ 4F⁴ [$4(−4D4) signed, roman numerals; missigning 3B1 as BBb (for Bbb)]; 468 leaves; pp [*40*] 1—51 38 53—92 83 94—449 460 461 452—512 493 514—800 678 802—864 867 868 867—871 [*25*] [*variants*: misnumbering 167 as 165, 751 as 851, 814 as 714].

Contents: [Engraved title] ¶1: Printed title (verso blank); ¶2: Long Gournay preface, revised; 3¶4: *Au lecteur*; 3¶4ᵛ: Life; 3¶6: Table of contents; ã1: Dedicatory letter to Richelieu; ã2ᵛ: blank; A1: *Essais*; 4D4ᵛ: *Privilège*, Errata; 4D5: Index; 4F4ʳ⁻ᵛ: blank.

HT: ¶2   [headpiece: central lion's head, 2 female figures, 2 boys with spears] PREFACE | SVR LES | ESSAIS DE MICHEL, | SEIGNEVR | DE MONTAIGNE. | Par fa fille d'alliance.

   3¶4   [headpiece: central winged head, 2 fauns, 2 horses' heads and forelegs] L'AVTHEVR, | AV LECTEVR.

   3¶4ᵛ   [double row of 30 fleur-de-lis type-orns] SOMMAIRE | *RECIT, SVR LA VIE DE MICHEL* | *Seigneur de Montaigne, extraict de fes propres Efcrits.*

[1] An engraved tp with pedestals and cartouche blank has been pasted into BN7 by Payen, and is reproduced by Tchemerzine (viii, 427).

3¶6   [row of 31 fleur-de-lis type-orns sideways] TABLE DES CHAPITRES.

ã1   [headpiece: central winged figure with crown, fauns, deer] A | MONSEIGNEVR | L'EMINENTISSIME | CARDINAL, | DVC DE RICHELIEV.

A1   [headpiece=¶2] ESSAIS DE MICHEL | DE MON-TAIGNE. | LIVRE PREMIER.

X5   [as A1 except] LIVRE SECOND.

3F2   [as A1 except] LIVRE TROISIESME.

4D4ᵛ   [rule] *Extraict du Priuilege du Roy.* (Plate 11)

4D5   [headpiece=ã1] TABLE | DES NOMS PROPRES, | ET DES PRINCIPALES | MATIERES CON-TENVES | en ce Liure.

RT: ESSAIS DE MICHEL DE MONTAIGNE. | LIVRE PREMIER [SECOND] [TROISIESME]. [ESSAIS DE MICHEL DE MONT. LIVRE I. X4ᵛ; ESSAIS DE MICHEL DE MONT. LIV. II 3F1ᵛ; PREMIER (no stop) H1 I1, 5]

CW: Quire. ¶6ᵛ *les* 2¶6ᵛ *ne font* E6ᵛ Quoy Z6ᵛ tourments, 2G6ᵛ coquille: 2V6ᵛ de 3F6ᵛ mes 3T6ᵛ Vt palam 4B6ᵛ combien 4D6ᵛ Carneades 4E6ᵛ Peripateticiens

Measurements (F3): 44(+2) lines. 259 (272) × 149 mm. 20 lines = 117 mm. Width with sidenotes 164 mm.

Privilège: To the Damoiselle de Gournay for 6 years to publish *Les Essais de Michel Seigneur de Montaigne, Edition nouuelle, exactement corrigee selon le vray exemplaire, & enrichie à la marge du nom des Autheurs citez, & de la Version de leurs passages, mise à la fin de chaque Chapitre.* 13 September 1633, signed LE QVESNE. *Achevé d'imprimer*: 15 June 1635. (Plate 11)

SECOND ISSUE

Title-page: The engraved tp (*d*) differs from the first issue tp (*a*) in Camusat's imprint and the addition of two coats of arms on the plinths. Tp (*e*) is a resetting of (*b*) using the same orn but adding Camusat's imprint. For the second issue it seems likely that the printed tp on ¶1 in the first issue was deleted and replaced by a sheet bearing the new tps, both engraved and printed, which could be folded so that either tp could come first. Lines 2, 4, 6, 8, 10, 13, A PARIS, IEAN CAMVSAT and AVEC PRIVILEGE DV ROY in red on tp (*e*).

> (*d*) Engraved title, portrait, imprint of Camusat.
> (*e*) Jean Camusat, printed title.

Collation: 2°: π^2 ã² ¶⁶ (−¶1) 2¶—3¶⁶ A—4C⁶ 4D⁶ (±4D4) 4E⁶ 4F⁴ (−4F4); 468 leaves. Signing and pagination as first issue, except for 42 unnumbered pages in the prelims and 23 unnumbered pages at the end.

Contents: π1: Engraved title (verso blank); π2: Printed title (verso blank). Thereafter as first issue, except that ¶1 is deleted and the dedicatory letter to Richelieu precedes the Gournay preface. On 4D4ᵛ there is a longer version of the *privilège*, and the Errata is moved to the foot of the preceding page.

HT: As first issue except for the displacement of ã1, and 4D4ᵛ: PRIVILEGE DV ROY. (Plate 12)

RT, *CW*, *Measurements*: as first issue.

Privilège: Similar to first issue, but with preamble stressing the need for a new corrected edition to remedy the errors which have crept into the text. Place of signing given as 'devant Nancy'. *Privilège* transferred from Mlle de Gournay to Jean Camusat by an agreement dated 28 August 1635. *Achevé d'imprimer*: 15 June 1635. (Plate 12)

Notes: 1. In many places the text of this edition returns to the correct readings of No 7A: 1595, where intervening editions have departed from it, and Mlle de Gournay in her preface stresses that the correct text of the *Essais* is to be found in 'les seules impressions de l'Angelier depuis la mort de l'Autheur [. . .] notamment celle *in folio*, dont ie vis toutes les espreuues: & celle-cy, sa sœur germaine' (3¶3ᵛ). However, the modernisation of the text, which started in 1625, is carried further in this edition, so that whilst 1635 is purer in some respects, it is contaminated in others.[2] Mlle de Gournay's preface contains a statement about the modernisation similar to that which appeared in 1625 (see No 23, note 6).

---

[2] See P Bonnet, 'Le texte des *Essais*', *BSAM*, IV, 7 (1966), p 73; M. Ilsley, *A daughter of the Renaissance*, 1963, pp 255—7 (though she appears to have confused the corrections to the translations of quotations with the modifications to the text).

2. Besides the pagination variants indicated above, collation of selected pages reveals the following press corrections:

	1st state	*2nd state*
Y3ʳ (p 257 line 15)	choque (Tro)	choquent (BL, Bod, RAS)
(p 257 line 25)	il ne faut (Tro)	il faut (BL, Bod, RAS)
Y4ᵛ (p 260 line 39)	ἠθείειν.	ἠθείειν?
	(BN1, Ars1, Bord)	(BL, Bod, RAS)
2N2ᵛ (p 424 line 20)	*qualis*	*quali*
	(BN1, Maz, BL)	(Ars1, Bord)
3H1ʳ (p 637 line 32)	vivre qui (BN1, Ars 1, Bord)	vivre que (BL, RAS)

In each case the second state is the correct reading. The correction *quali* for *qualis* is indicated in the Errata.

3. In her preface Mlle de Gournay states: 'nous auons pris la peine de corriger la plus part des erreurs auec la plume, & recueillir en vn Errata bien exact le reste de celles qui peuuent importer' (3¶3ʳ). The majority of copies contain the following 19 ink-corrections mostly in the hand of Mlle de Gournay:

	Printed text	*Ink-correction*
2¶3ʳ (line 8)	mespriseray	mesprisay
A6ʳ (p 11 line 24)	le punit	les punit
B1ᵛ (p 14 line 12)	*soy*	*elle*
B3ᵛ (p 18 line 14)	*forte*	*haute*
B4ᵛ (p 20 line 22)	*& ià bondissante*	*& bondissante*
E6ᵛ (p 60 line 30)	peut	pet
F4ʳ (p 67 line 31)	plus	pas
G4ᵛ (p 80 line 15)	le recharge	la recharge
G5ᵛ (p 82 line 26)	presenter	representer
H2ᵛ (p 88 sidenote)	in Cicerone l 7.	Cicero l 7.
H3ʳ (p 89 line 1)	la malade	le malade
I2ᵛ (p 100 line 24)	*collum*	*callum*
I3ʳ (p 101 line 15)	rauissement	rauisement
K4ᵛ (p 116 line 33)	parenté:	parenté,
L2ᵛ (p 124 line 7)	au tour:	au tour,
L3ᵛ (p 126 line 13)	le vede	la vede
L5ᵛ (p 130 line 39)	imaginables	inimaginables
N2ʳ (p 147 line 3)	haut.	haut etage.
Q1ᵛ (p 182 line 30)	craindre,	craindre

These 19 ink-corrections occur in the first quarter of the book, and most of the errata in the remaining three-quarters.

This confirms Mlle de Gournay's statement that she first corrected most of the misprints in ink, and then listed the rest in the Errata. But, conscious that even this might not suffice, Mlle de Gournay adds: 'Or de peur qu'il n'en reste quelqu'vne, apres ma recherche precedente; ie te promets de la repeter encores, & d'en mettre apres vn Exemplaire en la Bibliotheque du Roy, & l'autre en celle de Monseigneur le Garde des Seaux, corrigez des derniers traicts de ma plume' (3¶3ʳ). Neither of these copies can be identified with certainty, but we have indirect evidence for this second series of ink-corrections. Charles-Etienne Jordan in the *Recueil de littérature, de philosophie et d'histoire*, Amsterdam, 1730, pp 38—42, gives a list of about 50 corrections made by Mlle de Gournay on a copy of the *Essais* of 1635 belonging to Ezechiel von Spanheim, and which may earlier have belonged to Séguier.[3]   BN4, which was presented by Mlle de Gournay to the Feuillants of Paris, has about 125 ink-corrections in addition to those of the first series, and BN5 has two leaves bound in at the end containing a list of approximately 300 corrections entitled 'Errata manuscrit de la Dlle de Gournay' (Plates 13—16). A number of corrections is common to all three sources, but each source contains corrections which are not found in the other two.

Copies: (second issue unless first issue is indicated): BN1 (Z 765, 'Bibl. du Roi' on flyleaf); BN2 (Z Payen 110, Jordan's list of corrections entered by Payen, see note 3); BN3 (Fol. Z 1581); BN4 (Rés. Z 360, first issue, 'Don de Madamoiselle de Gournay/Ex Bibl. S. Bern. Fulientinorum Parisiensium' on printed tp); BN5 (Rés. Z 359, two leaves of MS corrections bound in at end, see note 3); BN6 (Z Payen 112—114, first issue); BN7 (Z Payen 111, first issue, lacks usual engraved tp but engraved tp without imprint pasted in by Payen); Ars 1 (Fol. Sc. A. 267); Ars 2 (Fol. Sc. A. 268, first issue); Maz (first issue); Sorb (first issue); Stge; *Alen*; *Aut*; *Aux*; Avig; *Bayn*; Bord; *Caen*; *Carp*; Chan/F; Chau; Cler; Dij; Gren (first issue); Lem; *Lille 1* (BML 16814, first issue); *Lille 2*

---

[3] A note by Morf in *Sitzungsberichte der königlich-preußischen Akademie der Wissenschaften*, 37 (1917), p 517 indicates that the Spanheim copy was in the Königliche Bibliothek, Berlin in 1917, but all attempts to locate it have so far failed. See also A Salles, 'Les corrections à la plume de Mlle de Gournay', *BSAM*, II, 1 (1937), p 24, *ibid.*, II, 5 (1939), pp. 26—7 and 'L'exemplaire Spanheim', *BSAM*, II, 3 (1938), p 28 (extract from Moréri's *Dictionnaire*).

(BML 50107); Ly; *Meaux*; Monp/U; *Pau*; Péri; Ren/U; *Stde*; *Ste*; *Stq*; *Touln*; *Touls*; Tro; Vers; *Ves*. UK: BL (lacks 3G3.4, replaced by duplicate 2G3.4); *LUC*; Cam: Kings; Ed/N; Ed/NB; Eton; *Leeds* (first issue); Ox: Bod; Magd; RAS; Tay 1 (Arch. III D 3); Tay 2 (Skipworth E 9); Sta. DENMARK: *Cop*; *Thor*. GERMANY: *Aug*; *Erl*; *Han*; *Stut*; Wolf. ITALY: Pav; Vat. NETHERLANDS: *Hague*. POLAND: *Poz*. ROMANIA: *Buc*. SPAIN: *Barc*; *Madr*. USA: *Ariz*; Bost; Chap (first issue); Chic/N; Chic/U; Harv 1 (MON.16.35.2F); Harv 2 (MON.16.35.5F, first issue, lacks printed tp); Harv 3 (MON.16.35); Ill 1 (Baldwin g 4643); Ill 2 (g 842. M76. K 1635, lacks gathering ã); Prin; W/Folg; Yale. USSR: *Mosc/L*.

26: 1636

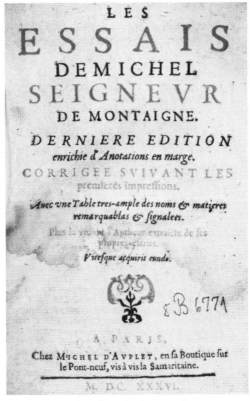

(*a*) M d'Auplet [149 mm]

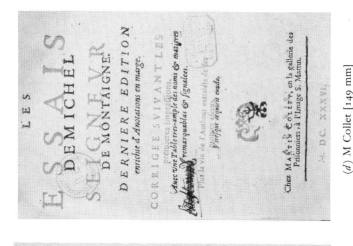

(d) M Collet [149 mm]

(c) L Boulanger [149 mm]

(b) P Billaine [149 mm]

(g) N and J de La Coste [149 mm]

(f) J Germont [149 mm]

(e) M Durand [149 mm]

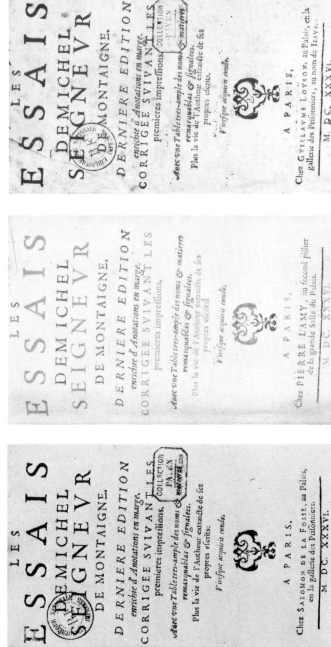

(b) S de La Fosse [149 mm]

(i) P L'Amy [149 mm]

(j) G Loyson [149 mm]

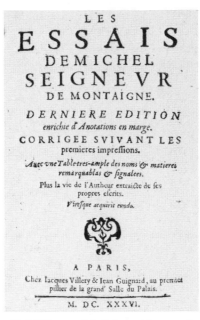

LES
ESSAIS
DE MICHEL
SEIGNEVR
DE MONTAIGNE.
DERNIERE EDITION
enrichie d'Anotations en marge.
CORRIGEE SVIVANT LES
premieres impressions.
*Auec vne Table tres-ample des noms & matieres
remarquablas & signalees.*
Plus la vie de l'Autheur extraicte de ses
propres escrits.
Virefque acquirit eundo.

A PARIS,
Chez Iacques Villery & Iean Guignard, au premier
pillier de la grand' Salle du Palais.
M. DC. XXXVI.

(*k*) J Villery and J Guignard [149 mm]

Title-page: The eleven tps differ only in the booksellers' imprints and all have the error *remarquablas* in line 11. Lines 2, 4, 8, 9, 12, 13, part of the orn, A PARIS and the date are in red. The words of the title are the same as in No 24: 1627 Rouen, except that *DERNIERE EDITION* replaces *EDITION NOVVELLE*, and *corrigee suivant les premieres impressions* replaces *corrigée & augmentée d'un tiers outre les precedentes Impressions*.

(*a*)   Michel d'Auplet (Bord, Wroc/U).
(*b*)   Pierre Billaine (BN1, Aber, Virg/U).
(*c*)   Louis Boulanger (BN2, Harv).
(*d*)   Martin Collet, black and red poorly registered (BN3, Boul).
(*e*)   Martin Durand, with tilde in ink added over DVRÃD (Tro, Vat).
(*f*)   Jean Germont (BN4).
(*g*)   Nicolas and Jean de La Coste (Dur, see note 2).
(*h*)   Salomon de La Fosse (BN5, 6).
(*i*)   Pierre L'Amy (BN7, 8, Châm, BL).
(*j*)   Guillaume Loyson (BN9, 10).
(*k*)   Jacques Villery and Jean Guignard (BN11, 12, 13, Mich).

Collation: 8°: ã⁸ A—4A⁸ [$4 signed, roman numerals; missigning B4 as F4, 2P3 as Pd iij, 2K1, 3, 4 as Kк, Kк iij, Kк iiij, 3K1—4 as Kкк, Kккк ij, Kккк iij, KKк iiij (*variants*: not signing D3, missigning 2G3 as Eg iij, 3C3 as Cce iij)]; 568 leaves; pp [*16*] 1—116 117n 114 119—142 145 144—155 158 157—181 s82 183—222 123 224 125 226—329 390 331—343 444 345 246 347—488 189 490—497 468 499—594 565 596—608 611—644 465 646—660 681 662—664 662 666—690 692 692—709 610 711—735 739 737 738 779—799 400 801—819 120 821—864 885 866—932 953 934—941 642 943—1005 984 1007—1015 1019 1017—1078 1097 1080—1108 1119 1110 111 1112—1129 [=1087] [*33*] [*variants*: 117n 78 119, misnumbering 161 as 61, 779 as 79].

Contents: ã1: Title (verso blank); ã2: *Au lecteur*; ã2ᵛ: Short Gournay preface; ã3: Table of contents; ã5ᵛ: Life; A1: *Essais*; 3Y8ᵛ: blank; 3Z1: Index.

HT: ã2   [double row of 14 fleur-de-lis type-orns, second row inverted] *AV LECTEVR.*

ã2ᵛ   [type-orns=ã2] ADVIS SVR LES ESSAIS | DE MICHEL SEIGNEVR | de Montaigne. | PAR SA FILLE D'AL-LIANCE.

ã5ᵛ   [type-orns=ã2, but last of top row inverted] SOM-MAIRE | DISCOVRS | SVR LA VIE | DE MICHEL, | SEIG. DE MONTAIGNE, | EXTRAICT DE SES | PROPRES ESCRITS.

A1   [headpiece: 2 horn-blowing satyrs, volutes] ESSAIS | DE MICHEL | DE MONTAIGNE, | LIVRE PREMIER.

T7   [as A1 except] LIVRE SECOND.

3B3   [as A1 except] DE MONTAIGNE. | LIVRE TROI-SIESME.

3Z1   [double row of 16 fleur-de-lis type-orns, second row inverted] TABLE | DES MATIERES, ET NOMS | PLVS MEMORABLES CONTENVS | aux Eſſais de Michel ſieur de Montaigne.

RT: ESSAIS DE MICHEL DE MONTAIGNE, | LIVRE PREMIER [SECOND] [TROISIESME]. [ESSAIDE 2S1ᵛ 2V4ᵛ; DEMICHEL D2ᵛ; DE MICHEL once or more in BDEGHKNOQ—XZ 2A—FHILOPRTVYZ 3BCEFHIL-MOQSTX; DE MICHEL DE MONTAINE, S2ᵛ; DEMONTAIGNE, N5ᵛ O8ᵛ 2B1ᵛ 2T8ᵛ 2V3ᵛ; DE MONTAIGNE, V6ᵛ Z1ᵛ 2A3ᵛ; MONTAGNE, 2M5ᵛ 2O3ᵛ

2Q1ᵛ 2S8ᵛ 2V6ᵛ; MONTIAGNE, 2D3ᵛ; LIRIVRE L2; LIRVE Q2; LIVRE once in TVY 2BDEGHK; LivrePremier. G2 I6 L5 N8 O7 P3; TITRE TROISIESME. 3S7; PREMIER. (for SECOND.) T8; PREMIER. G4 K8; REMIER. K6; SECOND! 2G1 2H2; SECOND. once or more in Y 2ACE—LN; TROSIESME. 3K8; TROISIESME. 3C6 3E5; TROISIEME. once in 3BDGHKMNPQV; TROISIESME. once or more in 3B—Y; TROISIESME, 3C7 3D8 3F1 3G2 3K3]

CW: Quire (−3T8ᵛ). I8ᵛ co-]gnoiſſoit T8ᵛ merueille 2I8ᵛ craignons 2X8ᵛ train 3I8ᵛ rage, 3K8ᵛ qu'el-]les 3Z8ᵛ Mariages

Measurements (P2): 41 (+2) lines. 138(144) × 70 mm. 20 lines = 67 mm. Width with sidenotes 87 mm.

Privilège: None.

Notes: 1. Set from No 24: 1627 Rouen, which has the same collational formula and shares seven pagination errors with this edition (145 for 143, 125 for 225, 189 for 489, 953 for 933, 642 for 942, 1097 for 1079, 1119 for 1109).

2. Dur has what appears to be a genuine 1636 tp but the rest of the copy is as No 14: 1608, including the erroneous text on p 938 (see No 14, note 3).

Copies: BN1 (Z Payen 115); BN2 (Z Payen 116); BN3 (Z Payen 117, lacks gathering 3E, F de Lamontaigne copy); BN4 (Z Payen 118, lacks gatherings 3Z, 4A); BN5 (Z 19579); BN6 (Z Payen 119); BN7 (Z 19580); BN8 (Z Payen 120); BN9 (Z Payen 121, MS notes by Payen); BN10 (16°Z 6358, MS notes by Armaingaud); BN11 (Z 19581); BN12 (Z Payen 122, tp remounted); BN13 (Z Payen 123—5, bound in 3 vols); Bord; *Boul*; Châm (bound in 3 vols with printed tps supplied for Bks II and III, probably in 18th cent); Péri (lacks tp); Tro (bound in 3 vols). UK: BL; Aber; Dur (tp only, see note 2). DENMARK: *Cop*. ITALY: Vat. POLAND: *Wroc/U*. SWITZERLAND: *Aar*; *Zür*. USA: Harv; *Mich*; *Prin*; Virg/U.

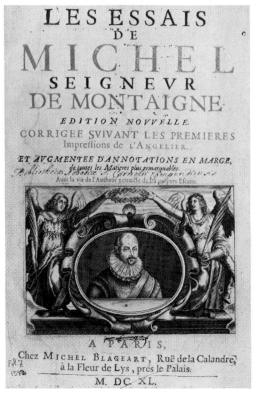

(*a*) M Blageart (Ruë, prés) [311 mm]

Title-page: The five tps differ only in the booksellers' imprints. There are
two states for Blageart (*a*) and (*b*) and one copy has Courbé overprinted
with Blageart (*d*). A significant innovation in the title are the words
corrigée suivant les premières impressions de L'Angelier and the omission of
the epigraph *Viresque* (see note 1). Lines 3, 5, 7, 8, 11 and A PARIS, are
in red.

- (*a*) Michel Blageart, with capital in 'Ruë' and accent on 'prés' (BN2,
  Ed/NB).
- (*b*) Michel Blageart, with 'ruë' and 'pres' (BN3, Châm, BL, Newc,
  Qu, RAS).
- (*c*) Augustin Courbé (BN5, Ill, Mich).
- (*d*) Courbé imprint (*c*) overprinted with Blageart imprint (*b*),
  probably in error (BN1).
- (*e*) Robert Denain (Laon).

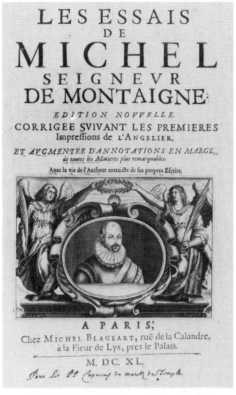

(*b*) M Blageart (ruë, pres) [311 mm]

Collation: 2°: ã⁶ A—3P⁶ 3Q—3T⁴ [$4 signed (3Q—3T $3 signed), roman numerals; missigning 3R2 as 3Q2 (*variant*: missigning F4 as D4)]; 388 leaves; pp [*12*] 1—38 63 40—201 102 103 204—207 210 209—229 229 231—283 288 285—388 379 390—394 394—395 397—452 451 454—456 461 458—493 492 495—596 598 599 599—694 694 696—715 786 717—745 747 747—750 [*14*] [*variants*: misnumbering 204 as 104, 515 as 513, 717 as 787, 742 as 747].

Contents: ã1: Title (verso blank); ã2: *Au lecteur*; ã3: Table of contents; ã5: Life; A1: *Essais*; 3S2: Index.

HT: ã2   [headpiece: central winged head, 2 fauns, 2 horses' heads and forelegs] ADVERTISSEMENT | AV LECTEVR.

      ã3   [headpiece: central winged head spouting water, volutes]

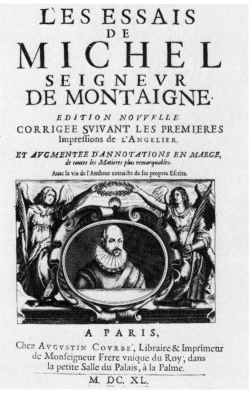

(c) A Courbé [318 mm]

TABLE | DES CHAPITRES | DV PREMIER LIVRE.

ã4   [double row of 24 arabesque type-orns, colons between 2
and 3, 12 and 13, 22 and 23] TABLE | DES CHAPITRES |
DV SECOND LIVRE.

ã4ᵛ   [double row of 24 arabesque type-orns, different arrangement from ã4, colons between 2 and 3, 4 and 5, 8 and 9, 12
and 13, 16 and 17, 20 and 21, 22 and 23] TABLE | DES
CHAPITRES | DV TROISIESME LIVRE.

ã5   [headpiece: central head, 2 birds, 2 putti] SOMMAIRE |
DISCOVRS | SVR LA VIE | DE MICHEL | SEIG-
NEVR | DE MONTAIGNE, | EXTRAICT DE SES |
propres Efcrits.

A1   [headpiece=ã5] ESSAIS | DE MICHEL | DE MON-
TAIGNE. | [rule] | LIVRE PREMIER.

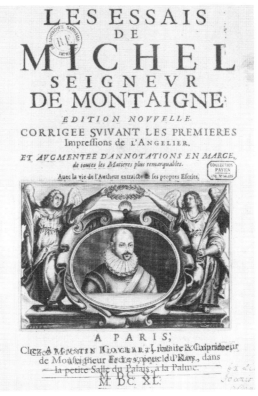

(*d*) A Courbé overprinted with M Blageart [318 mm]

S1 [headpiece: central winged figure with crown, fauns, deer, inits ID] [as A1 except] LIVRE SECOND.

2X2 [headpiece: central lion's head, 2 female figures, 2 boys with spears] [as A1 except] LIVRE TROISIESME.

3S2 [headpiece=S1] TABLE | DES MATIERES | PLVS REMARQVABLES | contenuës en ce Liure.

RT: ESSAIS DE MICHEL DE MONTAIGNE. | LIVRE PREMIER [SECOND] [TROISIESME]. [MONTAIGNE (no stop) C4^v D6^v E5^v F4^v 2A2^v 2B3^v 3O1^v, 5^v, 6^v 3P2^v,5^v 3Q2^v,3^v; MONTAINGE. 2H1^v 2Q4^v,6^v 2R1^v]

CW: Leaf. G5^v ne le faut N3^v nous S6^v c'eft 2G6^v iours 2Q2^v il s'en 3B6^v chacun 3I2^v arriué 3R2^v (signed 3Q2^v) *ô fortes* [*variant*: G5^v en faut]

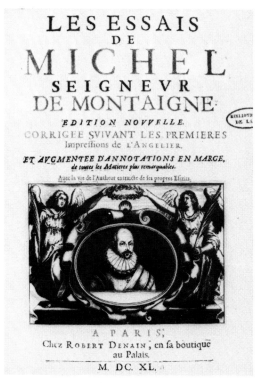

(*e*) R Denain [305 mm]

Measurements (Y5^v): 45(+2) lines. 264 (277)×150 mm. 20 lines=117 mm. Width with sidenotes 170 mm.

Privilège: None.

Notes: 1. The tp advertises this edition as 'corrigée suivant les premières impressions de L'Angelier', and it is indeed a close resetting of 7A: 1595. Misprints apart, it is therefore more faithful to the posthumous text of the *Essais* than any other seventeenth-century edition, including those of 1617, 1625 and 1635 supervised by Mlle de Gournay. It omits the epigraph *Viresque* which is not present in 1595, and in places it even follows the alignment of 1595, e.g. 1595, 3B1, lines 22—29=1640, 2Y2, lines 38—45.

2. On 3T4^v a head and snakes orn is found in about one third of the copies examined (BN3, 5, Gren, Mers, Qu, Mil/A, Ill). It is present in all

of the copies on ã4ᵛ, R6ᵛ, 2X1ᵛ, and is very close to the orn on the 1635 tps No 25 (b) and (e). The headpieces on ã2, S1 and 2X2 appear to be copies of the headpieces in 1635 on 3¶4, ã1 and ¶2.

Copies: BN1 (Z Payen 126); BN2 (Fol. Z 1582); BN3 (Z 763); BN4 (Z Payen 127, lacks tp); BN5 (Z Payen 128, lacks 3S3); *Ars*; *Sorb*; *Albi*; Ami; *Bayx*; Bes; Bord (5 copies); Châm (tp remounted); *Chan/F*; *Colm*; Gren; *Laon*; *Lep*; Ly; *Sél*; *Vers*. UK: BL; Cam: Trin; Ed/N; Ed/NB; *Lich*; Mers; Newc; Ox: Qu; RAS; *Wind*. GERMANY: *Pom*; *Tüb*. ITALY: Mil/A. NORWAY: *Oslo*. SWITZERLAND: *Bas*; *Bern*. USA: Chic/N; Chic/U; Harv; Ill; *Mich*. USSR: *Len/N*.

28: 1641 Rouen

[145 mm]

Title-page: The Honervogt engraving is as No 22: [1619] Rouen B and No 24: 1627 Rouen (g) (h), but with Jean Berthelin's imprint and the date in letterpress in the circular cartouche.

Collation: 8°: ã⁸ A—4A⁸ [\$4 signed, arabic numerals; missigning V3 as T3, 2G3 as Cg3, 2O4 as O4, 2S4 as S4, 3G3 as Cgg3, 3I3 as Iij 3 (for Iii 3), 3I4 as Iij 4 (*variants*: missigning 3T3 as Tts 3, not signing 3Z3)]; 568 leaves; pp [*16*] *1* 2—87 78 89—136 173 138—142 145 144—203 104 205—222 213 224—254 55 256—460 419 462—478 679 480—514 315 516 417 518—537 53e 539—570 571ᵗ 572—608 611—633 614 635—637 712 639—738 779—836 873 838—871 272 873—884 883 885 887—891 692 893—926 827 928—932 953 934—938 839 940—952 951 954—956 927 958 959 660 961—978 479 980—1034 1025 1036—1078 1097 1080—1096 1077 1098—1108 1119 1110—1118 1116 1120—1129 [=1087] [*33*] [*variants*: misnumbering 1075 as 5701, 1110 as 1011].

Contents: ã1: Title (verso blank); ã2:*Au lecteur*; ã2ᵛ:Short Gournay preface; ã3: Table of contents; ã5ᵛ: Life; A1: *Essais*; 3Y8ᵛ: blank; 3Z1: Index.

HT: ã2   [row of 12 arabesque type-orns, colon between fourth and fifth] *AV LECTEVR*.

     ã2ᵛ   [headpiece: top portion of frame with arabesque decoration] ADVIS SVR LES ESSAIS | DE MICHEL SEIGNEVR | de Montaigne, | PAR SA FILLE D'ALLIANCE.

     ã3   [double row of 12 fleur-de-lis type-orns] TABLE DES CHAPITRES | DV PREMIER LIVRE DES | Eſſais de Michel ſieur de | Montaigne.

     ã5ᵛ   [headpiece: central head, 2 crawling children] SOMMAIRE | DISCOVRS SVR LA VIE | DE MICHEL, SEIGNEVR | de Montaigne, extraict de | ſes propres eſcrits.

     A1   [headpiece=ã5ᵛ] ESSAIS | DE MICHEL | DE MONTAIGNE, | LIVRE PREMIER.

     T7   [as A1 except] LIVRE SECOND.

     3B3   [as A1 except] LIVRE TROISIESME.

     3Z1   [double row of 14 fleur-de-lis type-orns] TABLE | DES MATIERES, ET NOMS | PLVS MEMORABLES CONTENVS | aux Eſſais de Michel ſieur de Montaigne.

RT: ESSAIS DE MICHEL DE MONTAIGNE, | LIVRE PREMIER [SECOND] [TROISIESME]. [MCHEL once in 3EGHKMNP; DEMONTAIGNE, once in 3EFINPRTV; MONTAI NE, 3S5ᵛ; MONTAINE, 3T7ᵛ; SECGND. once in 2B—MOPX; TROISIEME. once in 3CE—LOSV—Y, twice in 3MNP, three times in 3Q; TROISIEME (no stop) 3F2 3I5; TROISIESME (no stop)

once in 3G—OSTVY] [*variants*: Premier. (for Second.) V5; Montagne, 3X]

CW: Quire. ã8ᵛ ESSAIS I8ᵛ ouuerts T8ᵛ merueille, 2I8ᵛ craignons
2X8ᵛ train 3I8ᵛ rage, 3K8ᵛ qu'el-]les 3T8ᵛ Philoſophes
3Z8ᵛ Mariages

Measurements (Q4): 41(+2) lines. 141(148)×73 mm. 20 lines=69 mm.
Width with sidenotes 89 mm.

Privilège: None.

Notes: 1. The Honervogt tp suggests that this edition is set from No 24:
1627 Rouen. This is confirmed by many shared errors in the text as well
as by the missigning of 2S4 as S4, which is not found in other editions.

2. There are two settings of gathering 3X. The setting with RT
Montagne, (for Montaigne,) found in BN1 is generally less correct.

Copies: BN1 (Z Payen 129, long MS note by Payen); BN2 (Z Payen 130,
lacks tp); *Ars*; *Sorb*; Bord; Nant. UK: BL; Ed/N; *Nott*; Ox: Wad
(bound in 3 vols). DENMARK: *Cop*. EIRE: Kilk. GERMANY:
Gött; *Han*; *Nür*; *Xant*. NETHERLANDS: *Gron*. SWITZER-
LAND: *Bas*; *Frau*. USA: *Prin*. YUGOSLAVIA: *Belg*.

LES ESSAIS
DE
MICHEL
SEIGNEVR
DE MONTAIGNE.

Derniere Edition.

ENRICHIE D'ANNOTATIONS
EN MARGE.

Auec vne Table tres-ample des Matieres.

Plus la Vie de l'Autheur, extraicte
de ses propres Escrits.

Vtriusque acquirit eundo.

A PARIS,
Chez MICHEL BLAGEART, au bout
du Pont-neuf, au coin de la ruë Dauphine.

M. DC. XLIX.

[150 mm]

Title-page: The wording of the title differs from that of the earlier Blageart edition, No 27: 1640. The epigraph reads erroneously *Vtriusque* for *Viresque*.

Collation: 8°: ã⁸ A—3Z⁸ ²3A⁸ [$4(−X4, 2K4) signed, roman numerals (¹3A signed AAa, ²3A signed Aaa); missigning 3T3 as 3T4, 2K1 as Kĸ, 2K2 as Kᴋ ij, 2K3 as Kĸ iij, 3K as KKᴋ, KKᴋ ij, Kĸĸ iij, ĸĸĸ iiij, 3Q3,4 as QQq iij, QQq iiij, 3X1 as Xxx (for XXx), 3Z2,3,4 as zzz ij, zzz iiij, zzz iiij (*variants*: missigning 2R3 as R3)]; 568 leaves; pp [*16*] 1—60 *61* 62—155 159 157—188 89 190—203 304 205—297 98 299—336 335 338—340 431 342—387 382 389—429 420 431—452 427 454—496 797 498—566 568 568—579 550 581—605 608—638 939 640—664 66 666—672 973 674—736 037 738 779—789 791 791 892 793—838 837 404 241 842—867 878 869—893 898 895—926 979 928—931 912 913 934—936 637 938—942 945 944—945 949 947—1008 1006 1010—1033 1014 1035—1057 1068 1059—1078 1077 1080 1091 1082—1129 [=1087] [*33*] [*variant*: misnumbering 921 as 121].

Contents: ã1: Title (verso blank); ã2: *Au lecteur*; ã3: Table of contents; ã5ᵛ: Life; A1: *Essais*; 3Y8ᵛ: blank; 3Z1: Index.

HT: ã2 [headpiece: central female head, 2 dolphins' heads, 2 cornucopiae] AV LECTEVR.

   ã3 [headpiece: central Indian head, 2 birds] TABLE | DES CHAPITRES | DV PREMIER LIVRE | des Eſſais de Michel, ſieur | de Montaigne.

   ã5ᵛ [headpiece: central shield with 3 fleurs-de-lis, foliage, 2 birds] *DISCOVRS SVR LA VIE* | *de Michel, Seigneur de Mon-* | *taigne, extraict de ſes propres* | *eſcrits.*

   A1 [headpiece=ã5ᵛ] ESSAIS | DE MICHEL | DE MON- TAIGNE. | LIVRE PREMIER.

   T7 [as A1 except] LIVRE SECOND.

   3B3 [headpiece=ã3] [as A1 except] LIVRE TROISIESME.

   3Z1 [headpiece: flowers and berries within frame] TABLE | DES MATIERES | ET NOMS PLVS MEMORA- | BLES CON- TENVS AVX ESSAIS | de Michel ſieur de Montaigne.

RT: Essais de Michel de Montaigne, | Livre Premier [Second] [Troisiesme]. [Esais once in 2TVY 3BD; ssais 3D8ᵛ; Essasi 3O8ᵛ 3Q3ᵛ 3S2ᵛ 3V7ᵛ; Essasis 3X6ᵛ; Essaisde 2Z6ᵛ 3A3ᵛ; Michelde once in 3HKLN—PR (no comma 3LNO); Mcheil 3Y1ᵛ; Michle de Monta- inge, once in 3KMNP—RV; deMontaigne, Q5ᵛ; deMontaigne. T3ᵛ; Montagne, 2X8ᵛ 2Y3ᵛ; Montaign 3Q3ᵛ; Montaigne. 3X5ᵛ; Premier, F1 G4 I5 K4 M7 P1 Q8 S7; prmiere. G6 I1 K2; Second, T8; Second (no stop) once in VXZ 2ACDFGIKMNPRTVYZ; second. once in 2LNOQSYZ 3A, 2X4,5; ꟻSecond. once in 2RTV; Livr troisiesme. 3SV7; Ttoisiesme. 3C1 3E3; troisiesme. once or twice in 3CE—X and also 3Y1, 3,5,6,7; TROISIEME. once in 3DF—HKLN; TROSIESME 3P1 3Q7 3R8; TROISIESM 3Q1 3R4; TROISISIESME. 3X1,6 3Y8]

CW: Quire. C8ᵛ roolle P8ᵛ *Nec* 2B8ᵛ *Bellua* 2R8ᵛ l'ame 3E8ᵛ Mais 3N8ᵛ m'allegue, 3Z8ᵛ Laideurs

Measurements (K4): 42(+2) lines. 143(150)×71 mm. 20 lines=68 mm. Width with sidenotes 88 mm.

Privilège: None.

Notes: 1. This edition belongs to the family of octavos with the last numbered page 1129. A large number of shared pagination errors show that it is unmistakeably derived from No 16: 1611, e.g. 304 for 204, 797 for 497, 979 for 927, 913 for 933, 1014 for 1034, 1068 for 1058. Moreover many of the alignments in the index of 1649 agree with 1611 against No 14: 1608. The short Gournay preface and the portrait are, however, omitted.[1]

2. There is a clear pattern in the occurrence of the RT SECOND (no stop), suggesting two compositors.

Copies: BN1 (Z 19582); BN2 (Z Payen 131); BN3 (Z Payen 132—133, bound in 2 vols); BN4 (Z Payen 134, lacks tp, prelims, index and other leaves); *Ars*; Cass; Stge (prelims muddled); Aix; Bord; *Chas*; Cler; *Colm*; Dôle (lacks tp, Leu portrait tipped in); Lav; Ly; Mars (bound in 2 vols); Ren; Tro. UK: Ox: RAS. GERMANY: Würz. ITALY: Regg. POLAND: *Wars/N*. SPAIN: *Madr*. SWITZERLAND: Gen; *Laus/P*; *Laus/U*.

---

[1] See P Bonnet, 'L'édition de 1649 des *Essais*', *BSAM*, IV, 3 (1965), pp 3—5.

(*a*) Engraved title and portrait [330 mm]

LES
ESSAIS
DE MICHEL, SEIGNEVR
DE MONTAIGNE.
NOVVELLE EDITION
EXACTEMENT PVRGE'E DES DEFAVTS

des precedentes, selon le vray original:

Et enrichie & augmentée aux marges du nom des Autheurs qui y sont citez, & de la Version de leurs Passages; Auec des Obseruations tres-importantes & necessaires pour le soulagement du Lecteur.

Ensemble la Vie de l'Autheur, & deux Tables, l'vne des Chapitres, & l'autre des principales Matieres, de beaucoup plus ample & plus vtile que celles des dernieres Editions.

A PARIS,
Chez AVGVSTIN COVRBE', Imprimeur & Libraire de M. le Duc
d'Orleans, au Palais, en la Gallerie des Merciers, à la Palme.

M. DC. I I I.
AVEC PRIVILEGE DV ROY.

(*b*) A Courbé; palm-tree and putti device [296 mm]

LES
ESSAIS
DE MICHEL. SEIGNEVR
DE MONTAIGNE.
NOVVELLE EDITION
EXACTEMENT PVRGEE DES DEFAVTS
des precedentes, selon le vray original.

Et enrichie & augmentée aux marges du nom des Autheurs qui y sont citez, & de
la Version de leurs Passages: Avec des Observations tres-importantes &
necessaires pour le soulagement du Lecteur.

Ensemble la Vie de l'Autheur, & deux Tables, l'vne des Chapitres, & l'autre des principales
Matieres, de beaucoup plus ample & plus vtile que celles des dernieres Editions.

A PARIS,
Chez la Vefue MATHVRIN DV PVIS, ruë Sainct Jacques,
à la Couronne d'Or.

M. DC. LII.

AVEC PRIVILEGE DV ROY.

(e) Veuve M Du Puis [289 mm]

LES
ESSAIS
DE MICHEL. SEIGNEVR
DE MONTAIGNE.
NOVVELLE EDITION
EXACTEMENT PVRGEE DES DEFAVTS
des precedentes, selon le vray original.

Et enrichie & augmentée aux marges du nom des Autheurs qui y sont citez, & de
la Version de leurs Passages: Avec des Observations tres-importantes &
necessaires pour le soulagement du Lecteur.

Ensemble la Vie de l'Autheur, & deux Tables, l'vne des Chapitres, & l'autre des principales
Matieres, de beaucoup plus ample & plus vtile que celles des dernieres Editions.

A PARIS,
Chez EDME COVSTEROT, ruë Sainct Jacques, prés les Machurins,
à l'enseigne du Bon Pasteur.

M. DC. LII.

AVEC PRIVILEGE DV ROY.

(d) E Cousterot [289 mm]

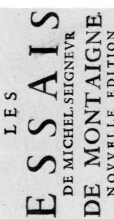

LES
ESSAIS
DE MICHEL. SEIGNEVR
DE MONTAIGNE.
NOVVELLE EDITION
EXACTEMENT PVRGEE DES DEFAVTS
des precedentes, selon le vray original.

Et enrichie & augmentée aux marges du nom des autheurs qui y sont citez, & de
la Version de leurs Passages: Avec des Observations tres-importantes &
necessaires pour le soulagement du Lecteur.

Ensemble la Vie de l'Autheur, & deux Tables, l'vne des Chapitres, & l'autre des principales
Matieres, de beaucoup plus ample & plus vtile que celles des dernieres Editions.

A PARIS,
Chez AVGVSTIN COVRBE, Imprimeur & Libraire de M. le Duc
d'Orleans, au Palais, en la Gallerie des Merciers, à la Palme.

M. DC. LII.

AVEC PRIVILEGE DV ROY.

(c) A Courbé; olive-tree and old
man device [289 mm]

(f) Veuve S Huré and S Huré [289 mm]

(g) T Joly [289 mm]

(b) P Le Petit [289 mm]

(i) J-B Loyson

LES
ESSAIS
DE MICHEL, SEIGNEVR
DE MONTAIGNE.
NOVVELLE EDITION
EXACTEMENT PVRGEE DES DEFAVTS
des precedentes, selon le vray original:

Et enrichie & augmentée aux marges du nom des Autheurs qui y sont citez, & de la Version de leurs Passages; Avec des Observations tres-importantes & necessaires pour le soulagement du Lecteur.

Ensemble la Vie de l'Autheur, & deux Tables, l'vne des Chapitres, & l'autre des principales Matieres, de beaucoup plus ample & plus vtile que celles des dernieres Editions.

A PARIS,
Chez IEAN BAPTISTE LOYSON, au Palais, sur le Perron royal, deuant
la porte de la Grand Chambre, à la Croix d'or.
M.DC.LII.
AVEC PRIVILEGE DV ROY.

(i) J-B Loyson [289 mm]

(j) S Piget

LES
ESSAIS
DE MICHEL, SEIGNEVR
DE MONTAIGNE.
NOVVELLE EDITION
EXACTEMENT PVRGEE DES DEFAVTS
des precedentes, selon le vray original:

Et enrichie & augmentée aux marges du nom des Autheurs qui y sont citez, & de la Version de leurs Passages; Avec des Observations tres-importantes & necessaires pour le soulagement du Lecteur.

Ensemble la Vie de l'Autheur, & deux Tables, l'vne des Chapitres, & l'autre des principales Matieres, de beaucoup plus ample & plus vtile que celles des dernieres Editions.

A PARIS,
Chez SIMEON PIGET, ruë Sainct Iacques, à l'enseigne
de la Sereine.
M.DC.LII.
AVEC PRIVILEGE DV ROY.

(j) S Piget [289 mm]

(k) P Rocolet

LES
ESSAIS
DE MICHEL, SEIGNEVR
DE MONTAIGNE.
NOVVELLE EDITION
EXACTEMENT PVRGEE DES DEFAVTS
des precedentes, selon le vray original:

Et enrichie & augmentée aux marges du nom des Autheurs qui y sont citez, & de la Version de leurs Passages; Avec des Observations tres-importantes & necessaires pour le soulagement du Lecteur.

Ensemble la Vie de l'Autheur, & deux Tables, l'vne des Chapitres, & l'autre des principales Matieres, de beaucoup plus ample & plus vtile que celles des dernieres Editions.

A PARIS,
Chez PIERRE ROCOLET, Imprimeur & Libraire ordinaire du Roy
& de la Maison de ville, au Palais, aux Armes du Roy & de la Ville.
M.DC.LII.
AVEC PRIVILEGE DV ROY.

(k) P Rocolet [289 mm]

Title-page: The engraved tp is similar to No 25: 1635 (*d*), and the ten printed tps differ in the booksellers' imprints. The olive-tree and old man device is found with all imprints except (*b*), which is an alternative Courbé device. Lines 2, 4, 6, A PARIS and date in red.

- (*a*) Engraved title, portrait, and imprint without name of bookseller.
- (*b*) Augustin Courbé, palm-tree and putti device signed 'Daret Sc'. (BN1, BN2, Ami, Blo, Ly, CUL, Ed/U, Liv, Stj, Dub/M, Ham, Wolf, Chic/U, Hunt, W/Cong).
- (*c*) Augustin Courbé, olive-tree and old man device (Tours).
- (*d*) Edmé Cousterot (Ang, Mel, Metz, Worc, Bru, Pra/S, Lucc, Prin).
- (*e*) Veuve Mathurin Du Puis (Avig, Chas, Laf, Flo, Oslo).
- (*f*) Veuve Sébastien Huré and Sébastien Huré (BN4, Bord 1, Brg, Lep).
- (*g*) Thomas Joly (Gren, Poi, Sal).
- (*h*) Pierre Le Petit (Bord 3, Chamb, Orl, BL2, RAS, Wroc/U, Len/N).
- (*i*) Jean-Baptiste Loyson (Belg).
- (*j*) Simeon Piget (Vals, BL1).
- (*k*) Pierre Rocolet (BN3, Cass, Bord 2, Cler, Touls).

Collation: 2°: a⁴ b—c⁶ A—4D⁶ [$4 signed, roman numerals];   454 leaves; pp [*32*] 1—208 193 210—334 355 336—343 342 341 346—436 457 438—439 450 451 442—448 459 450—532 503 534—627 608 629—832 839 840 [=834] [*42*] [*variant*: misnumbering 442 as 452].

Contents: a1: Printed tp (verso blank); a2: Engraved tp (verso blank); a3: Henri Estienne's preface; a3ᵛ: End of Estienne's preface, *Au lecteur*; a4: End of *Au lecteur*, Gournay's dedication to Richelieu; b1: Long Gournay preface; c4: End of long Gournay preface, Life; c6: Table of contents; A1: *Essais*; 4A4: Index; 4D5ᵛ: *Privilège*; 4D6ᵛ: blank.

HT: a3 [headpiece: central naked torso with headdress, snakes, birds, fruit, volutes] L'IMPRIMEVR | AV LECTEVR. (Plate 17)

b1 [headpiece: 2 central shields, one with 3 fleurs-de-lis, 2 putti holding crowns, fruit at edges] PREFACE | SVR LES | ESSAIS DE MICHEL | SEIGNEVR | DE MONTAIGNE. | Par fa fille d'alliance.

A1 [headpiece similar to b1] ESSAIS | DE MICHEL | DE MONTAIGNE. | [rule] | LIVRE PREMIER.

V4   [as A1 except] LIVRE SECOND.
3C4   [as A1 except] LIVRE TROISIESME.

RT: ESSAIS DE MICHEL DE MONTAIGNE, | LIVRE PREMIER [SECOND] [TROISIESME]. [MONTAIGNE. A4ᵛ; MONTAIGNE (no comma) R3ᵛ,5ᵛ; MONT AIGNE, 2S5ᵛ; SECOND (no stop) X3,6; SECOND. (for TROISIESME.) 3C6]

CW: Quire. a4ᵛ PREFACE   b6ᵛ *arracher*   c6ᵛ ESSAIS   H6ᵛ les   V6ᵛ mal   2F6ᵛ—*confueta*   3F6ᵛ fufcite   4A6ᵛ Charles   4B6ᵛ Lucullus   4C6ᵛ Liberalité.

Measurements (H2): 45(+2) lines. 264(277) × 137 mm. 20 lines = 117 mm. Width with sidenotes 169 mm.

Privilège: To Henri Estienne for 7 years to print *Essais de Montaigne, Histoire Romaine de Coëffeteau, & Estats & Empires*. Paris, 3 May 1651, signed SAVARY. Ceded by Estienne to Courbé and Le Petit for this edition only. *Achevé d'imprimer*: 28 December 1651.

Notes: 1. Set from No 25: 1635 with which it shares the modernisations of language.

2. Printed by Henri Estienne whose preface (Plate 17) advertises the novelty of this edition, namely both summaries of the text and translations of the Latin quotations in the margins. However, the preface is mistaken in attributing the marginal summaries to the L'Angelier editions since these did not appear until No 14: 1608, and the last edition bearing L'Angelier's name was No 13: 1604.

Copies: BN1 (Z 766); BN2 (Z Payen 135); BN3 (Z Payen 136); BN4 (Rés. Z 361); Ars 1 (Fol. S 270); Ars 2 (Fol. S 271); Cass; *Cath*; Inst; *Sorb*; Stge; Ami; Ang; Avig; Blo; Bord 1 (D 896); Bord 2 (GF 1544); Bord 3 (GF 744); Brg; *Chamb*; *Chas*; Cler; Gren; *Laf*; *Lep*; Ly; *Mel*; *Metz*; Nant (2 copies, Cousterot and Le Petit); Orl; *Pau*; *Perp*; Poi; *Roa*; *Sal*; Touls; Tours; *Vals*; *Vers*. UK: BL1 (720.m. 11—13); BL2 (1485.dd. 10); Cam: CUL; Ed/U; Liv (some sheets from No 31: 1657); Ox: New; RAS; Stj; Tay (lacks printed tp); Worc. BELGIUM: Bru. CZECHOSLO-VAKIA: *Pra/S*. EIRE: Dub/M. GERMANY: Ham; Wolf (tp remounted). ITALY: Flo; Lucc; *Mil/B*; *Mod*. NETHERLANDS:

Ams; *Hague.* NORWAY: *Oslo.* POLAND: *Krak/N*; *Wars/U*; *Wroc/U* (2 copies, Courbé and Le Petit). SPAIN: *Madr.* SWITZER-LAND: *Laus/P.* USA: Chic/U; *Harv*; Hunt; Prin; W/Cong; *Yale.* USSR: *Len/N*; *Mosc/G*; *Mosc/H.* YUGOSLAVIA: *Belg.*

31: 1657

(*a*) Engraved title and portrait [330 mm]

LES ESSAIS DE MICHEL, SEIGNEVR DE MONTAIGNE. NOVVELLE EDITION
EXACTEMENT PVRGÉ DES DEFAVTS des precedentes, selon le vray original.

Enrichies d'augmentations aux marges du nom des Autheurs qui y sont citez, & de la Version de leurs Passages Grecs & Latins; Auec des Observations tres-importantes & necessaires pour le jugement du Lecteur.

Auec augmentation de la Version Françoise des Passages Italiens.

A PARIS, Chez PIERRE LAMY, au second Pillier, de la grand Salle du Palais, au grand Cesar.

M.DC.LVII.

AVEC PRIVILEGE DV ROY.

LES ESSAIS DE MICHEL, SEIGNEVR DE MONTAIGNE. NOVVELLE EDITION
EXACTEMENT PVRGÉ DES DEFAVTS des precedentes, selon le vray original.

Enrichies & augmentées aux marges du nom des Autheurs qui y sont citez, & de la Version de leurs Passages Grecs & Latins; Auec des Observations tres-importantes & necessaires pour le jugement du Lecteur.

Ensemble la Vie de l'Autheur, & les Tables, auec des Chapitres, & ... des principales Matieres...

Auec augmentation de la Version Françoise des Passages Italiens.

A PARIS, Chez P. ROCOLET, Imp. ord. du Roy, & de la Ville de Paris, en la Gallerie des Prisonniers, aux Armes du Roy & de la Ville.

M.DC.LVII.

AVEC PRIVILEGE DV ROY.

LES ESSAIS DE MICHEL, SEIGNEVR DE MONTAIGNE. NOVVELLE EDITION
EXACTEMENT PVRGÉ DES DEFAVTS des precedentes, selon le vray original.

Enrichies & augmentées aux marges du nom des Autheurs qui y sont citez, & de la Version de leurs Passages Grecs & Latins; Auec des Observations tres-importantes & necessaires pour le jugement du Lecteur.

Ensemble la Vie de l'Autheur, & les Tables, l'vne des Chapitres & l'autre des principales Matieres...

Auec augmentation de la Version Françoise des Passages Italiens.

A PARIS, Chez CHARLES ANGOT, rüe Sainct Iacques; à la Ville de Leyden.

M.DC.LVII.

AVEC PRIVILEGE DV ROY.

(b) P L'Amy; Caesar's head device [290 mm]

(c) P Rocolet; ship and fleur-de-lis device [292 mm]

(d) C Angot; olive-tree and old man device [292 mm]

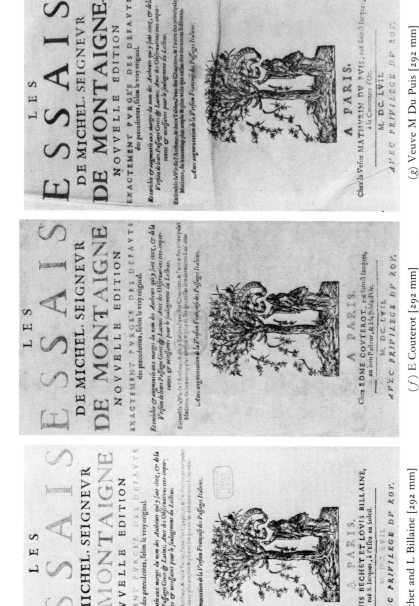

(e) D Bechet and L Billaine [292 mm]

(f) E Couterot [292 mm]

(g) Veuve M Du Puis [292 mm]

(h) S Huré and F Léonard [292 mm]

(i) J and E Langlois [292 mm]

(j) P Le Petit [292 mm]

(l) J Piot [292 mm]

(k) J-B Loyson [292 mm]

Title-page: The engraved tp is the same plate as No 30: 1652 with the date changed to 1657. In BN1 the scratched out 2 can be faintly seen. The twelve printed tps differ in the booksellers' imprints. All have the olive-tree device except (*b*) L'Amy and (*c*) Rocolet. The text of the title follows 1652 closely but adds *Auec augmentation de la Version Françoise des Passages Italiens*. Lines 2,4,6,11,12, A PARIS and the date are in red.

(*a*) Engraved title, portrait, and imprint without name of bookseller.

(*b*) Pierre L'Amy, Caesar's head device (Cass, Trent, Wars/N).

(*c*) Pierre Rocolet, ship and fleur-de-lis device, inits PR (BN4, Etam, Vien/N, Reg).

(*d*) Charles Angot, olive-tree and old man device (BN1, Arr, Caen).

(*e*) Denis Bechet and Louis Billaine (BN2, Man, Chic/U, Prin 2).

(*f*) Edmé Couterot (Drag, BL, Tay, Harv).

(*g*) Veuve Mathurin Du Puis (Boul, Diep, Vie, Pra/M 2, USC).

(*h*) Sébastien Huré and Frédéric Leonard (Ly, Monb, Nev, Nîm, Sto, Liv, Pra/M 1, Dub/T, Gött, Len/S, Mosc/L).

(*i*) Jacques and Emmanuel Langlois (Evr, Pau, Graz, Prin 1).

(*j*) Pierre Le Petit (Châm, Colm,Hy, RAS, Vien/U, Chap, W/Cong).

(*k*) Jean-Baptiste Loyson (Aut, Pad/U).

(*l*) Jean Piot (BN3, Sal).

(*m*) Thomas Jolly (no copy seen, but reproduced by Tchemerzine, viii, 435).

Collation: 2°: a⁴ b—c⁶ A—4D⁶ [$4 signed, roman numerals; missigning 2E2 as E2, 2F3 as F3, 3K as Kkk (*variants*: missigning 2R2 as R2, 4A1 with r in middle of direction line)]; 454 leaves; pp [*32*] 1—17 24 19—37 238 39—94 71 96—111 212 113—162 169 164—220 121 122 223—238 2Z9 240—252 353 254—344 341 346—356 757 358—431 532 433—439 450 451 442—467 168 469—480 489 482—533 354 535—543 542 545—553 556 555—600 501 602—627 608 629—651 402 653—662 693 664—742 762 744—765 762 767—788 783 790—801 800 803—832 839 840 [=834] [*42*] [*variants*: misnumbering 269 as 219, 288 as 88].

Contents: a1: Printed tp (verso blank); a2: Engraved tp (verso blank); a3: Henri Estienne's preface; a3ᵛ: End of Estienne's preface, *Au lecteur*; a4: End of *Au lecteur*, Gournay's dedication to Richelieu; b1: Long Gournay preface; c4: End of long Gournay preface, Life; c6: Table of contents; A1: *Essais*; 4A4: Index: 4D5ᵛ: *Privilège*; 4D6ᵛ: blank.

HT: a3   [headpiece: 2 central shields, one with 3 fleurs-de-lis, 2 putti holding crowns] L'IMPRIMEVR | AV LECTEVR.

  b1   [headpiece=a3] PREFACE | SVR LES | ESSAIS DE MICHEL | SEIGNEVR | DE MONTAIGNE, | Par fa fille d'alliance.

  A1   [headpiece=a3] ESSAIS | DE MICHEL | DE MON-TAIGNE. | [rule] | LIVRE PREMIER.

  V4   [as A1 except] LIVRE SECOND.

  3C4   [as A1 except] LIVRE TROISIEME.

RT: ESSAIS DE MICHEL DE MONTAIGNE, | LIVRE PREMIER [SECOND] [TROISIESME]. [MONTAIGNE (comma inverted) S3^v; MONTAINGE, 3Q1^v; MONTAIGNE (no comma) once or more in 2H 3ABD—K; IVRE 2S2,3 2T6 2X1 2Y4 2Z5; SECOND. (for PREMIER.) E2; PREMIER. (for SECOND.) V6 Z2,3,4 2B4 2C2,5; SECOND. (for TROISIESME.) 3C6 3K6; TROISIESME (no stop) 3F1,5 3H3; TROISIESME, 3G2 3H4,6 3I5; TROISIEME. 3G5; TROISIEME 3E1] [*variants*: MONTAIGNE (comma inverted) X5^v; MONTAIG N or MONTAI G N or MONTAIG or MONTAIGN 2G4]

CW: Quire. Selected CWs as No 30: 1652 except 4C6^v Liberali-

Measurements (2A2): 45(+2) lines. 265 (281)×137 mm. 20 lines=117 mm. Width with sidenotes 169 mm.

Privilège: As No 30: 1652, dated Paris, 3 May 1651, signed SAVARY. Ceded by Estienne to Le Petit and Huré for this edition only. *Achevé d'imprimer pour la seconde fois*: 1 October 1657.

Notes: 1. A mainly paginal resetting of No 30: 1652.

2. At the end of his preface Henri Estienne adds his title *Imprimeur de sa Majesté* (a3^v), which is not in 1652.

3. On some copies the engraved tp has not been printed on a2 (Liv, Dub/T, Pad/U). Sometimes it is placed before the printed tp.

Copies: BN1 (Fol. Z 195); BN2 (Z Payen 137, lacks engraved tp); BN 3 (Fol. Z 1071); BN4 (Z 767); *Ars*; Cass; *Inst*; *Arr*; *Aut*; *Boul*; *Caen*; *Chamb*; *Colm*; *Diep*; *Drag*; Etam; *Evr*; *Hy*; *Ly* (lacks engraved tp);

Monb; *Nev*; *Nîm*; *Pau*; *Sal*; *Sto*; *Verd*; *Vie*. UK: BL; *LUC*; Liv (lacks engraved tp, a2 blank); *Man*; Ox: RAS; Tay. AUSTRIA: *Graz/L*; *Vien/N*; *Vien/U*. BELGIUM: *Bru*. CZECHOSLOVAKIA: *Pra/M 1* (11.A.3.); *Pra/M 2* (8.A.3). EIRE: Dub/T (lacks engraved tp, a2 blank). GERMANY: Gött (lacks engraved tp); *Reg*. ITALY: Pad/U (lacks engraved tp, a2 blank); Trent. POLAND: *Wars/N*. USA: Chap; Chic/U (tp torn and remounted, lacks engraved tp); *Harv*; Prin 1 (Ex 3273. 1657.q); Prin 2 (Ex 3273. 1657. 2q, lacks engraved tp); USC (printed tp remounted); W/Cong. USSR: *Len/S*; *Mosc/L*.

32: 1659

(*a*) C Journel; vol i [136 mm]

(b) C Journel; vol ii [136 mm]

(c) C Journel; vol iii [136 mm]

(d) J-B Loyson; vol iii [136 mm]

Title-page: The three volumes have the same engraved tp signed 'N. De Larmessin jn. et fc' with the imprint of Christophe Journel, and differ only in LIVRE PREMIER, SECOND, TROISIESME. A paste-on cancel slip with the imprint of Jean-Baptiste Loyson is found on vol iii of BN9.

   (*a*) Christophe Journel, vol i.   (*c*) Christophe Journel, vol iii.
   (*b*) Christophe Journel, vol ii.   (*d*) Jean-Baptiste Loyson, vol iii.

Collation: 12°: i: ã^{12} ẽ^{12} ĩ^{10} A—2A^{12} 2B^2; ii: ã^2 A—2N^{12} 2O^4; iii: ã^2 A—2C^{12} 2D^8 2E^2 [\$6 signed, roman numerals; missigning i S5 as S6; ii S3 as S4; iii ã2 as ã, B3 as B2, T3 as T4 (*variants*: missigning i N4 as N6; iii K3 as iij, T5 as R v)]; i 324 leaves; ii 438 leaves; iii 324 leaves; pp i [*68*] 1—475 472 477—556 [*24*]; ii [*4*] 1—289 280 291—503 506—521 512 513 524 525 516 517 528 529 520 531—827 [=825] [*47*]; iii [*4*] 1—114 113 116 117 116 117 120—574 576 576—610 [*34*].

Contents: i: ã1: Title (verso blank); ã2: *Au lecteur*; ã3: Gournay's dedication to Richelieu; ã5: Long Gournay preface; ĩ4: Life; ĩ9^v: Table of contents Bk I; A1: *Essais* Bk I; 2A3: Index to Bk I; ii: ã1: Title (verso blank); ã2: Table of contents Bk II; A1: *Essais* Bk II; 2M5^v: Index to Bk II; iii: ã1: Title (verso blank); ã2 (signed ã): Table of contents Bk III; A1: *Essais* Bk III; 2C6: Index to Bk III.

HT: i: ã2   [headpiece: central head, volutes, 2 snakes] ADVERTISSEMENT | DE L'AVTHEVR. | Inferé en toutes les precedentes Editions.

       ã3   [headpiece: central head, 2 grotesque animal heads] Epiſtre de Mademoiſelle de Gournay, | inferée en ſon Impreſſion de 1635. | [rule] | A MONSEIGNEVR | L'EMINENTISSIME | CARDINAL DVC | DE RICHELIEV.

       ã5   [headpiece: central horned head, fruit] PREFACE | SVR | LES ESSAIS | DE | MICHEL | SEIG-NEVR | DE MONTAIGNE, | Par ſa Fille d'alliance.

       ĩ4   [row of 11 type-orns, colon after fourth and eighth] *SOMMAIRE RECIT,* | *Sur la Vie de Michel Seigneur* | *de Montaigne, extraict* | *de ſes propres Eſcrits.*

       ĩ9^v [double row of 4 type-orns, colon after first and

	third] TABLE | DES CHAPITRES. | [rule] | *LIVRE PREMIER.*
A1	[headpiece=ã5] ESSAIS | DE MICHEL | DE MONTAIGNE. | [rule] | LIVRE PREMIER.
2A3	[double row of 11 type-orns, colon after sixth] TABLE | DES MATIERES | PLVS REMARQVABLES, | Contenuës dans la premiere Partie | des Eſſais de Montaigne.
ii: ã2	[double row of 12 type-orns] TABLE | DES CHAPITRES. | [rule] | *LIVRE SECOND.*
A1	[as i A1 except] LIVRE SECOND.
2M5ᵛ	[as i 2A3 except] DES CHOSES | PLVS REMARQVABLES, | Contenuës en la ſeconde Partie | [. . .]
iii: ã2 (signed ã)	[double row of 10 type-orns] TABLE | DES | CHAPITRES. | [rule] | *LIVRE TROISIESME.*
A1	[as i A1 except] LIVRE TROISIESME.
2C6	[as i 2A3 except] DES MATIERES | PRINCIPALES, | Contenuës en la troiſieſme Partie | [. . .]

RT: ESSAIS DE MONTAIGNE, \| LIVRE PREMIER [SECOND] [TROISIESME]. [i: PREMIER, B6; IIVRE H7; iii: TROISIESME, V5; MONTAGNE, 2C4ᵛ]

CW: Quire. i: E12ᵛ Ce O12ᵛ mettent Q12ᵛ penſent S12ᵛ hu-]mains, 2A12ᵛ morts,   ii: A12ᵛ maladie, N12ᵛ en Q12ᵛ attendu Z12ᵛ que 2M12ᵛ Les   iii: D12ᵛ eſtude. E12ᵛ ancien N12ᵛ voir 2D8ᵛ creé (*sic*)

Measurements (i: D4): 33(+2) lines. 109(116) × 47 mm. 20 lines = 66 mm. Width with sidenotes 65 mm.
  (ii: D6): 33(+2) lines. 111(118) × 48 mm. 20 lines = 67 mm. Width with sidenotes 66 mm.
  (iii: D4): 33(+2) lines. 110(116) × 48 mm. 20 lines = 67 mm. Width with sidenotes 66 mm.

Privilège: None.

Notes: 1. This is the first edition of the *Essais* in three volumes. It shares with No 30: 1652 and No 31: 1657 sidenotes containing both summaries of the text and translations of the Latin quotations. It also reproduces Mlle de Gournay's dedication to Richelieu and her preface.

2. BN3,6 and 9 are bound as a set but are in fact vols i, iii and iii. BN10 has mixed sheets from 1659 and 1669. Some sets contain vols from Nos 33, 34 or 35, e.g. Monp, Ren/U, Mod, Bost, Chic/U.

Copies: BN1 (Z 19583—19585); BN2 (16° Z 6391, vol i only); BN3 (Z Payen 142, vol i only); BN4 (Z Payen 145, vol ii only); BN5 (Rés. p. R. 57, vol ii *Apologie* only); BN6 (Z Payen 143, vol iii only); BN7 (Z Payen 146, vol iii only); BN8 (Z Payen 147, vol iii only); BN9 (Z Payen 144, vol iii only, Loyson); BN10 (Z Payen 148, vol iii only, lacks tp); *Ars*; *Cath* (vol i only); *Maz*; Avig; *Châm* (vol i only); *Chau* (vol iii only); Monp (vol ii only with vols i, iii of No 34: 1669); Poi; Ren/U (vol ii only with vol i of No 33: 1659 Amsterdam); *Sens*; *Vend*. (vol iii only).   UK: Ox: Tay 1 (HH 15—17 Finch); Tay 2 (Vet. Fr. IA. 385).   GERMANY: *Spe*; Wolf (vols i, ii only).   ITALY: Bol/U; Mod (vol ii only with vol i No 34: 1669 and vol iii No 35: 1669 Lyons); Parm.   POLAND: *Wroc/O*. ROMANIA: *Buc* (vol iii only).   SPAIN: *Madr*.   SWITZERLAND: *Bas*.   USA: Bost. (vols i, ii only with vol iii No 34: 1669). Chic/U (vol. i only with vol ii No 34: 1669 and vol iii No 35: 1669 Lyons); *Harv*. USSR: *Len/S* (vol ii only); *Mosc/H* (vol ii only); *Mosc/L*.

33: 1659 Amsterdam/Brussels

(*a*) Engraved title [135 mm]

Title-page: The first of the three volumes has an engraved tp signed 'P. Clouwet fe:' and a printed tp, which is repeated in vols ii and iii with LIVRE SECOND, LIVRE TROISIESME, and different ornaments. Two imprints are found: Amsterdam, Anthoine Michiels (*b*) to (*d*) and Bruxelles, François Foppens (*e*) to (*g*). The engraved tp does not occur with the Foppens imprint except in Monp 2 and Wad.

(*a*) Engraved title.	(*e*) F. Foppens, vol i.
(*b*) A. Michiels, vol i.	(*f*) F. Foppens, vol ii.
(*c*) A. Michiels, vol ii.	(*g*) F. Foppens, vol iii.
(*d*) A. Michiels, vol iii.	

LES ESSAIS DE MICHEL, SEIGNEUR DE MONTAIGNE.

NOUVELLE EDITION

EXACTEMENT PURGÉE DES DEFAVTS des precedentes, selon le vray original:

Et enrichie & augmentée aux marges du nom des Autheurs qui y sont citez, & de la Version de leurs Passages; Avec des Observations tres-importantes & necessaires pour le soulagement du Lecteur.

Ensemble la Vie de l'Autheur, & deux Tables, l'une des Chapitres, & l'autre des principales Matieres, de beaucoup plus ample & plus utile que celles des dernieres Editions.

LIVRE TROISIESME.

A AMSTERDAM,
Chez ANTHOINE MICHIELS, Libraire.

M. DC. LIX.

(d) A Michiels; vol iii [125 mm]

LES ESSAIS DE MICHEL, SEIGNEUR DE MONTAIGNE.

NOUVELLE EDITION

EXACTEMENT PURGÉE DES DEFAVTS des precedentes, selon le vray original;

Et enrichie & augmentée aux marges du nom des Autheurs qui y sont citez, & de la Version de leurs Passages; Avec des Observations tres-importantes & necessaires pour le soulagement du Lecteur.

Ensemble la Vie de l'Autheur, & deux Tables, l'une des Chapitres, & l'autre des principales Matieres, de beaucoup plus ample & plus utile que celles des dernieres Editions.

LIVRE SECOND.

A AMSTERDAM,
Chez ANTHOINE MICHIELS, Libraire.

M. DC. LIX.

(c) A Michiels; vol ii [125 mm]

LES ESSAIS DE MICHEL, SEIGNEUR DE MONTAIGNE.

NOUVELLE EDITION

EXACTEMENT PURGÉE DES DEFAVTS des precedentes, selon le vray original:

Et enrichie & augmentée aux marges du nom des Autheurs qui y sont citez, & de la Version de leurs Passages; Avec des Observations tres-importantes & necessaires pour le soulagement du Lecteur.

Ensemble la Vie de l'Autheur, & deux Tables, l'une des Chapitres, & l'autre des principales matieres, de beaucoup plus ample & plus utile que celles des dernieres Editions.

LIVRE PREMIER.

A AMSTERDAM,
Chez ANTHOINE MICHIELS, Libraire.

M. DC. LIX.

(b) A Michiels; vol i [129 mm]

(e) F Foppens; vol i [129 mm]

(f) F Foppens; vol ii [125 mm]

(g) F Foppens; vol iii [125 mm]

Collation: 12°: i: a⁸ b¹² c⁶ A—T¹² V⁶; ii: π² A—2F¹² 2G⁶; iii: π²
A—X¹² Y⁶ Z—2B¹² [$6 (−ii T4; −iii P3 Y2) signed, arabic
numerals; missigning ii Q3 as Q4, iii 2B4 as 2B2]; i 260 leaves; ii 356
leaves; iii 296 leaves; pp i [*52*] 1—468; ii [*4*] 1—238 230 240—411 312
313 414—420 321 422—669 970 671—708; iii [*4*] 1—510 [*78*] [*variants*:
misnumbering ii 178 as 182, 206 as 210].

Contents: i: a1: Engraved title (verso blank); a2: Printed title (verso
blank); a3: *Au lecteur*; a4: Gournay's dedication to Richelieu; a5: Long
Gournay preface; b11ᵛ: blank; b12: Life; c4: Table of contents Bk I; c6ᵛ:
Quotations from Lipsius; A1: *Essais* Bk I; ii: π1: Title (verso blank);
π2: Table of contents Bk II; A1: *Essais* Bk II; iii: π1: Title (verso blank);
π2: Table of contents Bk III; π2ᵛ: blank; A1: *Essais* Bk III; Y4: Index;
2B12ᵛ: blank.

HT: i: a3   [headpiece: central horned head, fruit] ADVERTISSE-
MENT | DE | L'AUTHEUR, | *Inſeré en toutes les*
precedentes | *Editions*.

a4   [double row of 15 vertical acorns, second row inverted,
3 horizontal acorns at each end] Epiſtre de Mademoiſelle
de Gournay, | inſerée en ſon impreſſion de l'année |
1635. | [rule]

a5   [headpiece: central nude female torso, cornucopia in
each arm, volutes] PREFACE | SVR LES | ESSAIS DE
MICHEL | SEIGNEVR | DE MONTAIGNE. | Par ſa
Fille d'alliance.

b12   [headpiece=i a3] SOMMAIRE RECIT, | SVR | LA
VIE | DE MICHEL, SEIGNEUR | DE MON-
TAIGNE, | *Extraict de ſes propres Eſ-*|*crits*.

A1   [headpiece=i a3] ESSAIS | DE MICHEL | DE |
MONTAIGNE. | [rule] | LIVRE PREMIER.

ii: A1   [as i A1 except] LIVRE SECOND.

iii: A1   [as i A1 except] LIVRE TROISIESME.

Y4   [headpiece=i a3] TABLE | DES MATIERES | PLVS
REMARQVABLES. | contenuës en ce Livre | [rule]

RT: ESSAIS DE MICHEL DE | MONTAIGNE. Lɪᴠ. I [II] [III]. [i:
Lɪᴠ. I. B4 D11; Lɪᴠ, I. B10; Lɪᴠ.I C9 E2 G5 I2,9 L1,5 P9 Q2 S3; Lɪᴠ. II.
V4; ii: ESSAS 2E7ᵛ; MONTAGNE. 2C12]

CW: Page. i: H8^v merveille, Q12^v Roys S12^v mais ii: F6^v Car N12^v ment Z12^v qui iii: E12^v pas K10^v exempté V12^v fongent

Measurements (i: G3): 34(+2) lines. 117(123) × 54 mm. 20 lines = 69 mm. Width with sidenotes 70 mm.

Privilège: None.

Note: Set from No 32: 1659, which it follows closely in contents, except for there being one index at the end of vol iii instead of a separate index for the three vols.

Copies (all Amsterdam except where otherwise indicated): BN1 (Z 19586—19588); BN2 (Z Payen 149—151); BN3 (Rés. Z 2774—2776); BN4 (Z Payen 153, vol ii only); BN5 (Z Payen 138—140, Brussels); BN6 (Z Payen 141, Brussels vol i only); *Cath*; Aix; *Arr*; *Bord 1* (PF 32985 Rés., Brussels, Racine copy); *Bord 2* (PF 17058 Rés.); *Châm* (vols ii, iii only); Ly (3 copies); Monp 1 (L 123); Monp 2 (44914, Brussels); Nio; Orl; Ren/U (vol i only with vol ii No 32: 1659 Paris); *Sal*; *Stra* (Brussels); *Touls*; Vers.   UK: BL (Brussels); *LI*; *Man*; Ox: Bod; RAS; Stj (Brussels, vol ii only); Wad (Brussels vols i, iii only); Worc (vol i Amsterdam, vols ii, iii Brussels).   BELGIUM: *Bru*.   CZECHOSLOVAKIA: *Pra/S* (vols i, iii only).   GERMANY: *Erl* (Brussels); *Frei*; Gött.   ITALY: Bol/A; Mil/A; Parm (vol i Amsterdam, vols ii, iii Brussels); Vat 1 (Ferr. V 2509, Brussels); Vat 2 (Chigi V 2419).   NETHERLANDS: *Ams*; *Nijm*. POLAND: *Krak/J 1*; *Krak/J 2* (Brussels, vol iii only).   SWITZER-LAND: *Sol*; Wint.   USA: Chap; Clark; *Harv*; *Virg/S* (Brussels, vol ii only, Jefferson copy); Virg/U (vols i, ii only with vol iii No 34: 1669). USSR: *Len/S*; *Mosc/H* (vol i lacks tp, vol ii Amsterdam, vol iii Brussels); *Mosc/L*.   YUGOSLAVIA: *Lju*.

34: 1669

Title-page: The three volumes have the same engraved tp signed 'Matheus f.' with the imprint of Laurent Rondet, Christophe Journel and Robert Chevillion and differ only in LIVRE PREMIER, SECOND, TROISIEME. The title is as No 32: 1659, but adds *Auec priuilege du Roy*.
(*a*) Vol i. (*b*) Vol ii. (*c*) Vol iii.

(*a*) Vol i [135 mm]

(*b*) Vol ii [135 mm]

(*c*) Vol iii [135 mm]

Collation: 12°: i: ã¹² ẽ¹² ĩ⁸ õ² A—2A¹² 2B²; ii: ã² A—2M¹² 2N⁸; iii: ã² A—2C¹² 2D⁸ 2E² [i Volume signature: I. Part. $6 signed; missignings: I. Part (no stop) A6 M6 O6 2A1; I.Patr. D3 F1; I.Pert. E2 T3 Y5; Part. (no I) Y4. i Quire signature: $6 signed, roman numerals; missigning H5 as G5, S2 as R2, S5 as Q5, Z4 as z iiij] [ii Volume signature: II.Part $1 (+2M1—6, 2N1—2) signed; missigning: I.Part. 2N2. ii Quire signature: $6 (−2N4) signed, roman numerals; missigning ã2 as ã, S3 as S4, 2N6 as N6] [iii Volume signature: III.Part. $1 signed. iii Quire signature: $6 signed, roman numerals; missigning ã2 as ã, F2 as E2, F4 as E4, Y3 as Y4]; i: 324 leaves; ii: 430 leaves; iii: 324 leaves; pp i: [*68*] 1—80 8s 82—247 148 249—277 s78 279—321 332 323—371 172 373—462 464 464—535 356 537—556 [*24*]; ii: [*4*] 1—289 280 291—492 943 494—503 506—758 719 760—798 796 800—827 [=825] [*31*]; iii: [*4*] 1—456 417 458—488 469 490—572 373 574—610 [*34*].

Contents: i: ã1: Title (verso blank); ã2: *Au lecteur*; ã3: Gournay's dedication to Richelieu; ã5: Long Gournay preface; ĩ4: Life; õ1: End of Life, *Privilège*; õ1ᵛ: Table of contents Bk I; A1: *Essais* Bk I; 2A3: Index to Bk I; ii: ã1: Title (verso blank); ã2 (signed ã): Table of contents Bk II; A1: *Essais* Bk II; 2M5ᵛ: Index to Bk II; iii: ã1: Title (verso blank); ã2 (signed ã): Table of contents Bk III; ã2ᵛ: *Privilège*; A1: *Essais* Bk III; 2C6: Index to Bk III.

HT: i: ã2	[headpiece: central head with arms held up, foliage] ADVERTISSEMENT | DE L'AV-THEVR | Inferé en toutes les precedentes Editions.
ã3	[headpiece: central female bust, fruit] Epiſtre de Mademoiſelle de Gournay, | Inferée en ſon Impreſſion de 1635. | [rule] | A MONSEIG-NEVR | L'EMINENTISSIME | CAR-DINAL DVC | DE RICHELIEV.
ã5	[headpiece: central horned head, fruit] PRE-FACE | SVR | LES ESSAIS | DE | MICHEL | SEIGNEVR | DE MONTAIGNE, | Par ſa Fille d'alliance.
ĩ4	[row of 9 type-orns with 4 colons] *SOM-MAIRE RECIT,* | *Sur la Vie de Michel Seigneur* | *de Montaigne, extraict* | *de ſes propres Eſcrits.*

õ1ᵛ	[double row of 12 type-orns with 2 colons after eighth pair] TABLE | DES CHA-PITRES. | [rule] | *LIVRE PREMIER.*
A1	[headpiece=ã5] ESSAIS | DE MICHEL | DE MONTAIGNE. | [rule] | LIVRE PREMIER.
2A3	[row of 12 type-orns with colon after eighth] TABLE | DES MATIERES. | PLVS REMARQVABLES, | Contenuës dans la premiere Partie | des Eſſais de Montaigne.
ii: ã2 (signed ã)	[double row of 11 type-orns with colon after ninth] [as i õ1ᵛ except] *LIVRE SECOND.*
A1	[headpiece: flowers, volutes] ESSAIS | DE MICHEL | DE MONTAIGNE. | [rule] | LIVRE SECOND.
2M5ᵛ	[row of 13 type-orns] [as i 2A3 except] DES CHOSES | PLVS REMARQVABLES, | Contenuës en la ſeconde Partie | [. . .]
iii: ã2 (signed ã)	[row of 10 type-orns in pairs] TABLE | DES | CHAPITRES. | [rule] | *LIVRE TROI-SIESME.*
A1	[headpiece=i: ã5] ESSAIS | DE MICHEL | DE MONTAIGNE. | [rule] | LIVRE TROI-SIESME.
2C6	[double row of 11 type-orns with colon after sixth] [as i 2A3 except] DES MATIERES | PRINCIPALES, | Contenuës en la troiſiefme Partie | [. . .]

RT: ESSAIS DE MONTAIGNE, \| LIVRE PREMIER [SECOND] [TROISIESME]. [i: MONTAIGNE1 S7ᵛ; MONTAIGNE. Z7ᵛ; FRE-MIER. D8; PREMIER, Z2; ii: MONTAIGNE. B8ᵛ C7ᵛ,9ᵛ E5ᵛ; MONTAIGNd, 2L10ᵛ; SEGOND, 2I12; SECOND (S inverted) 2L6; iii: MONTAICNE, A5ᵛ D5ᵛ F3ᵛ 2B1ᵛ; MONTAIGNE. D6ᵛ E3ᵛ; MONTAGNE, T3ᵛ; TROISSIEME. H9 I6 L6 N6; TROISISEME. D10 F8; TROISIESME, S4]

CW: Quire. i: E12ᵛ Ce L12ᵛ autres O12ᵛ mettent X12ᵛ reſolution 2A12ᵛ morts, ii: D12ᵛ eft-ce I12ᵛ leurs R12ᵛ corporelles. 2C12ᵛ plus 2K12ᵛ tortuë iii: C12ᵛ de L12ᵛ *Velauit*, R12ᵛ Du 2A12ᵛ delicateſſe 2D8ᵛ creé

Measurements (i: D4): 33(+2) lines. 112(119) × 48 mm. 20 lines = 68 mm. Width with sidenotes 65 mm.

(ii: D4): 33(+2) lines. 110(116) × 48 mm. 20 lines = 67 mm. Width with sidenotes 66 mm.

(iii: D4): 33(+2) lines. 110(117) × 49 mm. 20 lines = 67 mm. Width with sidenotes 68 mm.

Privilège: To Antoine Estienne for 7 years. Paris, 6 March 1666, signed MABOVL. Ceded by Estienne to L Rondet, C Journel, R Chevillion. Registered 5 April 1666, signed PIGET, Syndic. *Achevé d'imprimer*: 15 January 1669. Same wording in i: õ1 and iii: ã2ᵛ.

Notes: 1. Set from No 32: 1659 with which it shares an almost identical collational formula and the pagination jump 503 506 in vol ii.

2. Gathering ii: 2N is out of order in BN2, Bes, Ren, BL, probably because of unsigned 2N4.

3. In BN2 gathering õ is misplaced in the middle of gathering 2B. It seems therefore probable that õ and 2B were printed together, and with gathering ĩ this would make a whole sheet.

Copies: BN1 (Z 19589—19591); BN2 (Z Payen 164—166, see notes 2 and 3); BN3 (Rés. Z 2771—2773, Huet copy); BN4 (Z Payen 154—163, bound in 10 vols); BN5 (Z Payen 167, tp and Table of Bk III, text of Bk II only); BN6 (Z Payen 172 bis, vol i gatherings ã, ẽ and ĩ 1—3 only); BN7 (Z Payen 152, vol i only, lacking all before ĩ4 and also gathering õ); *Cath*; *Inst*; *Albi*; *Ami* (vol i only); *Ann*; Bes; *Bord*; *Bre*; *Chau* (vol iii only); Dij; *Foix*; Loch; *Metz*; Monp (vols i, iii only with vol ii No 32: 1659); *Neuf*; Ren; *Stb*; *Tro*; *Vend* (vol i only); *Vers*. UK: BL; Ox: Ch; RAS; Stj (vol iii only).   AUSTRIA: *Vien/N*. CZECHOSLOVAKIA: *Pra/S* (vol ii only).   DENMARK: *Cop*.   GERMANY: *Boch*; *Ulm*; Wolf (vols ii, iii only). ITALY: Mod (vol i only with vol ii No 32: 1659 and vol iii No 35: 1669 Lyons).   POLAND: *Byd*; *Wars/N*.   USA: Bost (vol iii only with vols i, ii No 32: 1659); *Harv*; Virg/U (vol iii only with vols i, ii No 33: 1659 Amsterdam).   USSR: *Len/N*; *Len/S* (vol i only); *Mosc/H* (vol iii only).

LES
ESSAIS DE MICHEL
SEIG. DE MONTAIGNE

QVE SCAY-IL

Nouvelle Edition
mis en III. Voll.
M. DC. LXIX.

N. Auroux fec.

(*a*) Engraved title [121 mm]

(d) A Olyer; vol iii [129 mm]

(c) A Olyer; vol ii [127 mm]

(b) A Olyer; vol i [128 mm]

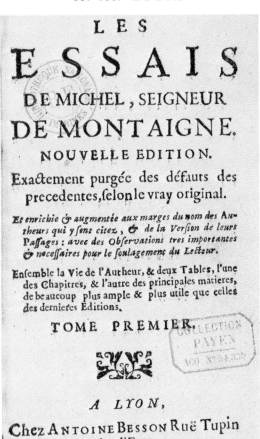

LES
ESSAIS
DE MICHEL, SEIGNEUR
DE MONTAIGNE.
NOUVELLE EDITION.
Exactement purgée des défauts des
precedentes, selon le vray original.

Et enrichie & augmentée aux marges du nom des Au-
theurs qui y sont citez, & de la Version de leurs
Passages: avec des Observations tres importantes
& necessaires pour le soulagement du Lecteur.

Ensemble la Vie de l'Autheur, & deux Tables, l'une
des Chapitres, & l'autre des principales matieres,
de beaucoup plus ample & plus utile que celles
des dernieres Éditions.

TOME PREMIER.

A LYON,
Chez ANTOINE BESSON Ruë Tupin
proche l'Empereur.

(e) A Besson, vol i [130 mm]

Title-page: The first of the three volumes has an engraved tp signed 'N. Auroux fec.' similar to tp (*a*) of No 33: 1659 Amsterdam, and a printed tp, which is repeated in vols ii and iii with LIVRE SECOND, TROISIE´ME. Lines 2,4,6, LIVRE PREMIER, A LYON and 1669 are in red in vol i but in black in vols ii and iii, which also differ in the swash caps in *A LYON*. All printed tps bear the imprint of André Olyer except BN4, which has Antoine Besson, no date and a different setting.

    (*a*) Engraved title.   (*d*) A. Olyer, vol iii.
    (*b*) A. Olyer, vol i.   (*e*) A. Besson, vol i.
    (*c*) A. Olyer, vol ii.

Collation: 12°: i: ã^{12} ẽ^{12} A—V^{12}; ii: π^4 A—2F^{12} 2G^8; iii: π^2 A—X^{12} Y^4 [$6 (−ii D6 Y4,6 iii D6) signed, arabic numerals; missigning i: M5 as M7; ii: H5 as G5, 2C3 as Ce3]; i: 264 leaves; ii: 360 leaves; iii: 258 leaves; pp i: [*48*] 1—310 312 312—454 445 456 [*24*]; ii: [*8*] 1—255 266 257—310 211 312—323 334 325—542 343 544—677 [*35*]; iii: [*4*] 1—206 107 208—348 34 350—403 304 405—430 231 432—487 [*25*].

Contents: i: ã1: Engraved title (verso blank); ã2: Printed title (verso blank); ã3: *Au lecteur*; ã4: Gournay's dedication to Richelieu; ã5: Long Gournay preface; ẽ8: Life; ẽ11: Table of contents Bk I; ẽ12^v: Quotations from Lipsius; A1: *Essais* Bk I; V1: Index to Bk I; ii: π1$^{r—v}$: blank; π2: Title (verso blank); π3: Table of contents Bk II; π4$^{r—v}$ blank; A1: *Essais* Bk II; 2F3^v: Index to Bk II; iii: π1$^{r—v}$: blank; π2: Title (verso blank); A1: *Essais* Bk III; X4^v: Index to Bk III; Y4: Table of contents Bk III; Y4^v: blank.

HT: i: ã3	[triple row of type-orns] ADVERTISSEMENT | DE L'AVTHEVR, | *Inferé en toutes les precedentes* | *Editions.*
ã4	[double row of 15 fleur-de-lis type-orns, second row inverted, colons after sixth pair] Epiftre de Mademoifelle de Gournay, | inferée en fon impreffion de l'année | 1635. | [rule] | A MONSEIGNEVR | L'EMINENTISSIME CARDINAL | DVC DE RICHELIEV.
ã5	[headpiece: volutes, flowers, foliage] PREFACE | SVR LES | ESSAIS DE MICHEL | SEIGNEVR | DE MONTAIGNE. | Par fa Fille d'alliance.
ẽ8	[triple row of type-orns as ã3] SOMMAIRE RECIT, | SVR | LA VIE | DE MICHEL, SEIGNEVR | DE MONTAIGNE, | *Extraict de fes propres Ef-* | *crits.*
ẽ11	[double row of type-orns as ã4] TABLE | DES CHAPITRES | DV LIVRE PREMIER.
A1	[headpiece: central bowl, 2 birds, fruit, inits PD] ESSAIS | DE MICHEL | DE | MONTAGNE. | [rule] | LIVRE PREMIER.
V1	[headpiece as ã5] TABLE | DES MATIERES | PLVS REMARQVABLES, | Contenuës en ce Premier Livre.
ii: A1	[double row of 5 arabesque type-orns] ESSAIS | DE MICHEL | DE | MONTAIGNE. | [rule] | LIVRE SECOND.
2F3^v	[as i: V1 except] Second Livre.

iii: A1   [headpiece: central head, foliage, volutes] [as ii: A1
          except] LIVRE TROISIESME.

X4ᵛ   [as i: V1 except] Troiſiéme Livre.

RT: ESSAIS DE MICHEL DE | MONTAIGNE. Lɪᴠ.I [Lɪᴠ.II.]
[Lɪᴠ.III]. [i: MONTAGNE. ABC2,4,6,8,10,12 D2; MONTAGNIE.
R5; Iᴠɪ. Q4 S4;   ii: EESSAIS 2E11ᵛ; MICHEEL K7ᵛ; MICHEL De
M11ᵛ P4ᵛ Q3ᵛ S2ᵛ; MICLEL 2D12ᵛ; MICHIEL O12ᵛ; MONTAIGNE,
once in B—EGI—NQST; MONTAIHNE. O5; MOMTAIGNE, X3
Y12; MONTANGE. O7,10 X9; MONTAGNE (no stop) V5 2B11;
Lɪᴠ, K2 M3 P4 Q2 R12; Lɪᴠ. (no II.) V9; Liv. once or more in 2B—E;
Lɪᴠʀ. L4 P5 R4 S8 V4 X10;   iii: ESAIS I11ᵛ; MONTAIGNE. Lɪᴠ. III.
(recto RT) F12ᵛ; MONTAIGNE, R7; Liv. T8 V7,10 X4]

CW: Unsigned pages. i: ã10ᵛ mot;   ẽ10ᵛ TABLE   ẽ12ʳ PRE   E12ᵛ eft
N12ᵛ creuer V6ᵛ Lâcheté   ii: H12ᵛ naiure: Q12ᵛ Mon 2E12ᵛ vous 2G1ᵛ
Mahomet   iii: E12ᵛ teſte   M12ᵛ comme   X12ᵛ Pont

Measurements (i: D8): 36(+2) lines. 120(126) × 55 mm. 20 lines=67 mm.
Width with sidenotes 66 mm.
    (ii: O12): 36(+2) lines. 124(130) × 55 mm. 20 lines=69 mm. Width
with sidenotes 67 mm.
    (iii: H7); 36(+2) lines. 121(126) × 56 mm. 20 lines=67 mm. Width
with sidenotes 67 mm.

Privilège: None.

Note: The engraved and printed tps are similar to No 33: 1659
Amsterdam, and the quotations from Lipsius also link it with that
edition. However, it differs in the index, which is at the end of vol iii in
1659 Amsterdam whilst 1669 Lyons has separate indexes for the three
vols as in No 32: 1659 and No 34: 1669 Paris.

Copies: BN1 (Z 19592—19594); BN2 (Z Payen 169—171); BN3 (Z
Payen 172, vol ii only); BN4 (Z Payen 168, vol i only, Besson imprint,
lacks engraved tp); *Sorb*; *Bord*; *Pau* (vol i only?); *Tarb* (vol ii only); *Val.*
UK: BL.   ITALY: Mil/B; Mod (vol iii only with vol i No 34: 1669, vol ii
No 32: 1659); Pad/U; Vero.   ROMANIA: *Buc.*   SWITZERLAND:
Frau.   USA: Chic/U (vol iii only with vol i No 32: 1659, vol ii No 34:
1669); *Harv*; NW.   USSR: *Mosc/H* (vol i only).

36: *L'Esprit des Essais* 1677

(*a*) Engraved title [148 mm]

Title-page: There is an engraved tp with a portrait bust in a laurel wreath frame, figures of muses, one holding QVE SCAY-IE on banderole, signed 'Le Doyen fe'. The printed tp has a crown and clasped hands device with inits CDS. Both tps bear the imprint of Charles de Sercy.

(*a*) Engraved tp. (*b*) Printed tp.

Collation: 8°: ã¹⁰ A—2X⁸⁻⁴ 2Y⁶ [$4(3) signed, roman numerals; missigning 2C2 as Cc ii (for ij)]; 280 leaves; pp [*20*] 1—243 242 243 246—539 [*1*].

Contents: ã1: Engraved title (verso blank); ã2: Printed title (verso blank); ã3: Publisher's preface; ã6: *Au lecteur*; ã7: Table of contents; ã10: *Privilège*; A1: *Essais*; 2Y6ᵛ: blank.

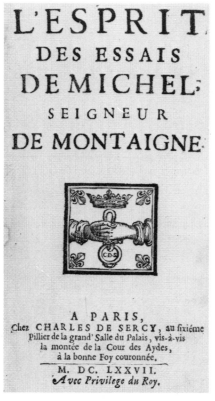

(*b*) Printed title [132 mm]

HT: ã3   [headpiece: central head, volutes] PREFACE.

ã6   [3 rows of type-orns, 19 in rows 1 and 3 with star after ninth, 11 in row 2 with colon after sixth] *L'AVTHEVR* | *au Lecteur.*

ã7   [double row of 20 type-orns] TABLE | DES CHA-PITRES. | [rule]

A1   [headpiece: central rose and 2 flowers, volutes] L'ES-PRIT | DE MICHEL, | SEIGNEUR | DE MON-TAIGNE. | *LIVRE PREMIER.* | [rule]

R6   [headpiece: crossed palms] [as A1 except] DE MON-TAGNE. | *LIVRE SECOND.* | [rule]

2M6   [headpiece: flowers and tendrils] [as A1 except] *LIVRE TROISIE'ME.* | [rule]

RT: L'ESPRIT | DE MONTAGNE. LIV. I [II] [III]. [MON-
TAIGNE. A8 2B—2X 2Y1—5; DE MONTAIGNE. (without LIV.
III.) 2Y6]

CW: Quire. ã10ᵛ L'ESPRIT B4ᵛ quelques K4ᵛ l'ame? V4ᵛ fuffiroient
2F8ᵛ exter-]minant 2O8ᵛ pour 2X4ᵛ decide

Measurements (E2): 30(+2) lines. 124(132)×68 mm. 20 lines=83 mm.

Privilège: For 10 years to Charles de Sercy. Saint-Germain-en-Laye, 26
November 1676, signed DESVIEUX. Registered 16 December 1676,
signed THIERRY, Syndic. *Achevé d'imprimer*: 8 May 1677.

Notes: 1. The text of the *Essais* has been abridged in the manner
explained in the preface. Critics, it is said, have censured Montaigne's
digressions and too frequent Latin quotations. The editor has removed
these so that Montaigne may appear 'dans toute la force & la vivacité de
son esprit' (ã5). He has retained only 'ce qui m'a semblé plus digne
d'estre retenu; c'est à dire, toutes les choses Historiques & divertis-
santes, que j'ay déchargé autant que j'ay pû, de leurs ornemens superflus'
(ã5). He has respected Montaigne's style except for 'ce qui est tout-à-fait
inconnu à nostre usage'. He has removed a few chapters and expanded
the titles of others. He is sure that this 'succincte reduction' will be better
than 'la vague estenduë de ses precedentes Editions' (ã5ᵛ).

2. Chapters omitted are I 17, 29, 35, 37, 53. Examples of changes of title
are I 44 *Du dormir* which becomes I 40 *Du sommeil*; III 5 becomes *Sur des
Vers de Virgile, ou plûtost de l'Amour, & du Mariage*; III 6 becomes *Des
Coches, ou plûtost des dépenses des Princes, & de l'industrie du nouveau Monde*.

3. The manner of the abridgement in I 8, at the beginning of II 12 and at
the end of III 13 may be seen in the pages reproduced in Plates 18—20.[1]

Copies: *BN* (3 copies); *Sorb*; *Châm*; Ren (lacks engraved tp); *Vals*. UK:
Gla; Ox: Bod; RAS (lacks engraved tp); Tay. ITALY: *Mil/B*; Mod;
Parm. POLAND: *Wars/U*. USA: *Harv*; *Ill*; *W/Cong*. YUGOSLA-
VIA: *Belg*.

---

[1] For a fuller discussion of this abridgement, see M Dréano, *La renommée de Montaigne
en France au XVIIIᵉ siècle*, pp 13—20.

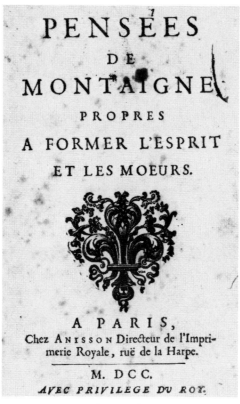

[121 mm]

Title-page: Imprint of Jean Anisson.

Collation: 12°: π² ã⁴ A—2E⁶ [$3(4) signed, roman numerals; missigning O2 as O3, R3 as R2, S2 as S3, Y2 as Y3, Y3 as V3]; 174 leaves; pp [*12*] *1* *2*—333 [*3*].

Contents: π1ʳ⁻ᵛ: blank; π2: Title (verso blank); ã1: Publisher's preface; A1: *Essais*; 2E5ᵛ: *Approbation*; 2E6: *Privilège* (verso blank).

HT: ã1   [3 rows of type-orns, rows 1 and 3 of 21 acorns] AVERTIS-
         SEMENT.
        A1 [headpiece: 2 seated putti, inits VLS] PENSÉES | DE |
        MONTAIGNE | PROPRES | A FORMER L'ESPRIT, | &
        les Mœurs.

RT: Pense´es | de Montaigne. [Psnee´es F3ᵛ K3ᵛ P5ᵛ V1ᵛ; Pensees (no accent) N4ᵛ Q4ᵛ R1ᵛ S2ᵛ Y2ᵛ 2C6ᵛ; Pens´ees H3ᵛ Z1ᵛ; Pense´es. 2B6ᵛ; deMontaigne (no stop) C5 G4 L4 O5 S3 X4 2B4; deMontaigne. E6; Montagne. T2 2A2]

CW: Quire. ã4ᵛ PENSE´ES C6ᵛ mafque, G6ᵛ ces L6ᵛ LIVRE R6ᵛ Il 2A6ᵛ forte

Measurements (F3): 19(+2) lines. 111(123) × 56 mm. 10 lines = 65 mm.

Privilège: For 6 years to Jean Anisson. Versailles, 20 March 1700, signed LE COMTE. Registered 19 April 1700, signed BALLARD, Syndic. *Achevé d'imprimer*: 16 October 1700. *Approbation*: 23 December 1699, signed PAVILLON.

Notes: 1. The text of the *Essais* has been abridged in the manner explained in the *Avertissement*. Montaigne is described as 'un Auteur fort équivoque & fort mêlé' (ã1); there is good and bad in all authors, but in the *Essais* 'ces bonnes choses se trouvent souvent gâtées par les mauvaises, & presque toûjours au moins, comme étouffées par beaucoup de fatras' (ã2). To suit the taste of the day 'pensées détachées' have been chosen from the *Essais*: 'il y en a de morales, d'enjouées, de sérieuses & de plaisantes' (ã2ᵛ). The editor, who shows some sympathy with Montaigne against the prevailing tastes of his day, says he has respected his style except where he is totally obscure or where words are completely archaic, e.g. détourbier, vastité, admonester, étriver.

2. The manner of the abridgement may be compared with that of *L'Esprit* of 1677 in Plates 18—20.[1]

Copies: *BN* (5 copies); *Châm*; *Hag*; *Laon*; *Monta*; *Ves*. UK: Gla; Ox: RAS; Tay. GERMANY: *Eut*; *Gött*; Wolf. NETHERLANDS: Utr. POLAND: *Poz*. ROMANIA: *Buc*. USA: *Prin*; *Yale*. USSR: *Len/S*. YUGOSLAVIA: *Belg*.

---

[1] For a fuller discussion of this abridgement, see M Dréano, *La renommée de Montaigne en France au XVIIIᵉ siècle*, pp 21—8. The abridgement is attributed to M Artaud.

PLATES

PLATE 1

Errata and press-corrections in No 1: 1580 Bordeaux, Vol i. Some of the errors listed in the Errata were corrected in the text during the course of printing, e.g. p 350, Y7^v, line 14. See No 1, note 5.

LES PLVS INSIGNES
FAVTES SVRVENVES
EN L'IMPRESSION
du premier liure.

Pag. 16. ligne, 14. oftez le point de la fin. pag. 11.
ligne, 4. pour les, lifez fe. pag. 3. l. 19. pour puif-
fant, lifez poifant. pag. 32. l. 3. pour prend, lifez
prenoit. pa. 34, l. 1. pour different, lifez defferent.
pag. 38. l. 12, pour vne virgule, metez vn point
pag. 40. l. 2. au lieu d'vn point, metez vne virgule.
pag, 54. l, 2, pour ne, lifez fi, pag. 60. l. 8. pour fe-
rons, lifez fuirons. pag. 8. l. 4. pour entierement,
lifez anciennement. pag. 116. l. 14. pour *primàm*
lifez, *prima*. pag. 133. l. 7. pour fa, lifez la. pag.
186. apres de l'auouer, metés vn point. pa. 190, l.
fi, apres il, mettez, me. pag. 240, l. 18. au lieu de
pour, mettez de. pag. 263. lig. 9. apres vous, oftez
l'interrogant, & li. 10. oftez l'interogant. pa. 298.
l. 19. pour font, lifez foint. pag. 325, l. 14. pour bié-
uaillance, lifez bienueillance. pag. 341. l. 6. pour,
reufe lifes renfe. pag. 345. 5. pour mettroient, lifés
metroit. pag. 346. l. 8. pour des hommes, lifes du
→ môde. pa. 350. l. 14. pour deffauts, lifes effects. pa. ←
357. l. 17 pour *adeo*, lifez, *odio*. pa. 424. l. 3. aioultes
au commencement, pris du. pag. 425. l. 9. pour,
d'vn, lifes, Vn. pag. 455. l. 18. pour *Pulfi* lifez *pufi*.
pa. 456. l. 11. pour *lautas*. lifés *lauti*. pa. 461. l. 10.
pour céte, lifés Cete. pag. 480. l. 8. apres trop, ad-
ioultes, ils trouueroint place entre ces deux extre-
mités

(a) Errata of 1580 Bordeaux; vol i: $\pi 4^v$ [131 mm]

PLATE 1 *(contd.)* 179

350 ESSAIS DE M. DE MONTA.
CHA. TRENTESETIESME.
Du ieune Caton.

I E n'ay point céte erreur cõmune de
iuger d'autruy felon moy, & de rap-
porter la condition des autres hommes
a la mienne. Ie croy ayféement d'autruy
beaucoup de chofes, ou mes forces ne
peuuent attaindre. La foiblefſe que ie
ſens en moy, n'altere aucunement les o-
pinions que ie dois auoir de la vertu &
valeur de ceux qui le meritent. Rampât
au limon de la terre ie ne laifſe pas de
remerquer iufques dans les nuës la hauteur d'aucunes ames heroiques. C'eſt
beaucoup pour moy d'auoir le iuge-
→ ment reglé, ſi les deffautz ne ſe peuuent
eſtre, & maintenir aumoins céte mai-
ſtrefſe partie exempte de la corruption
& debauche. C'eſt quelque chofe d'a-
uoir la volonté bonne, quand les iambes
me faillent. Ce ſiecle auquel nous vi-
uons au-

(b) First state of Y7ᵛ; line 14: deffautz
[134 mm]

350 ESSAIS DE M. DE MONTA.
CHA. TRENTESETIESME.
Du ieune Caton.

I E n'ay point céte erreur cõmune de
iuger d'autruy felon moy, & de rap-
porter la condition des autres hommes
a la mienne. Ie croy ayféement d'autruy
beaucoup de chofes, ou mes forces ne
peuuent attaindre. La foiblefſe que ie
ſens en moy, n'altere aucunement les o-
pinions que ie dois auoir de la vertu &
valeur de ceux qui le meritent. Rampât
au limon de la terre ie ne laifſe pas de
remerquer iufques dans les nuës la hauteur d'aucunes ames heroiques. C'eſt
beaucoup pour moy d'auoir le iuge-
ment reglé, ſi les effaitz ne ſe peuuent ←
eſtre, & maintenir aumoins céte mai-
ſtrefſe partie exempte de la corruption
& debauche. C'eſt quelque chofe d'a-
uoir la volonté bonne, quand les iambes
me faillent. Ce ſiecle auquel nous vi-
uons au-

(c) Second state of Y7ᵛ; line 14: effaitz
[134 mm]

PLATE 2   181

Two states of the Errata in No 1: 1580 Bordeaux, Vol ii: 4S7^{v}–8^{r}. See No 1, note 6.

LES FAVTES PLVS GRAN.
DES, QVI SE SONT FAITES
en l'impreſſion du ſecond liure.

page 7 ligne 8.oſtes ne. & ligne 9 liſes pas. pag. 9. lig. 3.
le. pag. 10.l.12. pour a, liſes, &. pag. 18.l.7.pour apres,
liſes aſpres.pag.21. l.22. pour depend, liſez depend.pag.
25.l.20. pour feracis, liſes fireci. pag. 25.l.fin.adiouſtez a
la fin,iuſtes.pag.36. l. 18. pour ſi y eſtois, liſez,ſi eſtoys.pag.
39.l.8 pour l'entreprise,liſez l'entremeſie pag.72.l.pour
auroint, liſez auoint pag.105.l.12. pour ées,liſez les.pag.
110.l.8. pour des, liſez les.pa.113.l.hn.oſtez,y pag.125.l.1
oſtez la parentheſe,& 7.ligne , apres l'ame,oſtez la paren-
theſe.10.ligne,apres maceſſible , metez la parentheſe. pag.
158.l.7 apres ie, metez le.pag.161.l.2. apres eſtu , metez
de &. En la 4. l. oſtez,de &. &ligne. 15. pour ideo metez a-
deo. pa.177. l.14. au lieu dehumeſtias, liſez, humeſtant. pag.
182.l.15. pour deſiregléement,liſez, regléement.ligne.18.
au lieu de Reſes, liſez Reſnes.pag.194.l.17. au lieu de re-
cite liſez recitoit.pag.202.l.17. oſtez ſe pag. 246.l.penulti-
tieſme,oſtez & & au lieu de maux,liſez biens.pag.253.l.18
au lieu de nommoient,liſez nemmoit.pa.270.l.13. au lieu
de celuy , liſez l'autre.pag. 271.l. 20.au lieu de ramenée,
metez ramené.pag.278 h.4 apres promeſſe,oſtez le point.
ligne.5.apres conccuoir,au lieu d'vne virgule metez coma.
pag.281.l.11.pour perte,metez portée.pag.283.l.13. pour
quel,metez,quelle ,po ur vniuerſel,v niuerſelle.pag.286.l.
antepenultieſme. pour cuiderons , metez prandrons. pag.
290.l.fin.pour aus liſez,au.pag.291.l.1.pour mouuemens,
liſez mouuemant ,pour plantes,liſez planetes pag.293.l.4
pour Et,liſez &, apres encore metez vn point.pag.316.l.3.
apres&,metez,ne ſe void point d'.pag.317,ligne3.apres les
mettez plus,pag.351.l.20.pour bien eſtre,metez bieneſtre.
pag.372.ligne.5.oſtez le coma.apres trouuons, metez le

coma. pag.374.l.4.pour combien de fois renuerſé , mettez
qui renuerſe tant de fois.pag.375.l.10.pour d'vn.metez du.
lig.20, au lieu d'amiable , metez aimable.pag.377.l.1.2.a-
pres pierre,metez vn point.pag.441.l.3.pour le, metez ſe
pa.485.l.1.apres mort,metez vn point.pa.486.l.2. au lieu
de partis,metez parts.lig.11. au lieu de correction , metez
coerction.pag. 502.ligne.18.apres deſlogement, metez vn
point.lig.19.apres ferme oſtez le point.pag.517.l. penultieſ
me,au lieu de Bedonius, metez Bedoins.pag.521.15.apres
que metez de. ligne penultieſme , au lieu de force,metez
farce.pag.524.l.6.au lieu de retenoit metez reieteroit. pa.
530.ligne 13.au lieu de a celuy,metez audit ſeigneur. pag.
538.l.16.apres puis,metez penſer.pag.552. au lieu de non,
mettez nom.pag 564.au lieu de pieds,metez pied.pag.573.
l.14,au lieu de a , metez auec.pag 575.l.12. au lieu dequoy
metez comment.pag.578.l penultime oſtez la memoire.&
on ſit.lig.2.apres toutes,metez ces.lig.6.au lieu de mais il,
metez qu'il.lig.15.au lieu de ces,metez ſes.lig.18.au lieu de
qu'ils, metez qu'elles ,au lieu de venus,venues. pag. 586.l.
5.apres vieilleſſe,metez la parentheſe.lig.7.au lieu de viſa-
ge.metez viſage.apres la vie , metez parentheſe page.645.
lig.14 pour en ,metez a.

(a) One state of the Errata in No 1: 1580 Bordeaux, Vol ii

LES FAVTES PLVS GRAN.
DES, QVI SE SONT FAITES
en l'impreſſion du ſecond liure.

page 7 ligne 8.oſtes ne. & ligne 9 liſes pas. pag. 9. lig. 3.
le. pag. 10.l.12. pour a, liſes, &. pag. 18.l.7.pour apres,
liſes aſpres.pag.21. l.22. pour depend, liſez depend.pag.
23.l.20. pour feracis, liſes fireci. pag. 25.l.fin.adiouſtez a
la fin,iuſtes.pag.36.l. 18. pour ſi y eſtois, liſez,ſi eſtoys.pag.
39.l.8 pour l'entreprise,liſez l'entremeſie pag.72.l.pour
auroint, liſez auoint pag.105.l.12. pour ées,liſez les.pag.
110.l.8. pour des, liſez les.pa.113.l.hn.oſtez,y pag.125.l.1
oſtez la parentheſe,& 7.ligne , apres l'ame,oſtez la paren-
theſe.10.ligne,apres maceſſible , metez la parentheſe. pag.
158.l.7 apres ie, metez le.pag.161.l.2. apres eſtu , metez
de &. En la 4. l. oſtez,de &. &ligne. 15. pour ideo metez a-
deo. pa.177. l.14. au lieu dehumeſtas, liſez, humeſtant. pag.
182.l.16. pour deſiregléement, liſez, regléement.ligne.18.
au lieu de Reſes, liſez Reſnes.pag.194.l.17. au lieu de re-
cite liſez recitoit.pag.202.l.17. oſtez ſe pag. 246.l.penulti-
tieſme,oſtez & & au lieu de maux,liſez nemmoit.pa.270.l.13. au lieu
de celuy , liſez l'autre.pag. 271.l. 20.au lieu de ramenée,
metez ramené.pag.278 h.4 apres promeſſe,oſtez le point.
ligne.5.apres conccuoir,au lieu d'vne virgule metez coma.
pag.281.l.11.pour perte,metez portée.pag.283.l.13. pour
quel,metez,quelle ,po ur vniuerſel,v niuerſelle.pag.286.l.
antepenultieſme. pour cuiderons , metez prandrons. pag.
290.l.fin.pour aus liſez,au.pag.291.l.1.pour mouuemens,
liſez mouuemant ,pour plantes,liſez planetes pag.293.l.4
pour Et,liſez &, apres encore metez vn point.pag.316.l.3.
apres&,metez,ne ſe void point d'.pag.317,ligne3.apres les
mettez plus,pag.351.l.20.pour bien eſtre,metez bieneſtre.
pag.372.ligne.5.oſtez le coma.apres trouuons, metez le

coma. pag.374.l.4.pour combien de fois renuerſé , mettez
qui renuerſe tant de fois.pag.375.l.10.pour d'vn.metez du.
lig.20, au lieu d'amiable , metez aimable.pag.377.l.1.2.a-
pres pierre,metez vn point.pag.441.l.3.pour le, metez ſe
pa.485.l.1.apres mort,metez vn point.pa.486.l.2. au lieu
de partis,metez parts.lig.11. au lieu de correction , metez
coerction.pag. 502.ligne.18.apres deſlogement, metez vn
point.lig.19.apres ferme oſtez le point.pag.517.l. penultieſ
me,au lieu de Bedonius, metez Bedoins.pag.521.15.apres
que metez de. ligne penultieſme , au lieu de force,metez
farce.pag.524.l.6.au lieu de retenoit metez reieteroit. pa.
530.ligne 13.au lieu de a celuy,metez audit ſeigneur. pag.
538.l.16.apres puis,metez penſer.pag.552. au lieu de non,
mettez nom.pag 564.au lieu de pieds,metez pied.pag.573.
l.14,au lieu de a , metez auec.pag 575.l.12. au lieu dequoy
metez comment.pag.578.l penultime oſtez la memoire.&
on ſit.lig.2.apres toutes,metez ces.lig.6.au lieu de mais il,
metez qu'il.lig.15.au lieu de ces,metez ſes.lig.18.au lieu de
qu'ils, metez qu'elles ,au lieu de venus,venues. pag. 586.l.
5.apres vieilleſſe,metez la parentheſe.lig.7.au lieu de viſa-
ge.metez viſage.apres la vie , metez parentheſe page.645.
lig.14 pour en ,metez a. pag. 646.lig.12.pour ie metez,ſi.

(b) Another state of the Errata in No 1: 1580 Bordeaux, Vol ii: one erratum added. The height of the tallest page is 121 mm

The *Au lecteur* of No 7A: 1595, ĩ4ᵛ, corrected by Mlle de Gournay. The printed text of No 7A: 1595 here corresponds neither to the text of No 4: 1588 nor to that of No 4†: The Bordeaux Copy. Mlle de Gournay's ink-corrections, made while she was at the Château de Montaigne, bring it close to the text of the Bordeaux Copy, but it still differs in three places. The MS note explains how Montaigne's *Au lecteur* was temporarily mislaid, and beneath are the instructions to the printer about the type to be used on this page. See No 7A†, note 3 and Plates 4 and 5.

[223 mm]

PLATE 4   183

The *Au lecteur* of No 8: 1598, ã4ᵛ. The printed text here corresponds almost exactly to that of No 7A: 1595 corrected in ink by Mlle de Gournay, and includes the note explaining how Montaigne's *Au lecteur* was temporarily mislaid. See No 8, note 1 and Plate 3.

AV LECTEVR.

'E s t icy vn Liure de bonne foy, Lecteur. Il t'aduertit des l'entree, que ie ne m'y suis proposé aucune
fin, que domestique & priuee: ie n'y ay eu nulle cō-
sideration de ton seruice, ny de ma gloire : mes forces ne sont
pas capables d'vn tel dessein. Ie l'ay voué à la commodité particuliere de mes parens & amis: à ce que m'ayans perdu (ce
qu'ils ont à faire bien tost) ils y puissent retrouuer quelques   ←
traicts de mes conditions & humeurs , & que par ce moyen
ils nourrissent plus entiere & plus visue, la cōnoissance qu'ils
ont eu de moy. Si c'eust esté pour rechercher la faueur du mōde,
ie me fusse mieux paré, & me presenterois en vne demarche   ←
estudiee. Ie veux qu'on m'y voye en ma façon simple, naturelle & ordinaire, sans contention & artifice: car c'est moy que
ie peins. Mes defauts s'y liront au vif, & ma forme naïfue,   ←
autant que la reuerence publique me l'a permis. Que si i'eusse
esté parmy ces nations qu'on dit viure encore soubz la douce
liberté des premieres loix de nature, ie t'asseure que ie m'y fusse
tres-volontiers peint tout entier, & tout nud. Ainsi, Lecteur,
ie suis moy-mesme la matiere de mon liure : ce n'est pas raison
que tu employes ton loisir en vn subiect si friuole & si vain.
A Dieu donq. De Montaigne, ce premier de Mars, mil cinq   ←
cens quatre vingts.

Cette preface corrigee de la derniere main de l'Autheur, ayant esté   ←
esgaree en la premiere impression depuis sa mort, a n'aguere esté re-
trouuee.

[143 mm]

PLATE 5

185

The inserted leaves of No 6: 1595 Lyons. These contain Montaigne's *Au lecteur* and a sonnet by Claude d'Expilly (see No 6, note 4). The text of *Au lecteur* corresponds to that corrected by Mlle de Gournay (see Plate 3). The height of the page signed *2 is 117 mm.

PREFACE
de l'Autheur,

AV

LECTEVR BENEVOLE.

'Est ici vn liure de bonne foy, Lecteur.Il t'aduertit, dés l'entree, que ie ne m'y suis proposé aucune fin, que domestique & priuee: ie n'y ai eu nulle consideration de ton seruice, ni de ma gloire : mes forces ne sont pas capables d'vn tel dessein. Ie l'ai voüé à la commodité particuliere de mes parens & amis;

*2

PREFACE.

à ce que m'ayans perdu (ce qu'ils ont à faire bien tost) ils y puissent retrouuer quelques traicts de mes conditions & humeurs, & que par ce moyen ils nourrissent plus entiere & plus viue, la cognoissance qu'ils ont eu de moi. Si c'eust esté pour recercher la faueur du monde, ie me fusse mieux paré, & me presenterois en vne desmarche estudiee. Ie veux qu'on m'y voye en ma façon simple, naturelle & ordinaire, sans contention & artifice : car c'est moi que ie peins. mes defauts s'y liront au vif, & ma forme naïfue autant que la reuerence publique

PREFACE.

que me l'a permis. Que si i'eusse esté parmi ces nations qu'on dit viure encore sous la douce liberté des premieres loix de nature, ie t'asseure que ie m'y fusse tres-volontiers peint tout entier & tout nud. Ainsi, Lecteur, ie suis moimesme la matiere de mon liure; ce n'est pas raison que tu employes ton loisir en vn suiet si friuole & si vain.

A Dieu donc.

De Montaigne, ce premier de Mars, mil cinq cens quatre vingts & dix.

SVR LES ESSAIS
du sieur de Montagne.

QVe tu es admirable en ce masle langage,
Mais plus en ces raisons qui diuent tes escrits!
Capables d'enhardir les plus lasches esprits
A desfier du temps l'inconstance & l'orage.
Montagne, qui nous peins ta vie & ton courage,
En quelle antique eschole as-tu si bien appris
De l'effroyable mort le glorieux mespris,
que tu soustiens sans peur l'horreur de son visage!
Magnanime Stoïcq', en ces braues ESSAIS,
Tes fideles tesmoins, en monstres que ie sçais
Fouler dessous les pieds le soin qui nous deuore.
Les siecles à venir chanteront à bon droict,
Montagne par lui-mesme enseigna comme on doit
Et bien viure & bien viure, & bien mourir encore.

CL. D'EXPILLY.

ESSAIS DE MICHEL DE MONTAIGNE.

LIVRE PREMIER.

Par diuers moyens on arriue à pareille fin.

CHAP. I.

A plus commune façon d'amollir les cœurs de ceux qu'on a offensez, lors qu'ayant la vengeance en main, il nous tiennent à leur mercy : c'est de les esmouuoir à commiseration & à pitié : toutesfois la brauerie, la constance, & la resolution, moyens tous contraires, ont quelquefois serui à ce mesme effect. Edouard, Prince de Galles, celui qui regenta si long temps nostre Guienne, personnage duquel les conditions & la fortune ont beaucoup de notables parties de grandeur, ayant esté bien fort offensé par les Limosins, & prenant leur ville par force, ne peut estre arresté par les cris du peuple, & des femmes, & enfans abandonnez à la boucherie, luy crians mercy, & se iettans à ses pieds, iusqu'à ce que passant tousiours ou-

Privilèges granted to Abel L'Angelier in 1594 and 1602. The same *privilège* dated 15 October 1594 (a) was used in 1595, 1598 and 1600, but with different settings. It reappeared in 1602 (b) but was cancelled, and a new *privilège* dated 1 April 1602 (c) mentioning the indexes was substituted. This 1602 *privilège* is found in 1604 (d) but with slight changes in the wording. See Nos 9, 10, 13.

Extraict du Priuilege du Roy.

PAr grace & Priuilege du Roy, il est permis à Abel l'Angelier, Marchant Libraire Iuré en l'Vniuersité de Paris, d'imprimer ou faire imprimer, vendre & debiter ce present liure, intitulé, *Les Essais de Michel , Seigneur de Montaigne, reueuz & augmentez de plus du tiers par le mesme Autheur.* Et sont faictes tref-expresses inhibitions & defenses à tous autres Libraires & Imprimeurs, d'imprimer, ou faire imprimer, vendre ou debiter ledit liure, sans le consentemét dudit l'Angelier: Et ce iusques au temps & terme de dix ans entiers & consecutifs: à peine de confiscation de tous lesdits liures qui s'en trouueront imprimez, & d'amende arbitraire. Et outre voulons qu'en mettant au commencement ou à la fin dudit liure ce present extraict, il soit tenu pour deuëment signifié, comme plus amplement est declaré & contenu ausdites lettres de Priuilege, donnees à Paris, le quinziesme iour d'Octobre, mil cinq cens quatrevingts & quatorze.

Signé, PAR LE ROY.

RAMBOVILLET.

(a) No 9: 1600; 4E3ᵛ [91 mm]

Extraict du Priuilege du Roy.

PAr grace & Priuilege du Roy , il est permis à Abel l'Angelier , Marchand Libraire Iuré en l'Vniuersité de Paris , d'imprimer ou faire imprimer , vendre & debiter ce present liure , intitulé , *Les Essais de Michel , Seigneur de Montagne , reueuz & augmentez de plus du tiers par le mesme Autheur.* Et sont faictes tref expresses inhibitions & defenses à tous autres Libraires & Imprimeurs , d'imprimer, ou faire imprimer, vendre ou debiter ledit liure, sans le consentement dudit l'Angelier :& ce iusques au temps & terme de dix ans entiers & consecutifs : à peine de confiscation de tous lesdits liures qui s'en trouueront imprimez, & d'amende arbitraire. Et outre voulons qu'en mettant au commencement ou à la fin dudit liure ce present extraict, il soit tenu pour deuëment signifié, comme plus amplement est declaré & contenu ausdites lettres de Priuilege, donnees à Paris, le quinziesme iour d'Octobre, mil cinq cens quatre vingts & quatorze.

Signé, PAR LE ROY.

RAMBOVILLET.

(b) No 10: 1602; Cancellandum 4E3ᵛ [91 mm]

PLATE 6 (*contd.*) 187

Extraiϛ du priuilege du Roy.

PAr grace & Priuilege du Roy , il eſt permis à
Abel l'Angelier , Marchand Libraire Iuré en
l'Vniuerſité de Paris , d'imprimer ou faire imprimer, vendre & debiter ce preſent liure, intitu-
lé, *Les Eſſais du Seigneur de Montaigne, reueuz, corrigez & augmentez
de deux tables & de la vie de l'Autheur, outre les Impreſſions cy deuant
faictes.* Et ſont faictes treſ-expreſſes inhibitions & defenſes à
tous autres Libraires & Imprimeurs, d'imprimer, ou faire imprimer, vendre ou debiter ledit liure, ſans le conſentement
dudit l'Angelier : & ce iuſques au temps & terme de dix ans
entiers & conſecutifs : à peine de confiſcation de tous leſdits
liures qui s'en trouueront imprimez, & d'amende arbitraire.
Et outre voulons qu'en mettant au commencement, ou à la
fin dudit liure ce preſent extraict, il ſoit tenu pour deuëment
ſignifié, comme plus amplement eſt declaré & contenu aux
lettres du Priuilege, donnees à Paris, le 1. d'Auril 1602.

Signé PAR LE ROY

RENOVARD.

(c) No 10: 1602; Cancellans 4E3ᵛ [91 mm]

Extraiϛ du Priuilege du Roy.

PAr grace & Priuilege du Roy, il eſt permis
à Abel l'Angelier Libraire iuré en l'vniuerſité
de Paris , d'imprimer ou faire imprimer , *Les Eſſais du Seigneur de Montaigne , reueus , corrigez &
augmentez de deux tables & de la vie de l'Autheur,
outre les Impreſſions cy deuant faictes.* Et ſont faictes
tres-expreſſes deffences à tous Imprimeurs & Libraires, ou autres de quelle qualité qu'ils ſoyent
d'imprimer ou faire imprimer, vendre ny diſtri-
buer en quelque ſorte & maniere que ce ſoit ledit liure , ſinon de ceux qu'aura imprimé ledict
l'Angelier, & ce iuſques au temps & terme de dix
ans , à peine de confiſcation de tous les liures qui
ſe trouueront imprimez , & d'amende arbitraire:
Et outre voulons qu'en mettant au commencement, ou à la fin dudit Liure ce preſent extraict, il
ſoit tenu pour deuëment ſignifié , comme plus
amplement eſt declaré ez lettres, donnees à Paris, le premier Auril 1602.

Signé PAR LE ROY,

RENOVARD.

(d) No 13: 1604; 3T4ᵛ [104 mm]

Montaigne's portrait by Thomas de Leu with the quatrain attributed to Malherbe. The portrait first appeared in 1608 (a) and was used again in 1611. In 1617 (b) the portrait is closely copied and there are variants in lines 2 and 4 of the quatrain. In 1617 Rouen (c) there is an inferior copy of the portrait, but no variants in the quatrain. See Nos 14, 18, 20.

(a) No 14: 1608 [148 mm]

PLATE 7 (*contd.*)   189

(b) No 20: 1617 [148 mm]

(c) No 18: 1617 Rouen [148 mm]

Cancels in No 14: 1608. Cancellandum 3K8ᵛ (c) carries the wrong text for p 938; the correct text is restored in the cancellans 3K8ᵛ (d). Cancellans 3K8ʳ (b) corrects several errors in cancellandum 3K8ʳ (a), e.g. 936 (937), line 9 Aaristote (Aristote), line 13 loüeurs (ioüeurs); it also adds a sidenote and adjusts the last lines to accord with the text on the following page. See No 14, note 3.

(a) Cancellandum 3K8ʳ [145 mm]

(b) Cancellans 3K8ʳ [145 mm]

PLATE 12   197

The *privilège* in the second issue of No 25: 1635, 4D4ᵛ. This longer version of the *privilège* and the record of its transfer from Mlle de Gournay to Jean Camusat displaces the Errata, which is moved to the foot of 4D4ʳ. See No 25 and Plate 11.

PRIVILEGE DV ROY.

OVIS par la grace de Dieu Roy de France & de Nauatre. A nos amez & feaux Confeillers les gens tenans nos Cours de Parlement Baillifs, Senefchaux, Preuofts, ou leurs Lieutenans, & autres nos Iufticiers & Officiers qu'il appartiendra, Salut. Noftre chere & bien amée la Damoifelle de Gournay nous a fait remonftrer, que le feu fieur de Montagne luy ayant de fon viuât recômandé le foin de fon liure des Effais, & depuis fon decez fes plus proches luy ayant donné toute charge de l'impreffion d'iceux, comme il eft notoire : & plufieurs fautes enormes s'eftans coulees en la pluspart des impreffions, en forte que tout le liure s'en trouue gafté, & plain d'obmiffions & additions apoftées, cô me l'expofante a fait voir à aucuns de nos amez & feaux Confeillers Maiftres des Requeftes ordinaires de noftre Hoftel, & autres nos Officiers. Elle a defiré rendre ce deuoir au public, & à la memoire dudit deffunt fieur de Montagne, d'empefcher que ce defordre n'afriue plus en l'impreffion dudit liure, qui eft d'importance, cô me eftant vn œuure tres excellêt, & qui fait hôneur à la France, Auquel en outre elle defire adioufter la verfiô de tous les paffages Latins, auec les noms & cottes des Autheurs d'iceux, qui font en grand nombre. Et pour pouuoir effectuer ce deffein elle nous a prié luy vouloir accorder vn priuilege perpetuel. A CES CAVSES, defirans gratifier ladite expofante : & fauorifer la bonne intention qu'elle a de conferuer ledit œuure des Effais, & en la façon qu'il a efté compofé par l'Autheur, fans qu'il y foit châgé aucune chofe qui le puiffe corrompre ; De noftre grace fpeciale, puiffance & authorité royale, auons à icelle expofante donné & octroyé, donnons & octroyons par ces prefentes priuilege pendant fix ans, de faire imprimer ledit œuure des Effais dudit fieur de Montagne par tels Libraires & Imprimeurs que bon luy femblera. Et faifons tresexpreffes deffences à tous autres Imprimeurs & Libraires d'entreprendre d'imprimer ledit Oeuure, fans le gré & confentement de ladite expofante, & fans s'adreffer à elle pour prendre aduis & adeu de la coppie & methode qu'ils doiuent choifir, pour faire fur icelle ladite impreffion, & s'obliger à elle d'y mettre bon ordre & bons correcteurs, pour euiter aux inconueniens & fautes qui peuuent ruiner ledit Liure : offrant auffi ladite expofante de fa part rendre cét office gratuitemêt au public, & aufdits Imprimeurs quand ils l'en requerront, & fans les obliger à aucune charge que de fuiure les anciens & meilleurs exemplaires, lefquels elle leur fournira, à peine à tous ceux qui contreuiendront au prefent priuilege, de confifcation de tous les exemplaires, defpens, dommages & interefts, amêde arbitraire, & de toute autre peine de droict & de nos ordonnances. Voulons en outre, qu'en faifant mettre au commencement ou à la fin dudit Liure cefdites prefentes, ou extrait d'icelles, elles foient tenuës pour fignifiees & venuës à la cognoiffance de tous, ceffant ou faifant ceffer tous troubles & empefchemens au contraire : Nonobftant oppofitions ou appellations quelconques. A la charge de mettre deux exemplaires dudit Liure en noftre Bibliotheque, premier que de l'expofer en vente, à peine d'eftre defcheu de l'effect de ces prefentes ; car tel eft noftre plaifir. Donné au Camp deuant Nancy, le treiziefme iour de Septembre, l'an de grace mil fix cents trente trois, & de noftre regne le vingt-quatriefme. Ainfi figné, par le Roy en fon Confeil LE QVESNE. Et feellé.

Ladite Damoifelle de Gournay a tranfporté le Priuilege cy-deffus à Iean Camufat, Libraire iuré à Paris, pour en iouyr conformement à l'accord fait entr'eux, le vingthuictiefme iour d'Aouft 1635.

Acheué d'imprimer le 15. Iuin 1635.
Les deux exemplaires ont efté fournis en la Bibliotheque du Roy.

[264 mm]

Corrections by Mlle de Gournay for the text of 1635. This is the first of four MS pages of corrections bound in at the end of No 25: 1635 BN5. The other three pages are reproduced in Plates 14, 15 and 16. The height of each page is approximately 250 mm. See No 25, note 3.

PLATE 14   199

Corrections for the text of 1635. See Plate 13.

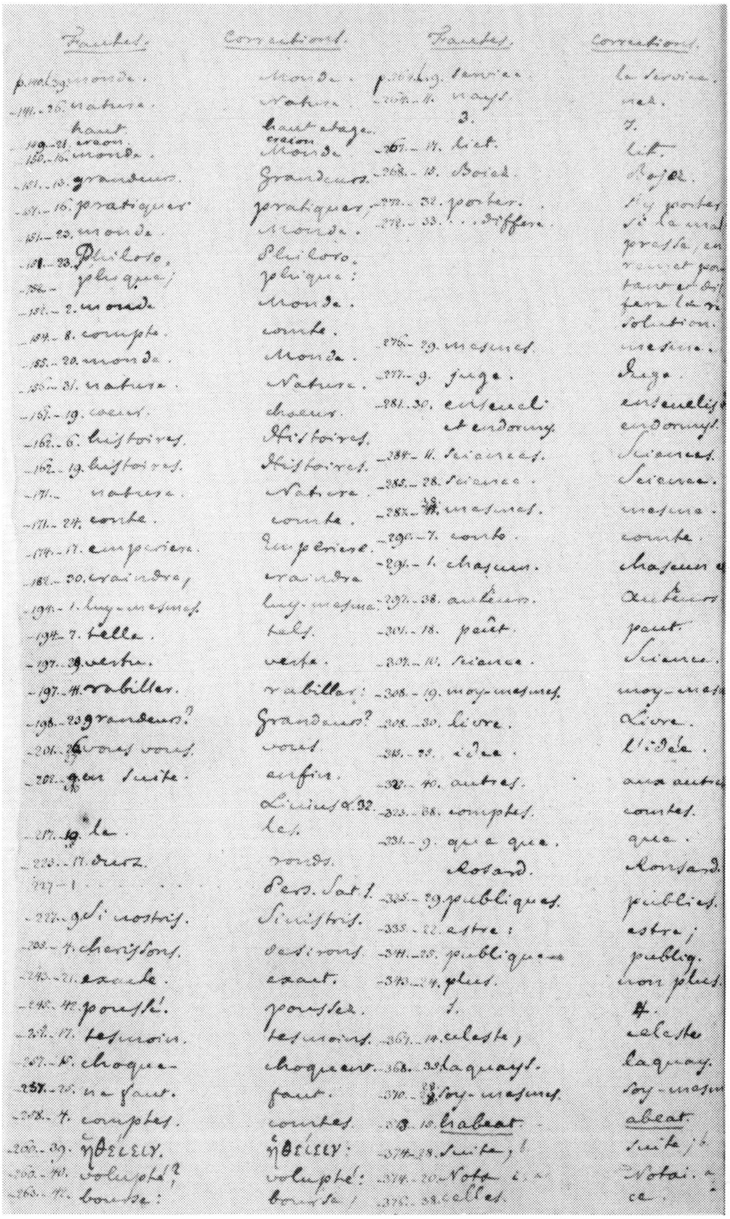

PLATE 15

Corrections for the text of 1635. See Plate 13.

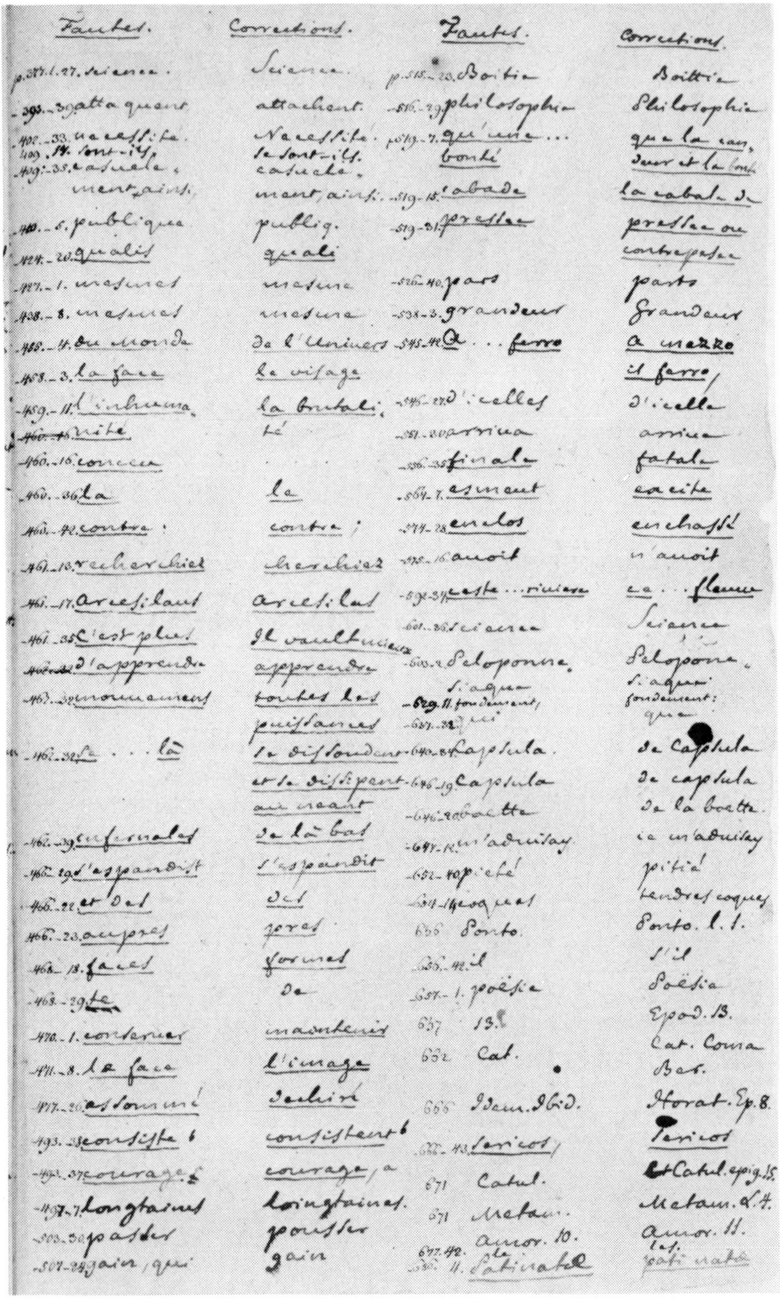

Fautes.	Corrections.
p.387.l.27. science.	Science.
393.-39. attaquent	attachent.
407.-33. necessité.	Necessité.
409. 14. sont-ils,	le sont-ils.
409.-35. casuelle- ment, ainsi,	casuelle- ment, ainsi.
410.-6. publique	publiq.
424.-20. qualis	quali
427.-1. mesures	mesura
438.-8. mesures	mesura
455.-41. du monde	de l'Univers
458.-3. la face	le visage
459.-11. l'inhumanité	la brutalité
460.-16. [illegible]	. .
460.-36. la	le
460.-42. contre:	contre;
461.-13. recherchiez	cherchiez
461.-17. Arcesilaus	Arcesilas
461.-35. C'est plus	Il vault mieux
462.-32. d'apprendre	apprendre
463.-32. mouvemens	toutes les puissances
462.-32. le . . . là	la dissoudent et la dissipent au neant
462.-39. infernales	de là bas
465.-19. s'espandist	s'espandit
466.-22. et des	des
466.-23. aupres	pres
468.-18. faces	formes
468.-29. le	de
470.-1. conserver	maintenir
471.-8. la face	l'image
477.-20. assommé	deschiré
493.-28. consiste à	consistent à
493.-37. courage à	courage, à
497.-7. longtaines	loingtaines.
503.-30. passer	pousser
507.-28. gain, qui	gain

Fautes.	Corrections.
p.515.-20. Boitie	Boittie
516.-29. philosophie	Philosophie
517.-7. qu'une . . . bonté	que la candeur et la bonté
519.-15. cabade	la cabale de
519.-31. presse	presse ou contrepresse
526.-40. pars	parts
538.-3. grandeur	Grandeur
545.-42. a . . . ferro	a mazzo il ferro,
546.-27. d'icelles	D'icelle
551.-30. arrive	arrive
556.-35. finale	fatale
564.-7. asiment	en cite
574.-28. enclos	enchassé
575.-16. avoit	n'avoit
598.-34. ceste . . . riviere	ce . . . fleuve
601.-26. science	Science
603.-2. Peloponnese.	Peloponne.
629.-11. s'acquiert fondement,	s'acquiert fondement:
637.-32. qui	que
640.-24. Capsula.	de Capsula
646.-19. Capsula	de capsula
646.-20. boette	de la boette.
648.-12. m'admiray	ie m'admiray
652.-40. piété	pitié
654.-14. coques	tendres coques
656 Ponto.	Ponto. l. 1.
656.-42. il	s'il
657.-1. poësie	Poësie
657 13.	Epod. 13.
662 Cat.	Cat. Coma Ber.
666 Idem. Ibid.	Horat. Ep. 8.
666.-43. Pericos,	Pericos
671 Catul.	et Catul. epig. 15.
671 Metam.	Metam. L. 4.
677.-42. Amor. 10.	Amor. 11.
680.-11. patinable	patinate

PLATE 16 201

Corrections for the text of 1635. See Plate 13.

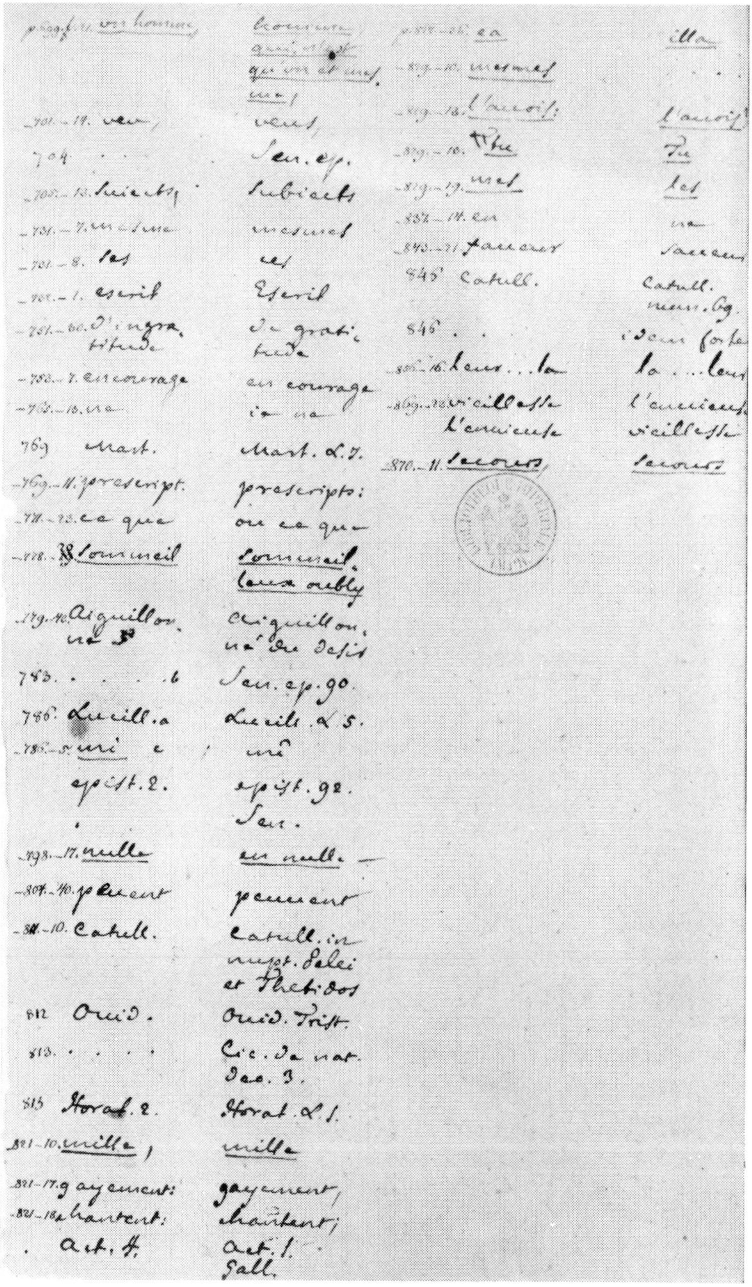

Henri Estienne's preface in 1652, a3ʳ⁻ᵛ. The printer draws attention to the convenient arrangement of the summaries, the references and the translations of quotations, all of which are placed in marginal notes. See No 30, note 2.

L'IMPRIMEVR
AV LECTEVR·

 NTRE le grand nombre des precedentes Impreſſions, i'oſe vous aſſeurer, TRES-CHER LECTEVR, que celle-cy eſtant la plus entiere & la plus parfaite, il ne faut point douter que par ſa recommandation elle n'enſeueliſſe toutes les autres. Ie l'ay purgée des defauts qui ont eſté cy-deuant recognus, & augmentée & enrichie de beaucoup d'ornemens tres-neceſſaires. Les Editions de l'Angelier & de Mademoiſelle de Gournay, ſ'eſtoient trouuées les plus conſiderables, quoy que ce qui eſtoit en l'vne ne fuſt pas en l'autre. En la premiere il y auoit aux marges, ſans aucune verſion, des obſeruations tres-vtiles & tres-importantes pour le ſoulagement du Lecteur; En l'autre, il y auoit ſans aucunes obſeruations, les noms des Autheurs Grecs & Latins qui y ſont citez, auec la verſion Françoiſe de leurs paſſages, fort frequents en cét Ouurage : laquelle verſion, au lieu d'auoir eſté inſerée à coſté deſdits paſſages, ne ſ'eſtant trouuée qu'à la fin de chaque Chapitre, partant fort incommode pour y auoir recours, interrompoit entierement vne lecture ſi agreable à ceux qui n'ont pas la connoiſſance de la langue Grecque & Latine. A preſent, LECTEVR IVDICIEVX, que leſdites verſions & obſeruations ſont conjointes & renduës inſeparables en toutes les pages de cette Impreſſion; & que par ce moyen, ceux qui n'ont pas cét aduantage d'entendre leſdites Langues, n'auront doreſnauant aucune difficulté, non plus que les ſçauans, de ſe rauir ſans interruption, des riches penſées de ce precieux Autheur; l'eſpere qu'vn chacun, & les Dames meſmes, y prendront tres-bonne part, puis qu'en cette Edition il n'y a plus rien de l'eſtranger, qu'elle eſt toute Françoiſe, & toute intelligible par le moyen de ladite traduction. Ie vous diray encore, qu'ayant eſté obmis à toutes les Tables precedentes des matieres, plus de la moitié des choſes remarquables, i'en

a iij

[272 mm]

PLATE 17 (contd.) 203

AV LECTEVR.

ay fait vne nouuelle qui est si exacte, que le Lecteur en toutes ren-
contres pourra à l'instant trouuer son entiere satisfaction, sans estre
obligé comme auparauant, de la chercher par vne trop longue & in-
certaine lecture. Il n'est pas à propos d'exalter le merite de Monsieur
de Montaigne: la quantité des Editions qui ont precedé celle-cy, de diuerses sortes de caracteres & de volumes, imprimez tant en cette Ville,
qu'aux autres de ce Royaume & des Païs estrangers, publient assez la
haute estime que toute l'Europe en a fait auec des applaudissemens
extraordinaires ; Ie diray seulement & auec verité, qu'il ne se peut
trouuer aucun entretien qui soit remply ny de plus d'erudition, ny de
plus d'vtilité, que ses doctes & rauissans Escrits. L'Aduertissement sui-
uant, auec la Preface de Mademoiselle de Gournay, cy-apres inserez,
vous en instruiront assez amplement. Ie n'ay plus rien à souhaiter, si
ce n'est, AMY LECTEVR, que vous receuiez cette Impression auec
autant d'indulgence, que i'ay eu de passion de m'en acquitter digne-
ment, tant en vostre faueur, que pour me rendre digne du Priuilege
dont il a pleu à Monseigneur le Chancelier de me vouloir gratifier,
comme d'vn moyen necessaire pour le restablissement des belles & cor-
rectes Impressions. Que si neantmoins le soin que i'ay pris ne peut éga-
ler en cét ouurage, l'obligation que i'ay à sa Grandeur, de laquelle les
bienfaits & l'approbation tournent à beaucoup de gloire, i'oseray pourtant esperer de sa bonté & de celle du public, qu'elles agréeront ce
trauail, & qu'elles me donneront lieu de continuer soigneusement ma
profession. HENRY ESTIENE.

ADVERTISSEMENT
DE L'AVTHEVR,
Inseré en toutes les precedentes Editions.

'EST icy vn Liure de bonne foy, Lecteur. Il t'aduertit dés l'entrée,
que ie ne m'y suis proposé aucune fin, que domestique & priuée : ie n'y
ay eu nulle consideration de ton seruice, ny de ma gloire ; mes forces ne
sont pas capables d'vn tel dessein. Ie l'ay voüé à la commodité particuliere de mes parens & amis : à ce que m'ayans perdu (ce qu'ils ont à faire bien-
tost) ils y puissent retrouuer quelques traicts de mes conditions & humeurs, & que
par ce moyen ils nourrissent plus entiere & plus viue la cognoissance qu'ils ont euë
de moy. Si c'eust esté pour rechercher la faueur du monde, ie me fusse mieux paré,
& me presenterois en vne desmarche estudiée : Ie veux qu'on m'y voye en ma façon
simple, naturelle & ordinaire, sans contention & artifice : car c'est moy que ie peinds.
Mes defauts s'y liront au vif, & ma forme naïfue, autant que la reuerence publi-

[272 mm]

PLATE 18

Two abridgements of Book I 8. See Nos 36 and 37.

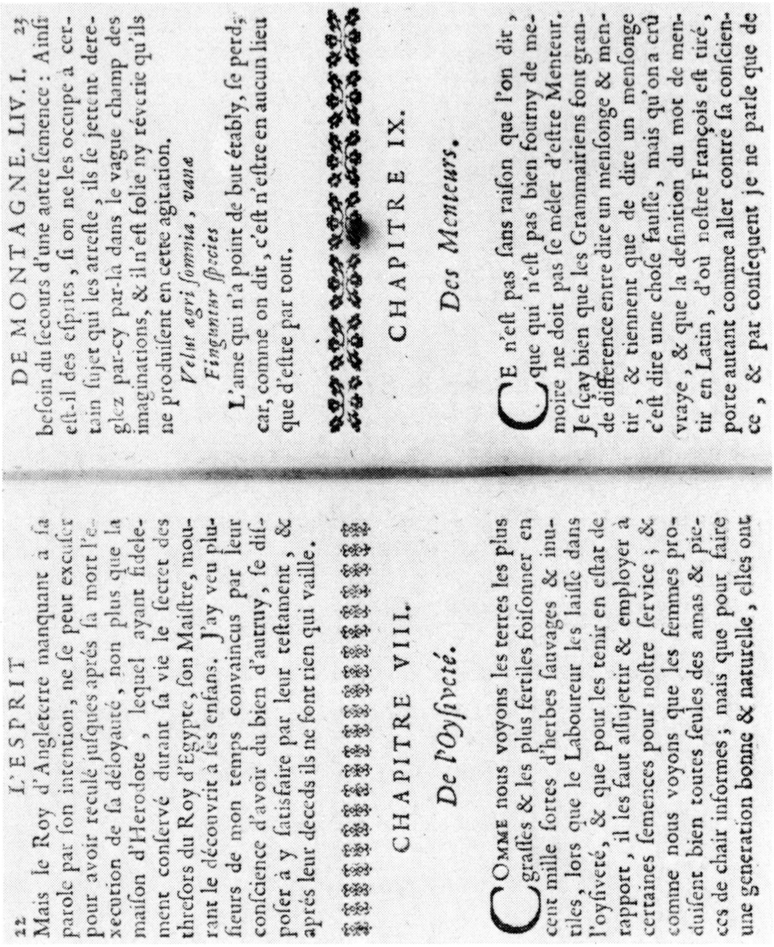

DE MONTAGNE. LIV. I. 23

befoin du fecours d'une autre femence : Ainfi eft-il des efprits, fi on ne les occupe à certain fujet qui les arrefte, ils fe jettent dereglez par-cy par-là dans le vague champ des imaginations, & il n'eft folie ny rêverie qu'ils ne produifent en cette agitation.

Velut ægri fomnia, vana
Finguntur fpecies

L'ame qui n'a point de but étably, fe perd; car, comme on dit, c'eft n'eftre en aucun lieu que d'eftre par tout.

CHAPITRE IX.

Des Menteurs.

CE n'eft pas fans raifon que l'on dit, que qui n'eft pas bien fourny de memoire ne doit pas fe mêler d'eftre Menteur. Je fçay bien que les Grammairiens font grande difference entre dire un menfonge & mentir, & tiennent que de dire un menfonge c'eft dire une chofe fauffe, mais qu'on a crû vraye, & que la definition du mot de mentir en Latin, d'où noftre François eft tiré, porte autant comme aller contre fa confcience, & par confequent je ne parle que de

22 L'ESPRIT

Mais le Roy d'Angleterre manquant a fa parole par fon intention, ne fe peut excufer pour avoir reculé jufques après fa mort l'execution de fa déloyauté, lequel ayant fidelement confervé durant fa vie le fecret des threfors du Roy d'Egypte, fon Maiftre, mourant le découvrit à fes enfans. J'ay veu plufieurs de mon temps convaincus par leur confcience d'avoir du bien d'autruy, fe difpofer à y fatisfaire par leur teftament, & après leur deceds ils ne font rien qui vaille.

CHAPITRE VIII.

De l'Oyfiveté.

COMME nous voyons les terres les plus graffes & les plus fertiles foifonner en cent mille fortes d'herbes fauvages & inutiles, lors que le Laboureur les laiffe dans l'oyfiveté, & que pour les tenir en eftat de rapport, il les faut affujettir & employer à certaines femences pour noftre fervice ; & comme nous voyons que les femmes produifent bien toutes feules des amas & pieces de chair informes ; mais que pour faire une generation bonne & naturelle, elles ont

(a) No 36: *L'Esprit* 1677; B₃ᵛ—4ʳ [127 mm]

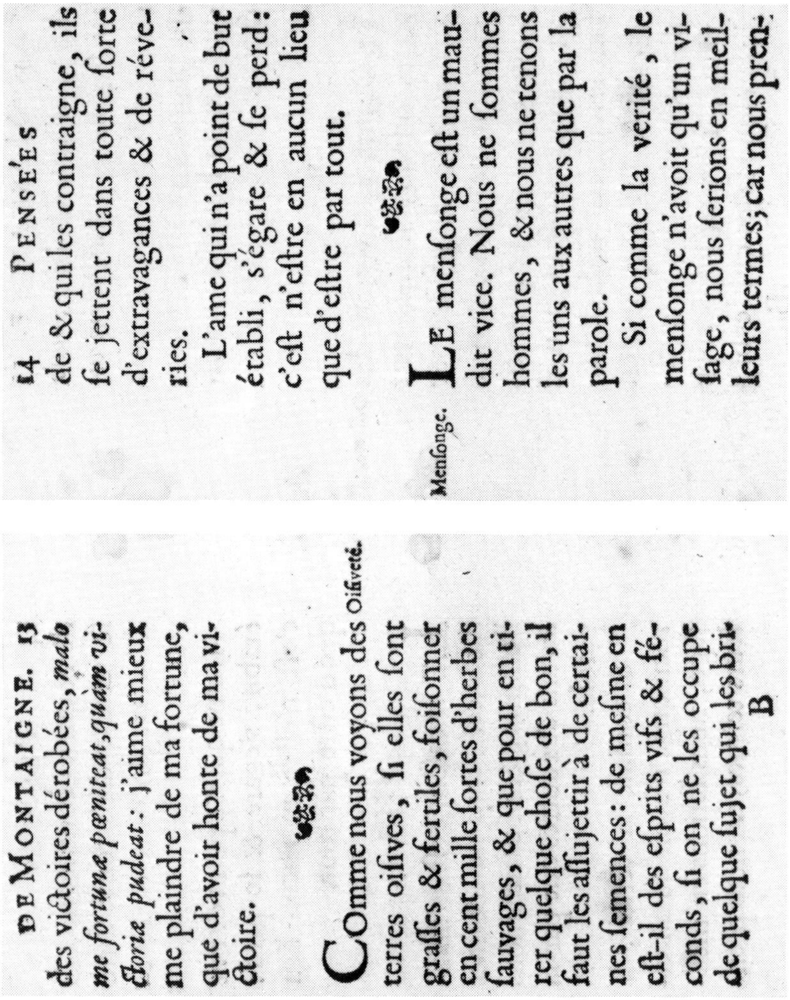

PLATE 18 (*contd.*) 205

14 PENSÉES
de & qui les contraigne, ils
se jettent dans toute sorte
d'extravagances & de réve-
ries.

L'ame qui n'a point de but
établi, s'égare & se perd :
c'est n'estre en aucun lieu
que d'estre par tout.

Menfonge. LE menfonge est un mau-
dit vice. Nous ne fommes
hommes, & nous ne tenons
les uns aux autres que par la
parole.

Si comme la verité, le
menfonge n'avoit qu'un vi-
fage, nous ferions en meilleurs termes ; car nous pren-

DE MONTAIGNE. 13
des victoires dérobées, *malo
me fortunæ pœniteat, quàm vi-
Étoriæ pudeat* : j'aime mieux
me plaindre de ma fortune,
que d'avoir honte de ma vi-
ctoire.

COmme nous voyons des oisiveté-
terres oisives, si elles font
grasses & fertiles, foifonner
en cent mille fortes d'herbes
fauvages, & que pour en ti-
rer quelque chofe de bon, il
faut les affujettir à de certaines femences : de mefme en
eft-il des efprits vifs & fé-
conds, si on ne les occupe
de quelque fujet qui les bri-
B

(b) No 37: *Pensées* 1700; B1ʳ⁻ᵛ [121 mm]

Two abridgements of the beginning of Book II 12. See Nos 36 and 37.

164 L'ESPRIT

je ne redonne les champs. Pythagore les achetoit des pescheurs & des oyseleurs pour en faire autant.

Les naturels sanguinaires à l'endroit des bestes, témoignent une propension naturelle à la Cruauté. Aprés qu'on se fût aprivoisé à Rome aux spectacles du meurtre des animaux, on vint aux hommes & aux Gladiateurs. Je crains que la Nature n'ait d'elle-même attaché à l'homme quelque instinct pour l'inhumanité. Personne ne prend plaisir à voir des bêtes s'entre-joüer & s'entre-caresser, & nul ne manque d'en prendre à les voir s'entre-déchirer & se demembrer; & afin qu'on ne se mocque pas de cette sympathie que j'ay avec elles, la Theologie mesme nous ordonne quelque faveur en leur endroit.

CHAPITRE XII.

Apologie de Raymond de Sebonde.

PIERRE Bunel homme de grande reputation de sçavoir en son temps, ayant arresté quelques jours à Montagne en la compagnie de mon pere, avec d'autres personnes de sa sorte, luy fit present, en

DE MONTAGNE. LIV. II. 265

en partant, d'un Livre intitulé, *Theologia naturalis, sive liber creaturarum magistri Raymundi de Sebonde*, & parce que la Langue Italienne & Espagnole estoient familieres à mon pere, & que ce Livre est bâty d'un Espagnol baragoüiné en terminaisons Latines, il esperoit avec un peu d'ayde, de pouvoir en faire son profit. Et le luy recommanda comme un Livre tresutile & propre à la saison: ce fut lors que les nouveautez de Luther commençoient d'entrer en credit, & ébranloient en beaucoup de lieux nostre croyance; en quoy il estoit d'un tres-bon avis; prevoyant que ce commencement de maladie declineroit aisément en un execrable Atheïsme.

Or quelques jours avant sa mort, mon pere ayant par hazard rencontré ce Livre sous un tas d'autres papiers abandonnez, me commanda de le luy mettre en François. C'estoit une occupation bien étrange & bien nouvelle pour moy; mais estant de fortune pour lors de loisir, & ne pouvant rien refuser au commandement du meilleur pere qui fut jamais; j'en vins à bout comme je pus; à quoy je pris un singulier plaisir, & donna charge qu'on le fist imprimer; ce qui fut executé après sa mort. Je trouvay les imaginations de cét Autheur fort belles, son ouvrage bien suivy, & son

Z

(a) No 36: *L'Esprit* 1677; Y4ᵛ—Z1ʳ [131 mm]

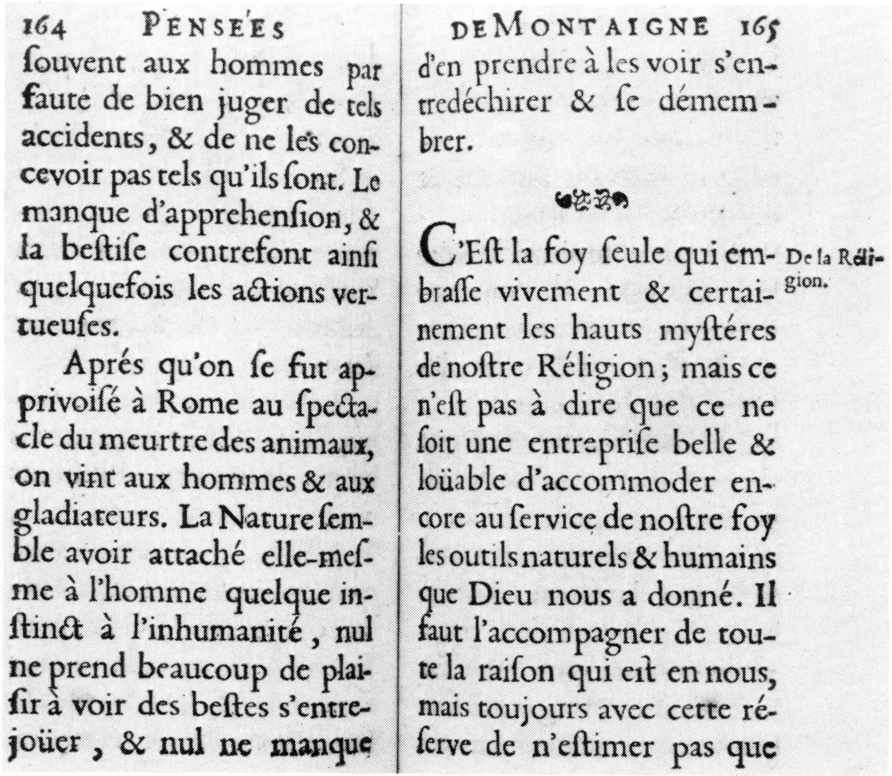

PLATE 19 (*contd.*) 207

164 PENSÉES
fouvent aux hommes par faute de bien juger de tels accidents, & de ne les concevoir pas tels qu'ils font. Le manque d'apprehenfion, & la beftife contrefont ainfi quelquefois les actions vertueufes.

Aprés qu'on fe fut apprivoifé à Rome au fpectacle du meurtre des animaux, on vint aux hommes & aux gladiateurs. La Nature femble avoir attaché elle-mefme à l'homme quelque inftinct à l'inhumanité, nul ne prend beaucoup de plaifir à voir des beftes s'entrejoüer, & nul ne manque

DE MONTAIGNE 165
d'en prendre à les voir s'entredéchirer & fe démembrer.

C'Eft la foy feule qui embraffe vivement & certainement les hauts myftéres de noftre Réligion; mais ce n'eft pas à dire que ce ne foit une entreprife belle & loüable d'accommoder encore au fervice de noftre foy les outils naturels & humains que Dieu nous a donné. Il faut l'accompagner de toute la raifon qui eft en nous, mais toujours avec cette réferve de n'eftimer pas que

De la Réligion.

(b) No 37: *Pensées* 1700; O4ᵛ—5ʳ [118 mm]

Two abridgements of the end of Book III 13. See Nos 36 and 37.

DE MONTAIGNE. 559

que celuy qui a pris des Empires & des Villes. Le glorieux Chef-d'œuvre de l'homme, c'est de vivre à propos ; toutes autres choses, regner, thesaurifer, bâtir, n'en font qu'appendicules & adminicules pour le plus. C'est aux petites ames, enfevelies du poids des affaires, de ne s'en sçavoir purement démêler, de ne les sçavoir & laisser & reprendre.

C'est une absoluë perfection, & comme divine, de sçavoir jouyr loyalement de son estre. Nous cherchons d'autres conditions pour n'entendre l'usage des nostres, & fortons hors de nous pour ne sçavoir pas ce qui s'y fait. Nous avons pourtant beau monter fur des échasses ; car fur des échasses, encore faut-il marcher de nos jambes : Et au plus élevé Thrône du Monde, nous ne sommes assis que fur noftre cul. Les plus belles vies font à mon gré celles qui se rangent au modele commun & humain avec ordre ; mais sans miracle & sans extravagance.

Fin du troisième Livre.

L'ESPRIT 558

558
ce. J'estime pareille injustice de prendre à contre-cœur les voluptez naturelles, que de les prendre trop à cœur. Xerxes estoit un fat, qui enveloppé en toutes les voluptez humaines, alloit propofer prix à qui luy en trouveroit d'autres. Mais non guere moins fat est celuy qui retranche celles que la Nature luy a trouvés. Il ne les faut ny fuivre ny fuyr ; il les faut recevoir. Quand je vois & Cefar & Alexandre, au plus épais de fa grande befogne, jouyr fi pleinement des plaifirs humains & corporels, je ne dis pas que ce foit relâcher fon ame, je dis que c'est la roidir, foûmettant par vigueur de courage à l'ufage de la vie ordinaire fes violentes occupations & laborieufes penfées. Sages s'ils euffent crû que c'eftoit là leur ordinaire vocation ; celle-cy l'extraordinaire. Nous sommes de grands fouz : Il a paffé fa vie en oifiveté, difons-nous ; je n'ay rien fait d'aujourd'huy. Quoy n'avez-vous pas vécu ? c'est non feulement la fondamentale, mais la plus illuftre de toutes vos occupations. Pour le montrer & exploiter, Nature n'a que faire de la Fortune : elle fe montre également en tous étages, & derriere comme fans rideau. Avez vous fçeu compofer vos mœurs ? Vous avez bien plus fait que celuy qui a compofé des livres. Avez-vous fçeu prendre du repos ? vous avez plus fait

(a) No 36: *L'Esprit* 1677; 2Y5ᵛ—6ʳ [127 mm]

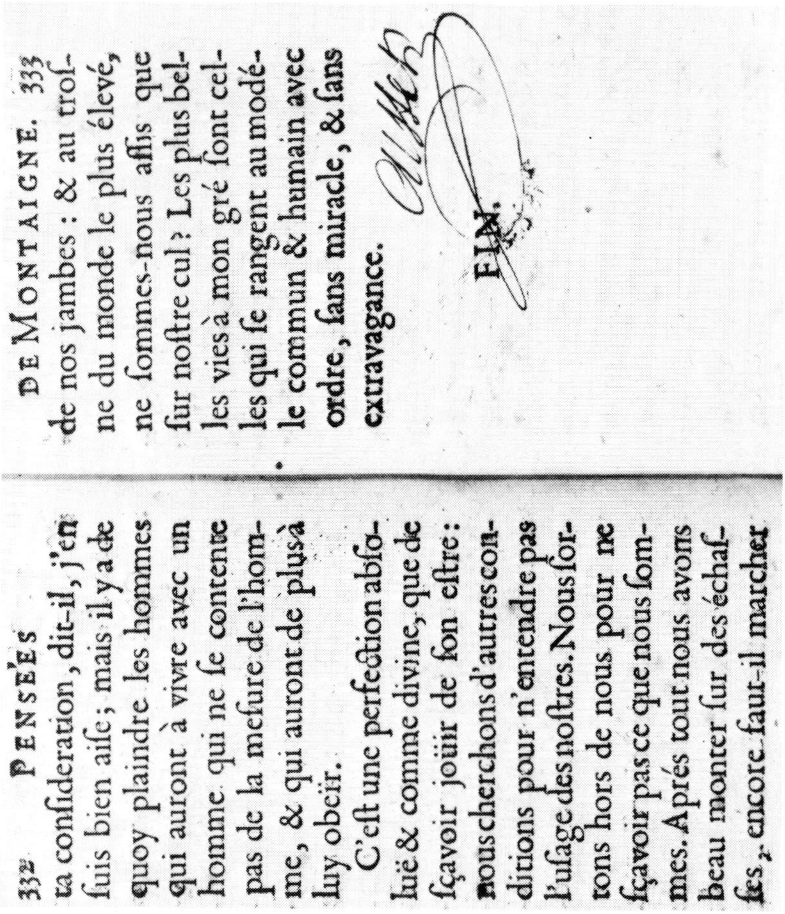

PLATE 20 (*contd.*) 209

332 PENSÉES

ta confideration, dit-il, j'en fuis bien aifé; mais il y a de quoy plaindre les hommes qui auront à vivre avec un homme, qui ne fe contente pas de la mefure de l'homme, & qui auront de plusà luy obeïr.

C'eft une perfection abfoluë & comme divine, que de fçavoir joüir de fon eftre: nous cherchons d'autres conditions pour n'entendre pas l'ufage des noftres. Nous fortons hors de nous pour ne fçavoir pas ce que nous fommes. Aprés tout nous avons beau monter fur des échaffes, encore faut-il marcher

DE MONTAIGNE. 333

de nos jambes : & au trofne du monde le plus élevé, ne fommes-nous affis que fur noftre cul ? Les plus belles vies à mon gré font celles qui fe rangent au modéle commun & humain avec ordre, fans miracle, & fans extravagance.

FIN.

(b) *Pensées* 1700; 2E4ᵛ—5ʳ [115 mm]

SOURCES OF ILLUSTRATIONS

Grateful acknowledgement is made to the following for supplying photographs and giving permission for their reproduction.

TITLE-PAGES

1: (*a*, *d*) Senate House Library, London University; (*b*, *e*) The John Rylands University Library of Manchester; (*c*) Bibliothèque municipale, Bordeaux.
2: Bibliothèque municipale, Bordeaux.
3: The Houghton Library, Harvard University.
4: (*a*) The Pierpont Morgan Library, New York; (*b*) Bibliothèque municipale, Bordeaux; (*c*) Senate House Library, London University.
4†: Bibliothèque municipale, Bordeaux.
5: (*a*, *b*) Mrs O. L. Sayce.
6: (*a*) Mrs O. L. Sayce; (*b*) The London Library.
7A: (*a*) Wadham College, Oxford; (*b*) The Trustees of the National Library of Scotland.
7†: Museum Plantin-Moretus, Antwerp.
7B: King's College, Cambridge.
8: Bodleian Library, Oxford, 8°M 217 Art.
9, 10, 11: Mrs O. L. Sayce.
12: (*a*) Oriel College, Oxford (*b*) Bibliothèque nationale, Paris.
12A, 12B: Bibliothèque nationale, Paris.
13: Mrs O. L. Sayce.
14: (*a*) Mrs O. L. Sayce; (*b*, *c*, *d*, *e*) Bibliothèque nationale, Paris.
15: Taylor Institution, Oxford.
16: (*a*, *c*) Bibliothèque nationale, Paris; (*b*) The Principal and Fellows, Jesus College, Oxford; (*d*) British Library, London; (*e*) University of Michigan, Dept. of Rare Books and Special Collections.
17: (*a*, *c*, *d*) Bibliothèque nationale, Paris; (*b*) British Library, London; (*e*) Biblioteka Narodowa, Warsaw.
18: (*a*) The President and Fellows, Corpus Christi College, Oxford; (*b*) Taylor Institution, Oxford; (*c*) University of Michigan, Dept. of Rare Books and Special Collections; (*d*) Mrs O. L. Sayce.
19: Bibliothèque nationale, Paris.
20: (*a*) British Library, London; (*b*) Bibliothèque nationale, Paris; (*c*) University of Michigan, Dept. of Rare Books and Special Collections; (*d*) Bodleian Library, Oxford, 4° Σ 406; (*e*) Illinois University Library.
21: (*a*, *b*, *c*, *e*) Bibliothèque nationale, Paris; (*d*) Bodleian Library, Oxford, Vet E 2 f 73; (*f*) Bibliothèque Mazarine, Paris.
21A: Bibliothèque nationale, Paris.
22: (*a*) Mrs O. L. Sayce; (*b*) Biblioteka Narodowa, Warsaw; (*c*) Bibliothèque nationale, Paris; (*d*) British Library, London.
23: (*a*, *f*, *i*, *k*, *l*, *m*, *n*) Bibliothèque nationale, Paris; (*b*) Bibliothèque municipale, Lyons; (*c*) Princeton University Library; (*d*) British Library, London; (*e*) Manchester College, Oxford; (*g*) Bibliothèque de l'Arsenal, Paris; (*h*) Muzeum Narodowe, Warsaw; (*j*) Ohio State University Library.
23A: The Houghton Library, Harvard University.

23B: Bibliothèque municipale, Nevers.

24: (*a, b, c, e, h, i*) Bibliothèque nationale, Paris; (*d*) Biblioteca Nazionale Marciana, Venice, 219 C 96; (*f*) Senate House Library, London University; (*g*) Bodleian Library, Oxford, Douce M 268.

24A: Bibliothèque nationale, Paris.

25: (*a, b*) Bibliothèque nationale, Paris; (*c*) The Brotherton Library, University of Leeds; (*d, e*) Bodleian Library, Oxford, Vet E2 c 12.

26: (*a*) Biblioteka Uniwersytecka, Wrocław; (*b, c, d, f, h, j*) Bibliothèque nationale, Paris; (*e*) Biblioteca Apostolica Vaticana; (*g*) The Lord Crewe Trustees, Durham University; (*i*) British Library, London; (*k*) University of Michigan, Dept. of Rare Books and Special Collections.

27: (*a, d*) Bibliothèque nationale, Paris; (*b*) Mrs O. L. Sayce; (*c*) Illinois University Library; (*e*) Bibliothèque municipale, Laon.

28: British Library, London.

29: Mrs O. L. Sayce.

30: (*a, h*) Mrs O. L. Sayce; (*b, f, k*) Bibliothèque nationale, Paris; (*c*) Bibliothèque municipale, Tours; (*d*) Worcester College, Oxford; (*e*) Universitetsbibliotek, Oslo; (*g*) Bibliothèque municipale, Poitiers; (*i*) Univerzitetska Biblioteka Svetozar Marković, Belgrade; (*j*) British Library, London.

31: (*a, j*) Mrs O. L. Sayce; (*b*) Biblioteka Narodowa, Warsaw; (*c, d, e, l*) Bibliothèque nationale, Paris; (*f*) British Library, London; (*g*) Bibliothèque municipale (section du fonds ancien), Dieppe; (*h*) Liverpool University Library; (*i*) Princeton University Library; (*k*) Biblioteca Universitaria, Padua.

32: (*a, b, c*) Bibliothèque municipale, Poitiers; (*d*) Bibliothèque nationale, Paris.

33: (*a, b, c, d*) Mrs O. L. Sayce; (*e, f, g*) Bibliothèque nationale, Paris.

34: (*a, b, c*) Mrs O. L. Sayce.

35: (*a, b, c, d*) British Library, London; (*e*) Bibliothèque nationale, Paris.

36: (*a, b*) Bodleian Library, Oxford, Vet E3 f 180.

37: Mrs O. L. Sayce.

PLATES

1. (a, c) Bodleian Library, Oxford, Arch B f 59, vol i, Errata and p. 350; (b) Senate House Library, London University.

2. (a) Bodleian Library, Oxford, Arch B f 59, vol ii, sigs 4S7^v and 4S8^r; (b) Senate House Library, London University.

3. Museum Plantin-Moretus, Antwerp.

4. Bodleian Library, Oxford, 8° M 217 Art, sig ã4^v.

5. Mrs O. L. Sayce.

6. (a, b, c, d) Mrs O. L. Sayce.

7. (a, c) Mrs O. L. Sayce; (b) Bodleian Library, Oxford, 4° Σ 406, sig ĩ4^v.

8. (a, b, c, d) Bibliothèque nationale, Paris.

9. (a) Mrs O. L. Sayce; (b) The Principal and Fellows, Jesus College, Oxford.

10. (a) Mrs O. L. Sayce; (b) Bibliothèque nationale, Paris; (c) The Principal and Fellows, Jesus College, Oxford.

11. The Houghton Library, Harvard University.

12. Mrs O. L. Sayce.

13, 14, 15, 16. Bibliothèque nationale, Paris.

17, 18 (a, b), 19 (a, b), 20 (a, b) Mrs O. L. Sayce.

BIBLIOGRAPHY

1. Bibliographies and lists of Montaigne's works

An asterisk indicates the works which are of most importance for the early editions of the *Essais*

*ARBOUR, R, *L'ère baroque en France: répertoire chronologique des éditions de textes littéraires*, 1st part: 1585—1615, 2 vols; 2nd part: 1616—1628; 3rd part: 1629—1643, Geneva, 1977—80

[ARMAINGAUD] *Bibliothèque du Dr Armaingaud: catalogue annoté de toutes les éditions des Essais de Montaigne (1580—1927)*, Paris, 1927

BAUDRIER, H L (continued by J Baudrier), *Bibliographie lyonnaise*, 13 vols, Lyons, 1895—1921 (reprinted Paris, 1964—5) (for editions of 1593, 1595 Lyons)

CLAUDIN, A and PLACE J, *Bibliographie des éditions originales d'auteurs français des XVIe, XVIIe et XVIIIe siècles réunies par M.A. Rochebilière*, Paris, 1930 (for editions of 1580, 1582, 1588, 1595, 1598)

COURBET, E, *Notice biographique et bibliographique sur Michel de Montaigne*, Paris, 1900

DESGRAVES, L, *Bibliographie bordelaise: bibliographie des ouvrages imprimés à Bordeaux au XVIe siècle et par S. Millanges (1572—1623)*, (Bibliotheca Bibliographica Aureliana, 37), Baden-Baden, 1971 (for editions of 1580, 1582)

*IVES G B, 'Bibliography of the Essays' in *Essays of Michael Lord of Montaigne*, 3 vols, Boston and New York, 1902—4 (iii, 415—92)

LABADIE, E., *Les Essais de Montaigne: variations des prix des éditions princeps*, Bordeaux, 1916 (for editions of 1580, 1582, 1587, 1588, 1595)

LE PETIT, J, *Bibliographie des principales éditions originales d'écrivains français du XVe au XVIIIe siècle*, Paris, 1888 (for editions of 1580, 1582, 1587, 1588, 1595, 1598)

**Les Essais de Montaigne: catalogue des éditions et des exemplaires présentés par la Bibliothèque municipale de Bordeaux à l'occasion du IVe centenaire de la première édition*, Bordeaux, 1980

*'Liste chronologique des éditions des *Essais* depuis l'édition originale (1580) jusqu'au 31 décembre 1912', *BSAM*, I, 1 (1913), pp 63—74

MICHEL, P, 'Bibliographie Montaigniste (1580—1950)', *BSAM,* III, 1 (1957), pp 62—80 (for editions of 1580, 1582, 1588, Bordeaux Copy, 1595, 1619 Rouen A, 1635 and after 1700)

MOUREAU, F, '*Libri manent* ou répertoire de quelques exemplaires précieux des *Essais*', *BSAM*, V, 25—6 (1978), pp 109—12 (for editions of 1580, 1582, 1588, 1595 Lyons, 1595 Paris, 1598 and after 1700)

*PAYEN, J-F, *Notice bibliographique sur Montaigne*, Paris, 1837 (supplements 1837 and 1860)

*RICHOU, G, *Inventaire de la collection des ouvrages et documents réunis par J.-F. Payen et J.-B. Bastide sur Michel de Montaigne*, Paris, 1878 (reprinted Amsterdam, 1972)

ROCHEBILIÈRE, see CLAUDIN.

SAINT-MARTIN, J DE, 'Sur quelques-unes des premières éditions des *Essais*', *BSAM*, IV, 4 (1966), pp 17—21 (for editions of 1598, 1602 Paris, 1602 Leiden A, 1608, 1619 Rouen, 1652, 1657)

SALLES, A, 'Les premières éditions des *Essais* dans les ventes publiques et chez les libraires', *BSAM*, II, 2 (1937), pp 89—90 (for editions of 1580, 1582, 1587, 1588, 1593, 1595)

—'Prix des exemplaires des *Essais* dans les ventes publiques et chez les libraires', *BSAM*, II, 3 (1938), pp 54—5 (for editions of 1598, 1635, 1659 Amsterdam/Brussels and after 1700)

—'Les éditions de Montaigne dans les ventes publiques et chez les libraires', *BSAM*, II, 4 (1938), pp 58—9 (for editions of 1580, 1582, 1587, 1588, 1595, 1602, 1635, 1652 and after 1700)

*TANNENBAUM, S A, *Michel Eyquem de Montaigne: a concise bibliography*, New York, 1942

*TCHEMERZINE, A, *Bibliographie d'éditions originales et rares d'auteurs* *français des XVe, XVIe et XVIIe siècles*, 10 vols, Paris, 1927—33 (viii, 402—46)

THORKELIN, F., *Katalog over Frederik Thorkelins Montaigne-samling*, Copenhagen, 1980 (for editions of 1588, 1595, 1635 and after 1700)

2. Facsimiles and principal modern editions of the 'Essais'

1580

DEZEIMERIS, R, AND BARCKHAUSEN, H (eds), *Essais de Michel de Montaigne: texte original de 1580 avec les variantes des éditions de 1582 et 1587*, 2 vols, Bordeaux, 1870—3

MARTIN, D (ed), *Montaigne, Essais: reproduction photographique de l'édition originale de 1580*, 2 vols, Geneva and Paris, 1976

1582

FRANÇON, M (ed), *Michel de Montaigne, Essais: reproduction photographique de la deuxième edition (Bordeaux, 1582)*, Cambridge (Mass.), 1969

1588 (THE BORDEAUX COPY)

COURBET, E, ARMAINGAUD, A, and DUPORTAL, J, (eds), *Les Essais de Montaigne: reproduction typographique de l'exemplaire annoté par l'auteur et conservé à la Bibliothèque de Bordeaux*, 3 vols, Paris, 1906—1931

STROWSKI, F, GEBELIN, F, and VILLEY, P, (eds), *Les Essais de Michel de Montaigne*, 5 vols, Bordeaux, 1906—33 (Edition municipale)

STROWSKI, F, (ed), *Reproduction en phototypie de l'Exemplaire avec notes manuscrites marginales des Essais de Montaigne appartenant à la ville de Bordeaux*, 3 vols, Paris, 1912

ARMAINGAUD, A, (ed), *Oeuvres complètes*, 12 vols, Paris, 1924—41 (the *Essais* are in vols I—VI)

1595

COURBET, E, and ROYER, C, (eds), *Les Essais de Montaigne*, 5 vols, Paris, 1872—1900

3. General

ABEL, A, 'Juste Lipse et Marie de Gournay: autour de *l'exemplaire d'Anvers* des *Essais* de Montaigne', *BHR*, 35 (1973), pp 117—29.

ARMAINGAUD, A, 'Editions des *Essais* de Montaigne de 1588 et de 1580', *Intermédiaire des chercheurs et des curieux*, 10 June 1902

BERNOULLI, R, 'La mise à l'Index des *Essais* de Montaigne', *BSAM*, IV, 8 (1966), pp 4—10

BOASE, A, *The fortunes of Montaigne: a history of the Essays in France 1580—1669*, London, 1935 (reprinted New York, 1970)

*BONNET, P, 'Le texte des *Essais* de Montaigne: évolution de sa structure des origines à nos jours', *BSAM*, IV, 7 (1966), pp 70—81 (also in M Françon, *Pour une édition critique*, 1965)

—'Reinhold Dezeimeris et son exemplaire des *Essais* de Montaigne', *BSAM*, IV, 4 (1965), pp 3—24

—'L'Exemplaire de Bordeaux et le texte définitif des *Essais*' in *Mémorial du 1er congrès international des études montaignistes* (ed. G Palassie), Bordeaux, 1964, pp 94—100

—'L'édition de 1608 des *Essais* de Montaigne et sa pagination réelle', *BSAM*, III, 27 (1963), pp 47—9

—'Une édition in-8° des *Essais* publiée *sans date* au XVIIᵉ siècle', *BSAM*, IV, 4 (1965), pp 29—31 (edition of [1617] Envers)

—'Sur un exemplaire des *Essais* portant l'adresse d'un libraire de Rouen et le millésime 1619', *BSAM*, IV, 8 (1966), pp 13—14 (edition of 1619 Rouen A)

—'Sur un exemplaire des *Essais* appartenant à une édition non datée du XVIIᵉ siècle [à l'adresse de: Rouen, J. Berthelin]', *BSAM* IV, 9 (1967), pp 46—8 (edition of [1619] Rouen B)

—L'édition des *Essais* de 1627', *BSAM,* IV, 8 (1966) pp 15—16

—'Les *Essais* à l'Index', *BSAM*, IV, 8 (1966), pp 11—12

—'L'édition de 1649 des *Essais*', *BSAM*, IV, 3 (1965), pp 3—5

Catalogue Drouot Rive Gauche: Livres rares et précieux composant la bibliothèque d'un amateur, 10 December 1976

CHAIX, P, DUFOUR, A, and MOECKLI, G, *Les livres imprimés à Genève de 1550 à 1600*, Geneva, 1966

COURTEAULT, P, 'L'exemplaire de Bordeaux au XVIIIe siècle', *BSAM*, II, 9 (1940), pp 54—6

DEZEIMERIS, R, 'Un nouvel exemplaire annoté des *Essais* de Montaigne' *La Gironde*, 31 August 1881 (edition of 1580)

—*Recherches sur la recension du texte posthume des Essais de Montaigne*, Bordeaux, 1866

DRÉANO, M, *La renommée de Montaigne en France au XVIIIe siècle*, Angers, 1952

DUPORTAL, J, *Contribution au catalogue général des livres à figures du XVIIe siècle (1601—1633)*, Paris, 1914

FRANÇON, M, *Pour une édition critique des Essais. Avant-propos de Pierre Bonnet: évolution et structure du texte des Essais*, Cambridge (Mass.), 1965 (P Bonnet's preface is reprinted in *BSAM*, IV, 7 (1966), pp 70—81

—'Notes sur l'édition de 1582 des *Essais*', *BSAM*, IV, 7 (1966), pp 82—3

—'L'édition des *Essais* de 1582', *BSAM*, IV, 14 (1968), pp 3—32 (reprinted as the preface to his fascimile edition of 1582 Bordeaux)

—'Notes de Miss Grace Norton dans l'exemplaire de l'édition des *Essais* de Montaigne (Lyon, 1595)', *BSAM*, IV, 4 (1965), pp 25—8

ILSLEY, M H, *A daughter of the Renaissance: Marie le Jars de Gournay, her life and works*, The Hague, 1963

JORDAN, C-E, *Recueil de littérature, de philosophie et d'histoire*, Amsterdam, 1730

'Manuscrit de Bordeaux', *BSAM*, II, 5 (1939), p 26

MARCHAND, J, 'Le Montaigne de la reine Elisabeth d'Angleterre (1580)' *BSAM*, III, 22 (1962), pp. 23—7

—*Hypothèse sur la quatrième édition des Essais de Montaigne (1587)*, Bordeaux, 1937

—'L'édition des *Essais* de 1587', *BSAM*, II, 9 (1940), pp 57—8

MASKELL, D, 'Quel est le dernier état authentique des *Essais* de Montaigne?', *BHR*, 40 (1978), pp 85—103

—'Montaigne correcteur de l'exemplaire de Bordeaux', *BSAM*, V, 25—6 (1978), pp 57—71

MASSON, A, 'Un exemplaire curieux des *Essais*', *BSAM*, II, 6 (1939), p 80 (edition of 1625)

MICHEL, P, 'Le problème des éditions', *BSAM*, III, 1 (1957), pp 16—19 (part of an article entitled 'Actualité de Montaigne')

MOUREAU, F, 'Sur des exemplaires des *Essais* en vente à la Foire de Francfort (automne 1581)', *BSAM*, V, 9 (1974), pp 57—9

SALLES, A, 'Quelques exemplaires annotés des *Essais* qui méritent attention', *BSAM*, II, 1 (1937), pp 39—40

—'La première édition des *Essais* de Montaigne (1580): corrections et retouches', *BBB*, 1931, pp 6—12

—'Un exemplaire de 1580 coté 600.000 fr.', *BSAM*, II, 2 (1937), pp 85—6

—'Les deux jumeaux de 1580', *BSAM*, II, 3 (1938), pp 23—4

—'Quelques notes sur l'édition princeps des *Essais* de 1580', *BSAM*, II, 10 (1941), pp 12—13

—'L'édition de 1582', *BSAM*, II, 4 (1938), pp 27—8

—'A propos de la troisième (?) édition des *Essais* jusqu'ici introuvable', *BSAM*, II, 1 (1937), pp 12—13; *ibid.*, II, 2 (1937), pp 53—4; *ibid.*, II, 6 (1939), pp 60—1

—'A propos de l'exemplaire Le Brun', *BSAM*, II, 3 (1938), p 29 (edition of 1588)

—'Quelques annotations de l'exemplaire Le Brun', *BSAM*, II, 5 (1939), p 28 (edition of 1588)

—'A propos du manuscrit de Bordeaux', *BSAM*, II, 1 (1937), p 19

—'Encore une petite énigme Montanienne (l'édition 1595 de Lyon)', *BSAM*, II, 2 (1937), pp 86—8

—'Le fameux carton de la page 63 (édition de 1595)', *BSAM*, II, 7 (1939), p 101

—'Le Montaigne de Montesquieu', *BBB*, 1930, pp 315—20 (edition of 1595)

—'Le Montaigne de Montesquieu', *BSAM*, II, 3 (1938), pp 24—5; *ibid.*, II, 6 (1939), p 84 (edition of 1595)

—'Le duel entre l'édition de 1595 et le manuscrit de Bordeaux', *BSAM*, II, 4 (1938), pp 29—32; *ibid.*, II, 5 (1939), pp 24—6

—'Mon exemplaire Petitpas 1617', *BSAM*, II, 5 (1939), p 38

—'Les corrections à la plume de Mlle de Gournay', *BSAM*, II, 1 (1937), p 24; *ibid.*, II, 5 (1939), pp 26—7 (editions of 1595, 1635)

—'L'exemplaire Spanheim', *BSAM*, II, 3 (1938), p 28 (edition of 1635)

Sayce, R A, *The Essays of Montaigne: a critical exploration*, London, 1972

—'L'édition des *Essais* de Montaigne de 1595', *BHR*, 36 (1974), pp 115—41

Thorkelin, F., 'Mon plus cher livre', *BSAM*, V, 10—11 (1974), pp 109—10 (edition of 1588)

Trinquet, R, 'Le cinquantenaire de l'édition Armaingaud: vers une édition critique des *Essais*', *BSAM*, V, 13 (1975), pp 37—42

Zeitlin, J., 'The relation of the text of 1595 to that of the Bordeaux Copy' in his translation *The Essays of Montaigne*, 3 vols, New York, 1934—6 (appendix to vol I)

INDEXES

Numbers refer to entries, not to pages: n refers to notes at the end of entries, not to footnotes.

1. PLACES OF PUBLICATION OF THE *ESSAIS*

Amsterdam, 33
Antwerp, 19

Bordeaux, 1, 2
Brussels, 33

Cologny, 12, 17

Geneva, 6 n1, 11 n3, 12 n4, 12A, 12B, 13 n3, 17

Leiden, 11, 12, 15
Lyons, 5, 6, 35

Paris, 3, 4, 4†, 7A, 7A†, 7B, 8, 9, 10, 13, 14, 16, 20, 23, 23A, 23B, 24A, 25, 26, 27, 29, 30, 31, 32, 34, 36, 37

Rouen, 18, 21, 21A, 22, 24, 28

2. BOOKSELLERS AND PRINTERS

Albert, Philippe, 12B, 17
Angot, Charles, 31
Angot, Nicolas, 22
Anisson, Jean, 37
Auplet, Michel d', 26

Bechet, Denis, 31
Bertault, Robert, 23
Berthelin, Jean, 22, 24, 28
Besongne, Jacques, 22, 24
Bessin, Nicolas, 23
Besson, Antoine, 35
Billaine, Louis, 31
Billaine, Pierre, 26
Blageart, Michel, 27, 29
Boulanger, Louis, 26
Boutonné, Rolet, 23

Caillouë, Jacques, 24
Camusat, Jean, 25
Can, Jean, 12A
Chevalier, Pierre, 24A
Chevillion, Robert, 34
Collet, Martin, 23, 26
Courbé, Augustin, 27, 30
Cousterot (Couterot), Edmé, 30, 31

Dallin, veuve Remy, 23
Daré, Pierre, 21
Daré, Thomas, 18, 21
Daré, veuve Thomas, 21
Daubin, Eustache, 23
Delas, Léger, 7A n2
Denain, Robert, 27
Doreau, Jean, 11, 12, 15
Douceur, David, 23B
Du Bray, Toussaint, 25
Du Carroy, Jean, 3 n2
Du Mesnil, Louis, 24
Du Puis, veuve Mathurin, 30, 31
Durand, Jean, 22 *achevé*
Durand, Martin, 26

Estienne, Antoine, 34 *privilège*
Estienne, Henri, 30 n2, 31 n2

Féron, Robert, 24
Foppens, François, 33

Germont, Jean, 26
Gueffier, François, 16, 20
Guignard, Jean, 26

3. GENERAL